Contemplations and Deliberations

between
Swami Vidyananda
and
John Brokaar

Copyright

The words in these writings and the content they encompass, originated from many a discussion, study, observation, and contemplative thought. As it is the authors' opinion that words cannot be 'owned' by any man or woman, just as a piece of earth that has been around since the beginning of time, cannot realistically be 'owned' by anyone either. The compilation of these words, thoughts, views, conclusions and ideas in this book, call it what you will, are based on the influence of preceding elements, which included the conscious intelligence of countless others, people and beings, and these can as such therefore, not realistically be 'owned' either. Gnosis is and remains the birthright of every man, woman and child, who has opted to choose consciously, and to enhance this and the self, through study, work and living a correct and fruitful life.

There is therefore no copyright on the contents of this book.

It is however stated that the 'authors', as the custodians of the book and its contents, authorize the use of these words by others as they wish, provided it is not for profit or material gain.

For comments and observations: johnbrokaar@yahoo.com

Printed by: PJ Bookbinders www.pjbookbinders.co.za

ISBN: 978-1-83492-015-3(pbk)   978-1-83492-016-0(e-book)

*The Dwar (gate) into the Labyrinth
at the Blue Butterfly retreat center*

The Wild Flowers

How can we call the flowers wild?
In comparison to us, they're mild!
Walk amidst them, but with care,
Find the hidden treasures there.

Daring colours mixed together,
Surrendering to wind and weather.
Taking nothing, simply giving
Showing us the art of living.

*Mother Yogeshwari   (1926 – 2021)
Co-Founder Ananda Kutir Ashrama
Cape Town, South Africa*

CONTENTS

DEDICATION	3
CONTENTS	5
PREFACE	11
ACKNOWLEDGEMENTS	12
INTRODUCTION	
by John Brokaar	13
by Swami Vidyananda	15
FOREWORD	
By Vani Mataji and Terri Brokaar	17

The Letters:

1 The Integral Flight of Starlings & the Interconnected State of All Things   **19**

25 March 2014	19
28 March 2014	21
5 April 2014	22
6 April 2014	25
14 April 2014	25
20 April 2014	27

2 Views on Causes and Connecting the Dots   **28**

12 April 2020	29
13 April 2020	30
Letter to Stuart	32
21 April 2020	34
6 June 2020	36
9 June 2020	38

3 Views on the News   **40**

2 June 2020	40
4 June 2020	42
7 June 2020	42
16 June 2020	46
Quote from the scripture of Srimad Bhagavatam	47
17 June 2020	48
23 June 2020	48
29 June 2020	53

4 Thoughts with a Friend — 55

    17 August 2020 — 55
    The first letter to Philip — 57
    20 August 2020 — 58

5 Our Trip — 60

    25 November 2020 — 60
    26 November 2020 — 61
    The second letter to Philip — 63
    28 November 2020 — 65

6 Your Christmas Talk — 67

    30 December 2020 — 67
    2 January 2021 — 68
    3 January 2021 — 68
    5 January 2021 — 71

7 An Interesting Development — 73

    8 February 2021 — 73
    9 February 2021 — 73
    9 February 2021 — 74

8 Reply — 75

    24 July 2021 — 75
    26 July 2021 — 77
    Statistical Diagram on Fatalities in South Africa — 78
    27 July 2021 — 79
    28 July 2021 — 81

9 Life for the Unvaccinated — 82

    3 November 2021 — 82
    8 November 2021 — 83
    8 November 2021 — 84
    10 November 2021 — 84

10 On Censorship — 85

    1 March 2022 — 85
    2 March 2022 — 88

11 Truth vs Hydra — 89

    4 April 2022 — 89
    5 April 2022 — 89
    6 April 2022 — 92

12 Imminent Visit — 93

    7 July 2022 — 93
    8 July 2022 — 94
    10 July 2022 — 95
    11 July 2022 — 96

13 On Possessions — 97

    31 July 2022 — 97
    19 August 2022 — 98
    20 August 2022 — 99
    21 August 2022 — 99
    24 August 2022 — 101
    25 August 2022 — 101
    29 August 2022 — 103
    31 August 2022 — 104

14 The Powers That Be — 105

    31 August 2022 — 105
    3 September 2022 — 105
    10 September 2022 — 107
    12 September 2022 — 108
    22 September 2022 — 110
    30 September 2022 — 112
    12 October 2022 — 113

15 Consciousness and the 4th Industrial Revolution — 115

    14 October 2022 — 115
    Consciousness and the 4th Ind. Revolution — 116
    The Reality of Dimensions — 118
    The Contemporary Definition of Consciousness — 120
    - *Science and Technology's Definition* — 121
    - *Religion and Spirituality's Definition* — 122
    - *The Trance and Psychedelic Definition* — 123

    The Definition of Consciousness as 'a Medium' — 124
    - *Water, Earth, Air, Fire, and Aether* — 125
    - *Water as a Medium of Consciousness* — 125
    - *Earth as a Medium of Consciousness* — 126
    - *Air as a Medium of Consciousness* — 126
    - *Æther as a Medium of Consciousness* — 127
    - *To Conclude: The Purpose of Fire* — 128

    15 November 2022 — 128

16 Delusions of Reality		**132**
	20 November 2022	132
	21 November 2022	134
	25 November 2022	135
	28 November 2022	137
17 Comments on the 'Ten Fundamental Principles for Establishing a New Paradigm'		**139**
	11 December 2022	139
	Letter to the Schiller Institute	141
	1. On Sovereignty	141
	2. On Eradicating Poverty	142
	3. On the Extending of Life-expectancy	143
	4. On Motivating Man on the Advance of Technocracy	143
	5. On the Proposed Systems of Finance	143
	6. On Advanced Infrastructure	144
	7. On Centralized Global Security	144
	8. On God as a Concept	144
	9. On the Settlement of Quarrelling Opinion	144
	10. On the Evil in Lack of Development	144
	An Ode to the Sage (and his Purpose)	145
	12 December 2022	147
	16 December 2022	148
	22 December 2022	150
	24 December 2022	152
	26 December 2022	153
18 Fate and the Depopulation Agenda		**155**
	13 January 2023	155
	16 January 2023	158
	19 January 2023	161
	21 January 2023	163
19 The Turkey Earthquakes		**166**
	9 February 2023	166
	10 February 2023	166
	- Technocracy	167
	- Cosmology	167
	- Spiritual Interconnectedness	167
	- Evidence of Historical Cycles	168
	- Knowing Geology and the 'Useful Crisis'	166
	- This Observer's Reality	166

14 February 2023	169
18 February 2023	171
21 February 2023	174
27 February 2023	176
11 March 2023	177

20 A Brief Update — 179

10 May 2023	179
11 May 2023	180
15 May 2023	181

21 On reports of Child Abuse and Sacrifice — 184

6 August 2023	184
11 August 2023	184
20 August 2023	185
22 August 2023	186
24 August 2023	190
26 August 2023	190
27 August 2023	191

22 Opinion — 193

23 August 2023	193
27 August 2023	194

23 A Backward & Forward Glance on Status Quos — 195

27 October 2023	195
28 October 2023	198
31 October 2023	200
16 November 2023	203

24 All the World's a Stage? — 207

28 November 2023	207
1 December 2023	208
26 December 2023	209
2 January 2024	212

25 Domination — 213

16 February 2024	213
3 March 2024	214
13 March 2024	216
17 March 2024	217

26 On the Automaton and the Religion of Science — 218

16 February 2024	218
Letter: Is Science a Religion?	218

5 March 2024	219
16 March 2024	221
7 March 2024	221
16 April 2024	223
24 April 2024	223
30 April 2024	225

27 Talk on AI — **226**

16 February 2024	226
6 March 2024	226
16 March 2024	227

28 Thoughts on the Astral World — **229**

20 June 2024	229
18 July 2024	231
2 August 2024	232
5 August 2024	235

AFTERWORD — **237**

"In the gardens of the Blue Butterfly, October 2013" 239

PREFACE

This book is a record of "conversations" between two friends, who are spiritual seekers. As seekers we acknowledge that we do not claim knowledge of the Truth. We are seeking. And in our seeking we may have opportunity to exchange our understanding with others.

In a series of emails we shared our understanding of various issues that face humanity. It is important to note that the book is therefore not a structured treatise. Our points of view were based on research, observations and personal reflection and our correspondence therefore included all three approaches, often within a single paragraph. Where possible we retrospectively inserted footnotes, which either clarify our points of view, share relevant information or give references. We were not able to do this for everything, since the idea of a book only emerged much later. As is usual in communication between friends, detailed references are not always included, so we have done the best possible in this regard.

Each chapter starts with a few introductory paragraphs to contextualise the correspondence for the reader. We wrote this in the third person.

We wish to point out that the sharing of these discussions with the reader is not meant to teach or convince the reader of our points of view, as these themselves are evolving. We hope that the reader will be stimulated to reflect on these topics with the same openness and respect with which they were written in our exchange. We hope that the reader will also be able to synthesise his or her viewpoints with those in the book and thereby reach a deeper understanding within him- or herself. And if certain viewpoints are not palatable to the reader, they can simply skip these.

The important thing is the evolution in each one of us. If we use communication wisely, then that will contribute to our growth. Hence our prayer is that the reader will read, reflect, contemplate and find a deeper level of truth within themselves. May we be blessed with wonderful insights in our ongoing journey and encounters with one another.

ACKNOWLEGDEMENTS

In the writing and publication of books of any nature, there are almost always a number of supporting elements involved, and we feel it is both important and necessary to acknowledge some of these.

First, we express our gratitude to the Divine for bringing the two of us together in a meaningful friendship, and to the many spiritual masters and mentors that influenced our respective paths.

Then, on the path of contemplation and deliberation that led to the contents of this book, we must acknowledge Terri, Vani and Uma, who were part of many a conversation prior to our email exchange. Their loving presence certainly contributed to our friendship and exchange.

For the compilation and finishes of this book, we thank Vani for providing a foreword; Terri for editing, putting together a beautiful cover, and providing a foreword; and we thank Uma, Maitri, Glynn and Carol for assisting us with proofreading.

Last, but not least, we feel it proper to acknowledge the many heroic persons that bring to light the facts regarding global events and who continue to do so. This naturally impacted our experiences and conversations; without these, the making of duly informed and contemplated decisions would have been mere guesswork!

INTRODUCTION
By John Brokaar

We live in extraordinary times. At least, when I observe the exponential changes in our complex and globally interconnected world, it seems so.

One could argue that every past generation may have thought similarly, but then, when we note how of late so much of our world's reported reality increased in absurdity, and often in plain sight, then to me it seems our times are quite unprecedented.

Still, I consider Life a beautiful gift, and to bear witness to the present times of change a great privilege. Yes, there is much darkness in the world, but this has always been so, as has the abundance of light. Perhaps some of the present contrasts enable us to see this more clearly! Whilst our media continues to paint a variety of human-caused end-of-the-world scenarios, it is not all doom and gloom. Poverty levels and literacy are both declining[1], our life expectancy is a lot higher than that of our forebears of only a few generations ago, and let us not forget the opportunity for learning that our times present. Naturally, this fantastic growth has brought a great many challenges too, however, balancing these is the proportional increase in the number of social structures[2], plus the element of individual choice! Where our dependence on our escalating technology may be of concern to some of the older generations, but we cannot forget that it also enables us to listen and learn from the wisest, and to access venerable teachings on Absolute Truth, without the need to travel to distant places, or back in Time!

Moreover the gift of life offers that which is most beautiful of all; love and friendship! Although we live in the world of people as individuals, we are not limited to being part of the crowd or alone. With very little effort we can choose to live on a path that confluences with, or is running parallel to that of others. Even when there are differences in ways or place of life, psyches and spirits can still be in sync. I always considered friendship as an essential building block in the process of life, to be comparable to DNA being a building block in its form. Where our respective journeys in search of meaning and truth rotate in parallel around each other, and every so often they connect in support of each other, or to simply exchange their findings. I feel my relationship with Swami Vidyananda is such a gift!

Our meeting was somewhat unexpected as I was not an Ashramite or a participant in yoga and its related activities. At the time when Swamiji and I met, my family and I lived on a beautiful piece of land where we had

---

[1] According to UN reports that, although our population grew by more than 400% over the past century, during this time the numbers on aspects of poverty and literacy dropped from around 75% of the global population to about 10 at present, and declining.

[2] According to UN, the coverage of social support structures expanded significantly in the past two decades, from approximately 30% in the early 2000s, to over 52% by 2023.

turned an old and neglected farm into a fauna and flora filled nature-reserve with guest and retreat facilities. We met 'by accident' when Swami Vidyananda hosted an unscheduled retreat there, one that had been scheduled elsewhere but which, due to flash floods, had become inaccessible. Although we just met for a cup of tea at the end of his retreat, I think our mutually inquisitive minds synchronized. Perhaps one could say we recognized the shared territory our respective life-journeys entered. This 'territory' is one that is hard to define as it has many descriptions, and I guess one can say 'the spiritual path', but that incorporates a large number of approaches, many of which do not synergize. I feel a more descriptive way would be to call it *'a place where truth seeking people from all walks of life find common interest and mutual ground on any and all things'*. Additionally present in this 'cup of tea' it seems, was that we were genuinely interested in learning about the activities and way of life of each other, which included gaining another perspective on all things in Creation, without judgement.

Today, with the mechanical encouragement to 'make friends' on the Social Media, the term 'friendship' is often diluted. One could consider incorporating comradeship, amity or companionship, and yet I feel these underrate my relationship with Swamiji, who I consider more than that. I also see him as one of my mentors and balancer or illuminator of things, and not just on the spiritual path!

Having had the privilege of more than 15 years of extensive and substantial exchanges with Swami Vidyananda, it dawned on me that sharing some of our thoughts, reflections and our kind of relating may be of interest others. Hence it is my wish that the reader finds some substance in these letters, and if not in its content then perhaps in the harmony of the exchange.

Vela Luka, Croatia
November 2024

INTRODUCTION
By Swami Vidyananda

John and I met on his and his wife Terri's private nature reserve in 2008. We came from very different backgrounds. Our spiritual paths outwardly were (and still are) very different. And yet we found a profound resonance in our exchanges.

I believe that the foundation for this was an openness and a respect for one another. This enabled us to really listen to one another. Remaining in harmony was priority: it served as the basis of our communication. Communication means to commune (comme-une), to become one. In our exchanges this seemed to be the driving force. Hence, although we had different (not necessarily opposing) views on things, this spirit of communication enabled us to listen to one another and to synthesise our views, which led to a deeper understanding in each one of us. When two points of view synthesise, they give rise to a deeper level of understanding, which transcends yet includes the previous viewpoints. There is great joy in this. As the basis of our friendship was openness and respect (and therefore love), the discussions we had were food for the soul, very enriching and delightful.

I follow the teachings of yoga and Vedanta. These concern themselves primarily with the journey of self-discovery: realising one's essential true Self, which is, according to yoga and Vedanta, pure consciousness. In the journey of self-discovery one becomes aware of one's conditioning. Seeing the world through a conditioned mind leads to a kind of illusory living, which we are all caught up on. To recognise the conditioning is an important part of the inner journey so that we can free ourselves and realise our true Self. Coming into contact with John helped me see how we are individually and collectively conditioned and how we live in an illusion created by various political, societal and other dynamics (which are discussed in this book). I found this discovery freeing.

I need to mention that the discussions between John and I always included my fellow ashramite and friend Vani, John's wife Terri, and occasionally our friend Uma. Everyone contributed to a delightful and uplifting exchange of heart and mind.

After John and Terri sold the nature reserve and moved to Croatia, John and I continued our conversations through email and the occasional video call. The synthesis of our exchanges continued through the emails. It was John's incentive to publish these. I was surprised but readily consented.

Cape Town, South Africa
January 2025

FOREWORD
By Vani Mataji

In the book, 'The Road less Travelled', the author M. Scott Peck writes about how he was taking a Sunday walk, and he happened upon a neighbour who was in the process of repairing a lawn mower. He was full of admiration for his neighbour and said to him that he had never been good with fixing those kinds of things or do anything like that. The neighbour's quick retort was – That's because you don't take the time.

Now, this is what Swami Vidyananda and John Brokaar do. They take the time to deliberate, reflect, contemplate and meditate. Their mutual love for filling their lives with the pursuit of the eternal Truth is a joy to behold.

Many a happy time has been spent in the company of Swamiji, John and his wife Terri. I found the conversations to be lively and thoroughly engaging, with plenty of wit and humour. Moments of togetherness, sharing insights, different points of view, and the love for the other expressed through attentive listening and questioning.

This Foreword is rather unconventional as I was not always privy to their online communication since John and Terri's move to Croatia, which makes up a significant part of the content of this book. But, being quite struck by their depth of knowledge and wisdom I feel that this book is a gift, as it would be their wish for us all to travel along that road less travelled open-minded and informed, by which we can better reach the ultimate goal of life, Self-realisation.

By Terri Brokaar

This book contains exchanges between two friends; one is John, my husband for almost thirty years, and the other is Swami Vidyananda, my friend for almost twenty years. Whenever Swami Vidyananda was visiting the retreat centre, tea was arranged and at the given hour, he would wander across the lawn to our kitchen. During these times, I was present for many discussions between John and Swami Vidyananda on almost any subject-of-substance under the sun, and most of which would take copious amounts of tea, coffee, and a number of hours.

Whatever the topic, their respect for each other and their respective paths through life, set the tone, and created space for discussions on spirituality, religion, history, people or geopolitics. All aspects were investigated with the desire to understand. These occasions were extremely nourishing for both heart and mind. The treasure lay not so much in the topics being talked about, but in their open and honest exchanges which inevitably led to meaningful insights. I particularly enjoyed how their vastly differing backgrounds none-the-less pointed toward teachings of a strikingly similar nature. The teachings direct one inwards and through earnest investigation reveal the greater harmony we are seeking to be within us! As such, the conversations in this book can be used for contemplation and examination, for they are flowers upon the path of life, revealing treasure should you care to look.

1

The Integral Flight of Starlings and the Interconnected State of All Things

During an evening on Welbedacht Nature Reserve, where The Blue Butterfly Retreat Center was situated, we enjoyed dinner with Swami Vidyananda, Vani, and Uma. As was customary, our cordial conversation on light and casual topics soon ascended to a deliberation of the deeper roots that ultimately connect each little topic. Within the ever-present consideration of the company and environment, which was harmonious and pleasant, we discussed the interconnected state of all things within Consciousness. This was consequently followed up by the following correspondence.

On Tuesday, March 25th, 2014, John wrote:

My dear friend Swami Vidyananda,

It was great to see you, Vani, and Uma this past weekend.

I found a video clip *(on the flight of starlings* – link inserted below) and have added some thoughts on it as I found it interesting and relevant and wanted to share this with you. If you have the time, I would very much appreciate your thoughts and insight on this.

http://www.youtube.com/embed/88UVJpQGi88

My thoughts are as follows: What I find interesting about this Starling phenomenon is not that the Starlings fly 'like' a giant organism but that most who look at this do not realize that, although each bird is an individual, they are - when in a flock - at that same time a single organism as well. The same phenomenon can easily be spotted in species such as ants, fish, herd animals, etc.

What is even more interesting is that, in general, people will not recognize that humans behave in very much the same manner. To understand this, however, one would first need to look inward:

If we review that our bodies contain trillions of bacteria - individual organisms with important functions without which we would not be able to survive - one may wonder at the fact that although we see ourselves walking around as a single body or being, we are an assembly of trillions of co-existing organisms[1].

Consider that each human body is made up of tens of trillions of cells and

---

[1] The average 70 kg body has around 30 trillion cells and 38 trillion bacterial cells.

yet, when we observe a single cell on its own, we find that it pretty much behaves like an individual being. It does what every other bird, fish, human does. It is completely aware of its surrounds as it adapts and responds to impulses and changes in chemistry or temperature; it feeds, it excretes, it reproduces and it fulfils the particular tasks for which it was created. But this is not a mechanical process, as some old-schools might teach, because if the 'brain' or nucleus were to be taken out of a cell, it would still do everything it did before, with reproduction being the only exception as the DNA, found in its nucleus, is now missing[1].

Could this indicate an individual little spirit in each cell, with an awareness of itself and its purpose as part of the whole? Whatever one may think or believe, it poses an interesting question.

If we then zoom in even further, into the quantum world, we find that atoms and their electrons do not behave mechanically either. The inexplicable and bizarre behaviour of quantum particles under observation[2] and further, how entangled electrons that are separated still behave as if they are joined (like twins), even led Einstein to refer to this as "spooky action at a distance"[3].

Then, leaving the microcosm and entering the macrocosm, we look at the human being and zoom out:

Imagine one were to ascend in a hot-air balloon over a city - as one rises and looks down upon the world, people first look like ants and then like little cells, city blocks begin to resemble organs, and the roads and rivers begin to resemble veins and arteries. Vehicles, trains, and ships look like blood cells bringing in nutrition and taking away the waste. As the balloon rises higher, one sees that the perceived organism is connected to other organisms (cities and suburbs) through roads and rivers and the idea of a body of sorts begins to form.

One may then realize that, in heavily populated areas such as within cities, man functions in very much the same way as the Starlings do, and there is often a particular spirit that affects the beings living there and that makes them get together to build, heal, teach or go to war...

Our ego makes us believe the self is unique and that at any given time, only exists on one level. It seems that even our spiritual thoughts have a kind of egoic undertone, as they generally consider that the soul has a karmic journey through numerous incarnations and gets punished if it does wrong or elevated if it does good. While this is not necessarily 'wrong', how often is it considered that there may be a contradiction in this view; we, as individuals, wish to become one with God but yet want to retain the "I" that we are?

---

[1] The nucleus of a cell contains the DNA, without which the cell is cannot produce the proteins and enzymes it needs to sustain itself, and will not be able to divide. It doesn't necessarily mean that the cell is not functional. **(https://socratic.org)**
[2] This refers to the wave-particle duality (https://www.britannica.com/science/wave-particle-duality)
[3] An object's motion can be affected by another object without the two being in physical contact; that is, it is the concept of the non-local interaction of objects that are separated in space. https://en.wikipedia.org/wiki/Quantum_entanglement)

If we all originated from the Universal One, to eventually return to become One with Him, perhaps we should begin by trying to see that we are never actually 'away' from Him but that we are always with(in) Him. We are, throughout our earthly existence, simply an extension of the Universal Oneness, regardless of whether we do good or bad - perhaps they are simply different sides of the same coin. Perhaps our lives here are all only an expression of God?

This is a complex question, and one that will arouse differing emotional responses from many. However, it's useful if one can see beyond one's individuality and can see how we, when we pass through life and then move on, simply merge with the rest of Divine Creation. During life we follow a string of waves within Creation, identified as individual groups like flocks, herds, civilizations, etc, and within which there are a limitless number of individuals who also comprise limitless versions and quantities of living, co-existing organisms.

One may then realize that we are a lot more, and a lot more complex than a mere individual being, as God's creation lives and exists on many different levels in the physical, mental and spiritual worlds. If one can accept that, then the interconnectedness of the physical, mental, and spiritual to the Divine Godhead becomes evident.

Best wishes,
John

On Friday, March 28, 2014, Swami Vidyananda wrote:

Blessed John,
Hari Om.

We had previously observed this very phenomenon.

Yes, one can see that it is one 'organism'. What is it that makes these birds fly as one bird?

Consciousness.

Consciousness is the substratum of the whole of creation and is beyond creation. Consciousness is the stuff of creation. It is the one unifying force out of which all has come, into which all shall return, and in which all is.

We may also call it God.

There is a hymn called Purusha Suktam in which God is described as a person, and his veins are the rivers, his bones the mountains, his hairs the trees, and all beings are a part of him. Swami Venkatesananda[1] used to say that we are all cells (phonetically similar to soul) in the body of God.

---

[1] Swami Venkatesananda was a Yoga Master who was a disciple of Swami Sivananda (Founder of The Divine Life Society) and who travelled and taught throughout the world from 1961 until 1982. He was the guru of Swami Vidyananda's teachers.
https://en.wikipedia.org/wiki/Venkatesananda_Saraswati

But each cell is no different from God. The stuff of the cell is the stuff of God.

He who realizes his true nature realizes that he is God; except there is no 'he'.

With Prem and Om,
Vidyananda

On Saturday, April 5th, 2014, John wrote:

Dear Vidyananda,
Hari Om.

With such wise and pure observations, I can see why you are the Swami!

The deep understanding of Consciousness is indeed a blessing and surely a lifelong quest and even then, in most cases, multiple lives! I guess it starts with achieving awareness and I have taken great interest in finding the interconnectedness through finding the fingerprints of God in *all* things, including material things, events, and even time and space.

Many of these fingerprints have been known for a very long time, from long before our own recorded histories. They were recorded by ancient civilizations throughout millennia in scripture, but also in their monuments and temples through the use of symbolism, alignments, geographical location, as well as the use of astronomy and 'sacred' geometry in the architecture.

One can consider, for example, a few known 'obvious' observations:
- Our planet turns on its axis every 24 hours
- Our planet goes around the sun every 365 1/4 days (more or less - it is 365.256363004 days!)
- Our planet's position as it faces the sun, has a 'wobble' on its axis as it rotates like a spinning top. The circular motion is known as precession or a Great Year and takes 25,920 years to complete.
- Before the implementation of the current Gregorian calendar, there was the Julian calendar, which was preceded by a solar year measured as 360 days plus 5 days allocated for fasting, celebration, bad luck or other, depending on where / when one was.
- If one divides the 25,920 of a Great Year by 360, one concludes that each Great Year equals 72 Solar Years.

Here is where the interesting part begins:

As a number, 72 represents an average human life in years, the average human heartbeat, the average percentage of water in the human body, about the percentage of the Earth's surface that is covered by water, the number of hours in the life cycle of the ovule, and so on. These can all be considered as co-incidences, but none-the-less, 72 is still accepted as a sacred number and reflected in most faiths, such as:
Egyptian mythology:
- Thoth's games every 72nd day[1]

---

[1] Thoth is the Egyptian god of wisdom, knowledge, writing, hieroglyphs, science, magic, art and judgment.

- Number of evil accomplices of Seth[1]

Kabala (Jewish tradition):
- 72 Names of God
- 72 Old men of the Synagogue (Zohar)

Maya:
- 7,200 Days were the K'atun Cycle[2]

Old Testament:
- 72 Languages (Biblical): Spoken at Babylon

Islam:
- 72 Islamic warriors at the Battle of Badr (624 CE)
- 72 Companions for an Islamic martyr

Chinese:
- 72 = Confucius' number of disciples
- 72 Planets between Heaven and Hell in Cao Dai[3].

Then, in further 'coincidental' numerology:
- 72 x 1.5 = 108[4] (you already know that one!)
- 72 x 15 = 1080
- 1080 Miles = radius of the moon in Miles
- 1080 x 2 = 2160
- 2160 = diameter of the moon & total of the inside angles of a Cube
- 2160 x 400 = 864,000
- 864,000 = Diameter of the sun in Miles
- 864,000 = Number of seconds in 10 days
- 400 = the ratio between the diameters of the Sun and Moon
- 400 = the ratio difference between the average distance from the Earth to the Moon and the Earth to the Sun.
- 40,000 = the Earth - Polar circumference in kilometers
- 72 x 10 = 720 = total degrees on the inside angles of a Tetrahedron
- 72 / 3 = 24 = hours in 1 solar day
- The number 24 can take one further into other realms:
    - 24 Hour Solar day has 1440 minutes (144 x 10)
    - 144 = 12th Fibonacci number and 12 x 12 = 144
    - 144 sq. Inches make up a square foot
    - 144 Cubits[5] = size of the Holy city of New Jerusalem in Revelations 21:17 as shown by the 7th angel
    - 144,000 sons of Israel redeemed in revelations
    - 144,000 = total amount of prophets in Islam
    - Inside corners of the Octahedron
    - Measurements of the Star Tetrahedron
    - 144,000 Days were the Mayan Bak'tun Cycle
    - 24 Hours = 86,400 seconds
    - 864,000 = The solar years in the Vedic age of Dwarpa Yuga

---

[1] Seth is the Egyptian god of war and chaos, murderer of Osiris.
[2] A k'atun is a unit of time in the Maya calendar.
[3] Caodaism is a Vietnamese monotheistic syncretic religion
[4] There are 108 beads in the Japamala or Mala, as well as the Rosary
[5] An ancient unit of linear measure

- If one were to Google these numbers, one also finds some silly, but still very interesting co-incidences, for example:
  - 864,000 = The distance in English feet between the base of Silbury Hill to Stonehenge
  - 864,000 = The distance in meters from Roslin Chapel in Scotland to Notre Damme (Both built by the Templars who brought the gnosis from the East)
  - Then; 8640 x 25,920 = 223,948,800 solar years = 1 Galactic year[1]

Another interesting feature is that almost all the numbers above (except for 400 and 24) add up to 9 or their combined numbers will add up to 9. The number 9 leads to a continuation of numerological coincidences:

- 9 x 9 = 81
- 81 = the only number that, if one divides 1 by it, one gets all the numbers in sequence: 0.1234567890123456789.
- 81 = the total amount of stable elements in the universe (the other elements are either subject to radioactive decay, or in the case of element numbers 43 and 61, do not exist unless they are synthesized)[2]
- 81 = the moon moves through space 81 times faster than the earth and is 1/81 the mass of the earth
- 81 - 9 = 72.

The list goes on – and one can apply same to numbers such as 33, 108, 153, 273, etc, and find countless connections (for example: 273 degrees = absolute zero, 273 days is the period of gestation, the number of times the Earth spins while the Moon spins around its own axis = 27.3 days, and the moon's radius in comparison to that of Earth is 27.3%.

When one studies scripture as well as the numerous ancient structures, it is quite clear that these measurements and their significance were already known by ancient civilizations, and they knew them well. They knew how to measure the Earth, Sun, Moon, Precession, distances, circumferences, and periods - more than 5,000 years ago - with an accuracy that we have only been able to calculate since we started putting satellite's up to measure things properly, and since we got GPS (in 1995). If one studies monuments such as the Great Pyramid in Giza, one encounters a myriad of details. Besides many of the other facts, figures, and mysteries – the Great Pyramid is a scale copy of the Earth and the moon, at a ratio of 1: 43,200 (this number equals the radius of the sun). In addition:

- The exact geographic location of the Grand Gallery in the Great Pyramid is 29 degrees, 58 minutes, 45.28 seconds North.
- If this location is translated into decimals, one gets 29.9792458.
- Now consider that this nine-digit number is the same as the speed of light, which is 299,792,458 meters per second!

The fingerprints of God are everywhere and in everything, we need but look. One can also go into the Golden Ratio[3] found everywhere in living things and man-made architecture but I will leave that for another email -

---

[1] Also known as a cosmic year, is the duration of time required for the Sun to orbit once around the center of the Milky Way Galaxy.
[2] The Periodic Table of Elements
[3] The golden ratio of 1.618 was called the extreme and mean ratio by Euclid

if you are still awake by the time you get to this conclusion!

Thank you again for your wise words in your response - they have reverberated inside me since you sent them. I hope the above will create further interesting conversations or correspondence!

Very best wishes,
John

On Sunday, April 6th, 2014, Vidyananda wrote:

Blessed John,
Hari Om.

WOW!

I was wondering why I had not received a response but now I know!

As you pointed out, God's fingerprints are left all over; and I must say it is astounding how science and mathematics have captured this. And as you also mention, this is ancient knowledge.

Again, I reiterate another one of your points that almost all of the sacred numbers add up to 9. 9 is a special number: I believe that in numerology it is considered a spiritual number.

Also, if you multiply any number by 9, and then add up the digits of the result, then you will get a multiple of 9. Keep adding the digits of each result and finally, you end up with 9. There is a mathematical expression for this which I have forgotten.

The mala ('Hindu' rosary) has 108 beads. You can link this with all the other knowledge that you have described.

And the Yogic scriptures tell us that the human being takes 21600 breaths a day (in normal health). Again '9'.

So, what does this tell us? The fingerprint of God is in our breath; nay it is in our hearts; it is the very heart of our hearts.

With Prem and Om,
Vidyananda

On Monday, April 14, 2014, John wrote:

My dear friend Swami Vidyananda,

In your reply, you state: "the human being takes 21,600 breaths a day". This to me may not be accurate as a more realistic amount is somewhere between 10,000 and 16,000 depending on a variety of factors (having timed my own!). However, my immediate observation on this is of course that "21,600" also equals 300 x 72 'Great Year days'.

Either way, all these number-related findings have led me to question their evident presence in so many places. *Why were all these special or 'sacred' numbers and geometrical features inserted or used, symbolically and occultly, in both eastern and western scriptures and architecture, including on some of the most ancient structures?*

It seems that a message - more ancient than our written and recited histories/memories - was inserted in the divine scriptures and is, with recent findings shining through eons to an antediluvian time, an era before the big floods at the end of the last Ice Age.

Mainstream archaeologist and scholars will not easily acknowledge the existence of antediluvian civilizations based on Atlantean myths, but cannot otherwise explain the presence of highly advanced, astronomically aligned megalithic structures that were discovered over the past few decades. These range from the astronomically aligned Giza Sphynx with its clear signs of water erosion (from a time when Giza was not in a desert) to the 10,000 + year old temples such as the one found in recent years in southern Turkey (Gobleki Tepi). Further, there is the 20,000-year-old pyramid in Indonesia (Gunung Padang) and many other old temples and cities that were built on much, much older structures. There are also numerous structures found submersed in regions (Japan / India) that only became submerged after the end of the last ice age (19,000 - 9,000 BC) and which led to sea levels rising worldwide by up to 120 meters (400 ft.) to the levels found today. These numerous sites, found all over the planet, are indicators of advanced civilizations in our past, civilizations that may not have left a mark of our kind of technology but one of high knowledge of cosmic/divine forces and an understanding of mathematics, geology, and astronomy.

Indicators of how advanced these civilizations were can be summarized by their understanding of:

- The earth's movements and dimensions (geometry and geodesy);
- The great year cycle also known as the precessional cycle – a process that takes 25,920 years;
- Our planet's movement around the sun, our solar system, and its place and movements within our galaxy;
- The interconnectedness of mankind with nature, our planet, and the cosmos that surrounds it.

What is further not generally accepted is that this rise in sea levels did not take place gradually as previously thought, but rather was a series of enormous, cataclysmic tidal waves that, in places, scoured the world's coastal zones with waves ranging from 60 - 200 meters high over a front of hundreds of kilometers, and barrelling across the continents at speeds of 100 - 150 km/hr. Considering that these coastal zones were most probably the centers and portals of civilization due to their access to the oceans and favourable climates, the sudden rise in sea-levels would have had dramatic consequences. This, combined with the effects to the earth's crust caused by the weight-loss of the Northern Hemisphere's icecap of 3 - 4 km thick and which led to earthquakes and volcanic activity due to a meteor impact some 12,980 years ago and further led to another 1,000 yearlong 'mini' ice age! The combined events would most likely have ended a civilization, reducing the majority of the human race to tribal existence in a stone age.

The importance of this epoch is expressed in many ancient monuments that have their geographical position and alignment, their entrances, tunnels and passage alignments, and so on, positioned according to the cosmic alignments and precessional settings. Although there are many facets that can be expanded on, the one that stands out as most important (to me), is that it points to this era.

It seems clear to me that civilizations did rise and fall in the past - but that they were of the highest 'elevation' when it comes to learning and knowledge, and were, before the big meltdown, able to map the world's oceans, and potentially able to foresee such events.

If this is the case, what would be the purpose of letting us know they were who they were? Is there a message for mankind to heed, and of course, is our current civilization taking notes?

Something else to meditate on!

Best wishes to all,
John

On Sunday, April 20, 2014, Swami Vidyananda wrote:

Blessed John,
Hari Om.

You evidently have a very slow breath, as a good yogi should.

Civilizations come and go. According to the Yoga Vasistha[1] evolution is cyclical, consisting of creation, preservation, and destruction. It tells of a saint who had witnessed the cycle of the cosmos for the seventh time!

Knowledge however appears to come and go, but actually is eternal. It is waiting for us to tap into. That knowledge depends on consciousness. Without consciousness, there is no knowledge. And when that consciousness remains pure, then knowledge will be used for the benefit of all creation.

With Prem and Om,
Vidyananda

---

[1] The Yoga Vasishtha is a classic text on Vedanta which explores consciousness.

2

Views on Causes and Connecting the Dots

Due to the inability to travel, the following email exchange was initiated at the onset of the 2020 global 'Lockdown'. We bore witness to a clearly instigated, bizarre form of mass-psychosis, that led the vast majority of trusting people, to comply to an unsubstantiated and exaggerated COVID narrative.

The absurdity aside, it brought forth illuminating insights into the nature of the human collective, especially so among those who placed their innocent faith in news bulletins and self-proclaimed experts who had familiar faces, but no actual medical background. There were, as a result, so very many who, unable to apply their own conscious perspective and faculties of formulation, were not in control of their own thinking and reasoning. We saw that many preferred to accept the versions of reality from sources that they had known for years were biased, deceptive, and outright corrupt, and which followed political or corporate agendas.

John's perspective was one that was oriented around the historical and present geopolitical spheres, and by observing how propagandized trends of a sociological kind, altered the psychic nature of the unawakened individual to a grotesque perversion of his or her conscious, conscientious, and compassionate one. According to John, the 'COVID 19' event provided irrefutable proof of the existence of a conspiratorial organization, composed of states, organizations, and corporate associations, that had reached its control over large portions of every dominant department in governments and houses of power, globally. With control over information, law, money, and the military, they had been able to wield authoritarian power and mind-altering influences over a 21st-century civilization that found itself addicted to screens and processed forms of entertainment.

Swami Vidyananda pointed out that much of this phenomenon was indeed very old and that it had, in many ways, been foretold by his past teachers' teachers. Swami Vidyananda's perspectives were based on his considerable spiritual work, including the teachings of his guru, the venerable Swami Venkatesananda, as well as a vast grasp on the writings of many wise sages. These indicated that the rise and fall of the ways of the world are not without purpose. It seemed that in this, each individual's personal practices were the only thing that would allow him or her to prevail, and that the powerful effects of prayer should never be underestimated.

As such, Swami Vidyananda showed John the light that continues to shine brightly in the darkest of nights; John showed Swamiji an understanding of the world of the unconscious and unawakened man in his (or her) pursuit of transcendence through unabated accumulation of things, people, knowledge and power.

What both saw was that the source of civilization's corruption lies deeper than just material wealth and things. Further, the logic and reach of its manipulators, were, from the eyes of the contemporary man and woman's sincere goodness and light, a very complex thing to fathom and process.

On Sunday, April 12, 2020, John wrote:

The ultimate cause of all human suffering is laziness.

It is not desire as some religions may try to translate it, as desire is subject to suffering.

Nor is it corruption, as this is only as deep as the ignorance of those subjected. Neither came first, they appeared simultaneously among men.

The ultimate cause of laziness is the absence of consciousness[1]; preferring the easy and lukewarm option has put men to sleep and blinded them to the laws of Causality.

The absence of consciousness is caused by laziness, as it is laziness that lets others to do their thinking for them. This type of thinking is typically the 'opinion-based' kind that differs from one moment to the next and disrupts the process of thought that is in the pursuit of Truth.

Hence, laziness and the absence of consciousness are integrally connected.

As are the absence of a desire for Truth and the absence of consciousness, integrally connected.

The depth of man's sleep is determined by the intensity and duration of his exposure to falsehood. As such, he finds himself surrounded by a darkness that he co-created, but it is too late - he cannot un-create this as it would require a return to the world of its creation, which no longer exists. Today there is only the world in which it is already manifest.

Having freely given up his liberties it is easier to return to sleep, accepting what is and the spoon-fed information he has become unable to think through.

---

[1] Where the word 'Consciousness' has different meanings to different people, as it is between SV and JB, J's perspective is expanded on in Chapter 15.

Now however, he finds himself subordinated (enslaved) into a belief that he must give more, to support the system, even though he does not see or understand what the system is. Consequently, he is divided and lost for all his days, the weeping and gnashing of teeth becomes ever-present.

For those who remain asleep[1], the transition will eventually come at great suffering and pain.

The observant will study man's body, his sensory awareness and his capacity to think, and realize that unlike all other creatures on the earth, man is a manifestation of both form and formless. When this understanding is truthfully embraced, from a perspective of the whole, a third force is born.

Where-as both his physical and metaphysical elements are from the earth, this third force is not of the earth. Being neither form nor formless, this third force transcends time and space as the three-dimensional man knows it, and it is eternal.

Man, being unique from all other forms of life, then becomes subject to a law that differs from that of the earth and present in Great Nature. This process is hinted at in writings of old, that refer to those who become conscious, sincere and correct, and thus, having more, shall have more in abundance; but from whoever squandered and no longer has, more shall be taken.

Hence it is also written to be watchful and stay awake: Those who opt to sleep and submit, enable those who take; but from those who are awake, nothing can be taken.

On Monday, April 13, 2020, Swami Vidyananda wrote:

Dear John,
Hari Om.

Thank you for sharing this wisdom. Did you write it? I just read it now. It is strange that just this morning I talked about the 3 Purushas mentioned in the fifteenth chapter of the Bhagavad Gita. The first Purusha refers to the body-mind complex, which is perishable. The second Purusha refers to the consciousness, which is as if embodied, but is imperishable. But the third Purusha, the Supreme Purusha, transcends both!

We have been thinking of you and pray that you are all well.

Yours in Prem and Om,
Vidyananda

On Monday, April 13, 2020, John wrote:

Dear Vidyananda,
Hari OM.

---

[1] By being 'asleep' J. does not refer to the dream state, but to not being aware of the mechanical and reactive nature of one's ego.

It is very good to hear from you my friend, I think of you often, and especially how you perceive the madness that surrounds us?

There is an Orthodox Christian Monk in the United States, whose work, amongst others, I follow. He renounced his church (and his TV evangelical life) and who now lives in a monastery where he practices a form of Esoteric Christianity. He guides an on-line community through the teachings of the Armenian mystic Gurdjieff's Fourth Way, by which I came into contact with him. I occasionally correspond with him, and he referred to these days as 'Holy Times', which I suppose is reference to a phenomenon akin to the 'rapture' that is written about in the Bible. There does seem to be a very clear and noticeable divide between people - and this divide is not along lines of faith, race, nationality, qualification, financial status, intellectual or social status - but between those whose eyes and ears are open and those for whom they remain shut; the latter being oblivious to the artificial nature of their reality. I have written more about this further down.

As to your question; did I write it? Yes I did. Are they my words - is the wisdom mine? As we do not own wisdom, I cannot claim such, but I guess one could say that it (the words) found my 'pen' intuitively.

The way I see the Purushas or third force is in sequential layers - some of which we can also define as sequential dimensions or rather Higher Dimensions.

More importantly perhaps, is that I do not believe that there is a coincidence in your talking about the three Purushas and the receipt of similar writing from me to this effect. In fact, yesterday, when I was doing the final editing on my letter, Terri mentioned a part of a book she was re-reading (*The Road Less Travelled* by M. Scott Peck) where Peck speaks specifically about how the element of 'laziness' affects the Higher Being (this is in the conclusions of his last chapters).

To me it seems obvious that, when in search of Truth, we are all spoken to by the same Voice, or the same 'Guide(s)'. I find that this Voice is particularly vocal (or audible) at present, in these most interesting of days, days that will likely, unfortunately devolve exponentially, and globally, into a world as yet unheard of. I have to state here that I have, since before the beginning of this event, and in fact over the past +- 20 years, been watching and learning, and over the past decade especially, waiting for it. It was, in my view, as inevitable as the consequences of building a house on ice, at the onset of spring.

The tone of my writing, on this inherent laziness, refers to the spiritual path of 'man', and carries a glimmer of hope that some will look inwards and recognize that which is, and has been, lovingly waiting for them. I sent an old and worldly-wise colleague of mine an extended version of this letter - one with a more blunt and geopolitical perspective added to it and have inserted it below for you to read, if you have time and find this to be of interest.

All that aside, Terri & I are very well. Nick is with us and of truly great help monitoring and running the farm without staff. Things on Welbedacht are quite pleasant actually, and I could get used to the peace! Matthew, the champion in 'How to best ride out a quarantine'; has left the island of St Maarten last week as crew on an ocean racer type sailboat. They are in St Vincent at the moment (which is part of the Grenadine islands), and will sail from there to The Netherlands next week sometime, probably via the Azores for a little breather. This will take him about 4 - 5 weeks, by which (hopefully) the global waiting game will be mostly over!

It is always good to hear from you, and I look forward to seeing you again soon. Please stay in touch and also send my love to all at the Ashram.

Best wishes,
John

My letter to the colleague:

"Dear Stuart,

Your reports and views on the causes and consequences of the global economic catastrophe are solid research; the statistics are irrefutable and with your background and understanding of these things. Thank you for collating and copying me in on these - I find your selections very informative and of great interest.

Although I too share a sense of resentment with the architects of this COVID program, since we have known of them for some time and what they are capable of, there is no surprise here. The same can be said for the masses of 'Democracy-orientated' 'sheeple'[1], whose infinite suggestibility brought on by their inherent laziness is no surprise either.

All this, however, brings a deeper-seated realization to the fore.

It may be said that I am taking a fence position - where I am on neither side of this debate, although I am quite aware and reasonably well informed of both. The 'actors in this play' (a suitable analogy), are the Kakistocracy[2] (the criminal so-called heads of state), who were promoted by the Technocracy (media, IT, AI & related sciences & general Intelligentsia) and the Meritocracy[3] (the manipulators of financial and economic control) on one side, and the so-called Democracy, being a great many people with various opinions and various states of awareness or rather sleep-state, on the other.

These are all closely related to each other and in fact, they are, in a way, one and the same. Although these factions do not see it that way, they are energetically connected to the point that they cannot exist for very long without each other, and across time, they only change places to become what they once struggled with/against.

---

[1] The term 'sheeple' refers to those who tend to subject themselves to the herd instinct and blindly follow the masses.
[2] A kakistocracy is a government run by the worst, least qualified, or most unscrupulous citizens.
[3] A meritocracy is the notion of a political system in which economic goods or political power are vested in individual people based on ability and talent, rather than wealth, social class, or race.

In practice, none of these entities actually have any idea, besides material, physical & psychological profits or losses, what the true and ultimate consequences of their actions, or lack thereof are. They are ignorant of the Law of Unintended Consequences, and thus, what these consequences are. The 'clever' ones, who so cunningly enhanced the populace's common hypnosis to believe in their Kakistocracy, do not understand that they themselves are cogs within the same machine, and thus, their actions are equally mechanical and predictable.

Some (many) will prefer to lay the blame on greed and corruption, but these two symptoms are only as old and deep as the ignorance they feed on; ultimately, what came first is and always was laziness. (and herein lies the ultimate cause of all human suffering - it is not desire as some religions may say, as desire is subject to suffering).

Laziness is the consequence of an absence of consciousness and the absence of consciousness is caused by laziness - a vicious devolving cycle. This downward spiral is not broken by any kind of 'evolution' as long as lazy men allow others to do their thinking for them. And this is not the 'opinion-based' thinking, of which man has plenty, that differs from one minute to the next, and which consequently suppresses the process of thought that is in the pursuit of Truth.

Hence, laziness and absence of consciousness are integrally connected.

As is the absence of a desire for Truth and the absence of consciousness.

From the super-man to the over-man to the under-man[1]; when left unattended, this devolving motion is natural on the equilibrium-seeking Earth. The reverse movement, however, (from under-man to over-man, to super-man) is not. As such, the absence of consciousness is and always will be natural in most people and all animals. As an example, if one takes away a creature's brain it becomes like a plant, if one takes away the vital force, the plant becomes a mineral. While this process can be externally implemented as such, it cannot be reversed. The result in life is that the man absent of consciousness, will, like the animal, only do what is instinctively essential. This is a process the cunning under-man will criticize or manipulate, and yet, a more conscious mind will simply identify it as laziness.

As man does not simply grow a consciousness without work, a lazy person will stay the same for the remainder of his or her life and be drawn into idolizing the physical & material world of form. Others, who intentionally choose to ask, act, and seek, become conscious by accident or fate (which of course are the same).

Either way, the world works the way it does for a reason. Whatever happens from here on, it is unlikely any of these trends will ever change. 'Citizens' will predictably become aware that they were duped by a dis- and mis-information war, aimed at stimulating their secret fears (of death and loss). They will then predictably become shocked, which then sinks into states of self-pity and depression, and as most are and remain lazy, many will prefer to take the easy route which is to distract or submit and go back

---

[1] A term applied to the level of consciousness, by Friedrich Nietzsche.

to sleep (Food, Football, Facebook, Sex, Booze, etc). Some, however, will be enticed to turn to anger and seek justice or revenge. Being cowardly by nature, they will hide their fear by cloaking it in acts of wanton violence, but by which they simply allow the enhancement of the police state or, if victorious, the implementation of draconian reforms of their own to ensure this cannot occur again. All along playing into the hands of those who understand how to manipulate their pawns' suggestibility.

The only way that this vicious circle may find an end is to somehow enable people (on both sides of the divide) to awaken; but this may only be feasible by allowing the present calamity to now run its course. Imagine, for example, trying to convince a 'flat-earth' believer that the world is spherical: to do so verbally / intellectually one may end in an endless debate and, if the flat-earther understands the human psyche and ego, and if he is a good orator, then he may even convince the spherical proponent to change or at least doubt his own view. The best way would be to take the flat-earther by the hand and say "Great, let us walk east and see what the edge looks like" and send him on his way (or if you like him, even walk with him).

My point is that, if the Pied Pipers[1] behind this act have been able to convince so many 'people' to follow this tune, place themselves under voluntary house arrest whilst they happily allow their praised heroic Pipers to burn their wealth, livelihood, and their children's futures, then perhaps this is simply their destiny. There will always be those who, like us, were born and bred in Hamelin, and who will sooner embrace conscious awareness and begin to smell the coffee.

As for the motivations behind the Meritocracy and Technocracy; I understand their beliefs, ambitions, and visions, and neither agree nor disagree with them. They are however predictable; today they have joined forces, but tomorrow it will be different as only one can rule, and neither one will want to become subject to the other. As a consequence, they will likely start a mutually destructive war on each other; regardless of who wins this, the outcome will be one where the 'sheeple' will turn back to some or other form of Aristocracy.

Nothing is therefore likely to change, but perhaps, some of the Body Snatcher[2] types mentalities, will actually create a higher percentage of 'accidental or fateful' awakenings?"

On Tuesday, April 21, 2020, Swami Vidyananda wrote:

Dear John,
Hari OM.

I am sorry I took a while to respond but I wanted to have a little extra time to read your two emails again. Believe it or not, we are actually quite busy,

---

[1] The Pied Piper of Hamelin is fable, dating back to the Middle Ages. It describes a piper who is dressed in (symbolic) multicoloured clothing, who can lure rats (and children) with his magical pipe. The piper is symbolic for an orator, whose magical words sway an ignorant citizenry.
[2] A referral to a movie; *Invasion of the Body Snatchers*, within which people are transformed by an alien force, into docile replicates.

as we are also offering daily online teachings besides performing some of our usual ashram duties and keeping up our spiritual practices.

It is inspiring again to note the 'coincidence' of receiving your writings and my personal study: I was reading the book 'Christ, Krishna and You' by Swami Venkatesananda, in which he also emphasizes the problem of laziness. And this is also mentioned in the Yoga Sutras of Patanjali[1] as one of the obstacles to enlightenment. And, to be honest, I can detect it in myself as well, especially when it comes to trying to figure out what is happening on the world scene regarding this so-called pandemic. And in the context of our current world situation, it is definitely correct to say that many people are too lazy to think and simply gobble up what is presented to them.

However, the problem of desire should not be neglected, which is why it is mentioned in the scriptures. It relates to when we wish to apply ourselves wholeheartedly to the seeking of the Ultimate Reality, which requires our total focus. We may find that in that very moment when we try to muster our entire being for the ultimate search our desires raise their heads, and the intensity of the search wanes and gets distracted. When the scriptures use the word desire, it includes attachments and the deep longings and yearnings of our hearts. And it is at that point that we discover that our search has been abandoned.

Although spirituality is indeed an integration of Spirit and World, this integration can only really happen completely, when we have discovered Spirit fully. By Spirit I mean the Ultimate Reality, That beyond which nothing else is. That Itself is integrated with the world already and reveals Itself in that manner finally.

Also, it is quite likely that laziness and desire are interrelated. We are never lazy to pursue what we desire, but we are very lazy to pursue what we don't desire. And unfortunately the many have desire only for the pleasures of life. No wonder that they are lazy in regards to the pursuit of truth. So, I feel that both these obstacles to Truth have to be carefully observed and studied, as they both trip us up and are deeply interconnected to each other.

In regards to what is happening in world politics, I am still unclear as to details and who is doing what, except that it is clear to me that things are not as they are presented. And for the moment we may have to live with these lockdown restrictions, and may also follow protocols, but without buying into the so-called 'realness' of it. Maintaining our spiritual focus is the most important and all-important.

As you rightly mention in your email to your friend: politics will go back to what it was before. That is because the superficial unity is based on the perceived common enemy (whether real, created, or non-existent COVID-19). Once that enemy is gone, the superficial and fragile unity will crumble into the previous battles. All this is a repetition of world history and it will keep repeating itself. Probably the same 'demons' keep coming back to do their mischief.

---

[1] The Yoga Sutras of Patanjali is a classic text on yoga and meditation.

But as we awaken, each one has to take their particular path of awakening and get established in it: it may be an activist like Mahatma Gandhi or a silent sage like Ramana Maharshi, or something in-between. Most important, I feel, is to become aware of our true spiritual nature, which is ultimately unaffected and eternal. There alone is Peace.

So, my heart-felt prayer is that you, your family, and all beings may attain that peace, yes including the various 'crats'.

With Love and Blessings,
Vidyananda

On Saturday 06 June 2020, John wrote:

Dear Vidyananda,

I apologize for not responding to your review of my email (The Cause of All Suffering) sooner - it had been sitting in my 'to-do' file but somehow I did not get to it. Normally I am quite driven to respond or attend as soon as possible and yet at other times, sometimes, I find myself drawn back there only weeks or months later. It is my impression that, as we are all expressions of the Divine, and as such participants in His Grand Scheme of things, maturation for realization is seldom an instant process.

This 'Realization', I believe you may agree, is not an intellectual, or physical process, nor is it one which one can attain when emotions are brought into play; it seems more as a process of 'emergence' which occurs when mind-body-feeling are in truthful balance, and then time and external circumstances are accepted in their role. Realization is therefore, in my view, a Gift that one attains not just through focus, work or suffering for reward, but by something that is quite miraculous or magical - a process we as humans may try to attain but which we cannot control. (I 'realize' that this long review/ comment on why I did not respond in April may also seem like an excuse for not responding sooner...)

In your response, you wrote: "*The problem of desire should not be neglected, which is why it is mentioned in the scriptures. It relates to when we wish to apply ourselves wholeheartedly to the seeking of the Ultimate Reality, which requires our total focus. We may find that in that very moment when we try to muster our entire being for the ultimate search our desires raise their heads, and the intensity of the search wanes and gets distracted. When the scriptures use the word desire, it includes attachments and the deep longings and yearnings of our hearts. And it is at that point that we discover that our search gets abandoned.*":

Yes, I agree of course, but perhaps it is important to consider what is meant by 'desire'. Is the desire for knowledge or material things not the same as the desire to know or serve God? Should we not consider caution on the process of desire, such as the desire to enhance passion, as even this, when left unchecked[1], may lead our passion to become obsession? Even when we refer to our search for "Ultimate Reality"; can this too not be seen as an end goal, a desire so to speak, and even that which we see as the

---

[1] Meaning: without Consciousness

path or journey to it? When man replaces his material desires to a desire to serve God, depending on what he wishes to achieve here and why, does he not risk merely replacing one form of desire for another? And if so, could one then say that the 'problem of desire' lies in its degree or object of attachment? I guess it all comes down to Consciousness.

In my own studies I have observed, when reviewing differing religious scriptures and spiritual practices, that these predominantly began from the Source or Origin of Pure Truth and were then given to man. Man, by his Creator's very Design is a 'Being-with-choice' (because only by actually having a choice can he discover his unconditional love and appreciation for God). As such, he will either choose to use *the Truth his reason perceives* to serve himself, or he to use *It* in service to God/ others. From there, each option or version of Truth he has chosen will, by his assessment of it, divide again into how he conveys or chooses to perceive *It*, and again and so on. This process of reality formation will continue until, at the bottom of his created pyramid of versions of Truth, a collection of all possibilities of various degrees of 'purity' is found, intermingled with the 'horror' & 'suffering' within human civilization.

I concluded from my studies that, as each eventual effect at the bottom of this hypothetical 'pyramid of versions of Truth' is, by proxy, interconnected to all things within *It*, *It*[1] *must* as such be reversible or better expressed, refine-able! Thus, as God is All and in All, then the only '100% Pure Truth' one can find within this 'pyramid', must lie within a *truthful* awareness and acceptance of, all versions!

Naturally - by 'acceptance' one merely understands; it naturally does not mean one condones or supports, as this again would be each one's inner journey within his or her multi-dimensional realm of infinite possibilities. It has been my conclusion then, that to truthfully love All things unconditionally, one must learn to understand them, and this understanding in itself is a complex thing to accept, as it requires a desire to know that which does not necessarily agree with one's own values. Neither laziness nor deferral will therefore allow much room here.

You then wrote: *"... it is quite likely that laziness and desire are interrelated. We are never lazy to pursue what we desire, but we are very lazy to pursue what we don't desire."* and *"... both these obstacles to Truth have to be carefully observed and studied, as they both trip us up and are deeply interconnected to each other."*

Yes, I found this to be a profound observation! They are indeed deeply interconnected and in fact, I would even dare say they are the same. This may not always be logically or *intellectually* explained except perhaps, through the process of Emergence[2]. This process, man has tried to do intellectually as, unbeknownst to him, it appears in many things, but is only possible when, again through work, he begins to understand how things

---

[1] Referring to the attainment of absolute Truth
[2] The process of emergence occurs when, out of a complex system – meaning one with many components – a phenomenon is made manifest, that was not present in any of its parts individually or within its sum.

can be both form and formless, as in simultaneously, and yet either one or the other at the same time! ;-)

As to the present world of 'laziness', politics, and demons; I do believe there are Mahatma Gandhi's and Ramana Maharshi's, as well as other activities in the works. In the perfection of a divinely balanced and harmonious interconnected Divine Cosmos, there must be! In fact, I am personally aware of certain projects of immense potential, that have been in the making for several decades and their time for 'emergence' is just about due. These are passive projects aimed at empowering the people by by-passing the controls from the globalist cabal. This may change the destiny of our civilization before its otherwise inevitable collapse, into a new type of civilization, one where every man and woman is enabled to be sovereign unto him or herself (at least, from a financial & authoritarian control perspective).

The state of our civilization is clearly on a knife's edge though, and additionally, what is occurring in the world may also be connected to a larger cosmic or dimensional clockwork which, as you have mentioned yourself in previous conversations, has occurred several times in the past[1]. Therefore, to lament it is futile and unnecessary because, as Vani Mataji so eloquently stated, 'God cannot be conquered!' We will be witnessing some birthing pains though.

Lastly, you stated, *"... to become aware of our true spiritual nature, which is ultimately unaffected and eternal. There alone is Peace"*.

And in that I too find, lies the answer! If we consider the various 'dimensions' we exist in - we can only 'see' the existence of our 3rd dimension - the 1st and 2nd dimensions are invisible and only exist in theory, even though they form part of our 3rd dimension. Through invisible, indefinable, and un-measurable Spirit, we may become aware of Higher Dimensions, and consequently discover that our third dimension is, to these Higher Dimensions, like the 1st and 2nd dimensions are to us!

From such a view, our very existence in this world is questioned - and thus, what occurs, must occur. We stay present and tuned, do what we can, and when it is necessary, and as such, remain in tune with Truth and Light, and consequently connect with the Higher Dimensions, where "There alone is Peace"!

With high regards and best wishes,
John

On Tuesday, June 9, 2020, Swami Vidyananda wrote:

Dear John,
Hari OM.

No need for an apology. It would have been alright also if you had not responded. It would not alter our friendship. However, I much value your

---

[1] The four ages or yugas refer to cosmic ages that are referred to in the Vedic / Hindu system. These four ages are known as Satya, Treta, Dvapara, and Kali, and humanity at present, is in the most degenerate one, the Kali Yoga.

emails!:-)

I like your term 'emergence'. Yes, realization is definitely not an action of the ego or mind: something beyond allows it to emerge in our consciousness. If we can be aware of that we will remain humble, grateful, and in a state of wonder!

This problem of desire is always under discussion. My teacher Sri Gopiji explains it simply[1]. Is the desire taking us up the ladder or down the ladder of spiritual evolution? If it is taking us up the ladder, it is good because it will lead to the realization of the Ultimate Reality, provided that the desire is purely for the realization of That. Otherwise, it would be like any other desire, which leads us down the ladder, or at best stuck on the same rung. Down the ladder means that we become more materialistic (in the broad sense of the term).

As you mentioned the Truth becomes expressed in manifold versions. This is most probably because when Truth is expressed through the mind-intellect, a division arises. This is because the mind only thinks in terms of divisions. And so these divisions keep on multiplying (or rather dividing) until one can no longer be sure whether a particular version has any resemblance to Truth or not. But, as you rightly point out, each version (even if 'polluted') has the potential to discover the Truth because it is still in the fold of Truth. We would say that one can start with any point of view and if sincerely pursued, that seeker should arrive at Truth; possibly even discarding the point of view, should it be realized that it is not really valid. Sincerity seems to be the key. And here comes the big question: how do I know that I am truly sincere? This question cannot be answered but should remain a question of inward observation. And this is where certainly many of us become lazy!

I am glad to note that you also foresee a positive future and that there are also movements of goodness. Yes, there is always the counter-balancing. The thing to watch out for is that the movement of goodness or restoration often becomes corrupt when it gains power, and then itself becomes the source of oppression. We pray that mankind learns.

On a personal note, I pray that you are not too badly affected by the lockdown in terms of your finances, despite that there is no income from your cottages and the retreat center.

I am also interested to know what your view is on the status of South African banks. How secure are they?

Blessings to you and everyone.

Yours in Prem and Om,
Vidyananda

---

[1] Sri Gopiji is a senior monk at the Sivananda ashram in Rishikesh, India, who has kindly taken time to teach Swami Vidyananda scriptural knowledge.

3

Views on the News

The following exchange occurred in parallel to the "Cause of All Suffering" one, and is a topic separate to the philosophical one, and more relevant to what was occurring around the Covid incident.

In the midst of a supposedly deadly pandemic that had all the appearances of the traditional flu, it became remarkably difficult to use the main-stream news in order to inform oneself. The following exchange was subsequent to this and based on the clear and evident escalation of the main-stream media's mis- and disinformation. What made it confusing was that much of the often falsified news was based on factual causes, but within which, certain effects were often falsified or even entirely fabricated – including fatalities that had no relation to the pandemic and yet were blamed on it. As a result, the falsified reality that was broadcast by the news, negatively affected the perceived reality and actions of the great many.

On Tuesday, June 2, 2020, John wrote:

My dear friend Vidyananda,
Hari OM!

I *know* this finds you well!

I saw two questions in your email to Terri regarding me and my activities. The one was concerning my writings; it is a complex project that I have worked on for a number of years. It is organic in many ways and it is guided to the extent that some things are only emerging after a process of maturation and once a number of 'buttons' have been pushed / adjusted / identified.

As to the other question on the 'real' news, what is news..?

The 'news' is a rather complex matter which entails a wide spectrum of subjects and detail. There is so much available and so very much information one can share, but one needs to *knowingly* wade and filter through many (mostly) layers of intentional disinformation, with numerous and various Artificial Intelligence inserted distractions along the way[1].

It is complex because in doing this filtering, the proverbial baby can no

---

[1] Where news on certain and tragic incidents are placed in-between news related to celebrities, sport events and general advertisements.

longer be identified from the bathwater, and in fact, the bath itself sits within a sea of baths[1].

For example, without an understanding of the world's multi-faceted financial systems that have been developed to function as they do for centuries[2], one will not understand the principles of domestic and global economics. The same can be said of politics, real-politics, geo-politics, or the idea of geo-strategic politics. One can expand from these into the fields of psychology (individual and social), hypnosis and the conditioning of systems of belief, including branding and marketing (otherwise referred to as brainwashing and propaganda), history, and certain mystical influences. Then, in the current environment one would have to have a basic grasp on flu-type viruses and the function of our immune system, without which most people will only see the answers provided by corporate sponsors. The actual reality is lost on many, primarily because, due to their innocent but uninformed minds, it is too far off and contradictory to their contemporary beliefs.

Thus, the world of Media has to many become the new religion. I find that unless one is asked a question on some specific detail or other that interests or intrigues people, one cannot be certain of the harmony or disharmony that the provision of alternate news information will bring. I have, for example, stopped sending out my general informative reports after 3 or 4 months because I felt that if others are, at this time, still reverting to what politicians have to say on the television, newspaper or social media, then my reports will simply bring uninvited negativity. (There were also some who asked me to stop doing so, because they were sincerely concerned for my safety). For those who preferred to not inform themselves and look elsewhere, however, there is no easy-out or miracle pill. Civilization as we know it, will not again be as it was before and perhaps things will worsen over the coming months or years. This is not all bad though, on the contrary, perhaps whatever has occurred and is still to come will have consequences, many of which will only be discovered at a later stage, once one is able to know and accept *what* is, *how* it came to be and *why* it was meant to be...

As for the day-to-day news; I avoid reading any of the news reports, especially as much of what is reported is then often contradicted the next day. Subsequently, I prefer to read what supposedly, verifiably occurred, and I say 'supposedly' because even the 'verifiable' is often falsified. It is important for people to know the typical strategies used to shape or remake their perception of reality; a strategy that is narrated in some detail in George Orwell's classic '1984' (written in 1953).

Personally therefore, to inform myself, I obtain the basic bits by following specific sources from people whom I know to be correct, and have a good

---

[1] "Don't throw the baby out with the bathwater" is an idiomatic expression for an avoidable error in which something good or of value is eliminated when trying to get rid of something unwanted.
[2] From the take-over of the Bank of England by the bank of Rothschild in 1815, to the creation of the Federal Reserve Bank – a private entity that controls every one of the world's Reserve Banks.

grasp on most of the subjects mentioned above. I can fill in the blanks using focussed thought, meditation and contemplation.

As always, I hope to not have bored, or confused you with my thoughts, and if not, do let me know yours.

With high regards and best wishes,
John

On Thursday, June 4, 2020, Swami Vidyananda wrote:

Dear John,
Hari OM.

Thank you for responding to my questions.

Thank you for sharing the news. I must admit that although I can see the truth of what is being said, I find it difficult to comprehend how these few corporates and organisations can actually do what they do. It is quite astounding to think that almost the entire world is in their pockets. It seems to indicate that when governments are in debt to these corporates etc, that they became slaves. But if I owe someone money, how can I become their slave?

I should just walk away. Unless they can beat me up! So, does all this mean, that instead of Coronavirus we may have had a war?

The desire to rule the world seems to be their aim. Can such endeavours finally succeed? So many have wanted to conquer the world but no-one has ever achieved it.

But Vani Mataji said it well, "No-one can conquer God." And that is finally our salvation. Be one with God.

And in the meantime we can only navigate the best each one can, according to his/her capacity and understanding.

God bless us.

Yours in Prem and Om,
Vidyananda

On Sunday, June 7, 2020, John wrote:

Dear Vidyananda,
Hari OM.

Thank you for your thoughtful, considered reply.

Yes, God is in all Things, and He is naturally also referred to in these 'Views on news"; however, this heading takes more of a physical-material-geopolitical angle and I would like to take the initiative by responding to it along these lines.

It begins with an awareness of the entwined aspects (like a double helix) of the physical and the spiritual lives we lead, and it helps to understand both. I was often asked by spiritually aligned people, why I spent so much time studying geopolitical matters and history's greater conspiracies as, in the perceived harmony of life and the spiritual journey, these matters seemed to them somewhat irrelevant. My answer was and still is, that if one sincerely wishes to know what something truly is, one must acknowledge the existence of both sides of the coin, so to speak, and thus, also know what it is not. This work cannot be determined by simply taking what one is being told as gospel; it is like climbing a steep cliff on a mountain, and sometimes you have to look down to appreciate where your passage did not end!

To explain topics such as the state of banking or the psychological enslavement of people (which is part of 5th Generation Warfare[1]) is complex and cannot be answered in a single letter – simply because there are many factors involved, and some of these have a history that literally spans across millennia.

Take the state of banking and currency, such as the South African Reserve Bank, for example. Although its sounds like a country's national bank, it is like almost every other Reserve Bank in the world, a privately controlled entity like the US Federal Reserve and its conglomerates the BIS and CLS Banks[2]. The banking world is truly a very dark horse; it is murky and complex to understand for most, even for bank employees in senior management - and this is done intentionally[3]. Very few understand the official explanations on their websites and if one perseveres, and cross-checks their activities by tracing the origins, functionality and end-destination of money, one will find very little of the 'official explanations' to be factually true. Indeed, the truth is often completely the opposite.

Today, the world of banking is no longer the place where you can safely store your money. It is in fact the contrary, as actually a bank is not very safe and to use it costs you in both fees and the devaluation of currency – which is done intentionally. It is therefore more a place of facilitation that manages money, except of course that 'money in the bank' is not even something that is yours. This is because while it is in their system, the bank can use it and even lose it. Money in the form of currency is therefore only a symbolic account of something that banks enable, so you can trade with the world around you (and even this ability is limited to what *they* consider you are worth!). Thus, with a now globalised economy and a population that is completely dependent on this system, it has irreversibly bound the economic welfare *and* mental fascination of a great many!

As a result of this entangled situation, it is not complicated to see how the world of money and banking has become a very powerful and very weaponized tool. If one can see this potential as such, and to that add the

---

[1] Fifth-generation warfare is warfare that is conducted primarily through non-kinetic military action, such as social engineering, misinformation, cyberattacks, along with emerging technologies such as artificial intelligence and fully autonomous systems.
[2] Bank for International Settlements, and the CLS Banking Group
[3] Henry Ford (in 1938) wrote: "It is well enough that people of the nation do not understand our banking and monetary system, for if they did, I believe there would be a revolution before tomorrow morning."

knowledge that the system is controlled by a remarkably small and closed group of selected individuals, one can begin to see how this system is a veritable noose around the necks of most countries. This is because most countries are very deeply indebted to institutions such as the IMF and the World Bank, both of which are directly and indirectly controlled by the American Federal Reserve Bank.

The system of money and banking can however, only work as long as the majority of people believe in it – in that they will accept it as tender for goods and services. This type of belief is like a type of sectarian religion whose dogma is under strict control – control that is maintained by manipulating what it is that people know. When we next consider what it is that people think they know, by looking at the world through their sources of information, we encounter the next dark act of deception. Among these sources are the social and main-stream media as well as the government's announcements. It also includes our academia, wherein a very large part of our social narratives and history are re-written to suit certain narratives, which are largely designed by the controllers of finance and information, to maintain the docility of our thoughts and opinions.

The system that designs and distributes the news, as we discussed previously, finds its greatest powers of persuasion embedded in forms of fear mongering. It is a relatively simple design that works well in all countries because, of course, most people are afraid of death, but they are even more afraid of the unknown. They especially fear what they cannot see, such as, for example, an invisible virus or the prospect of being 'considered unsocial' if they were to follow a narrative that differs from what is socially accepted. With regards to the so-called pandemic, for example, we saw how every public website had some form of Covid-19 or Corona virus link or article attached to it, with which they intended to repeat the lie enough times until, inevitably, it became truth[1]. This process has a two-pronged consequence; besides being mis-informative on things that matter, having one's perspective of reality altered subconsciously this way in order to make one do, or act, or think in a certain way, is also a form of enslavement.

If one considers this last view, one may wonder what it is that drives this destructive process, and to what avail? One may detect how, behind all these schemes of money, banking and our sources of information, there are very large and often sinister entities operating in the background. Some of these entities are in the form of very large corporations, and even most countries that are indebted now function as such – wherein banks regulate a country's austerity measures, for example[2]. Many of these corporations have attained such absolute power, that they exist over and above governance and law. In a way, these entities mirror a type of dark spirituality, as they encompass a form of immortality. One may see, for example, how

---

[1] "A lie told once remains a lie but a lie told a thousand times becomes the truth": Joseph Goebbels.
[2] Austerity is a set of economic policies that aim to reduce a state's deficits through spending cuts, tax increases, or a combination of both. Austerity measures are often enforced by banks on governments that find it difficult to meet their existing obligations to pay back loans.

the design of the multi-national corporation becomes quite surreal, in that it is a non-human entity and yet has similar rights as those of a person.[1] This may be quite unsettling, especially if one considers that through its countless servants, it has the ability to see, think and protect itself, whilst enhancing a form of immortality through its endless supply of highly ambitious and easy to replace officers. It therefore does not have to care much for the individual mortal, because ultimately, its primary desire and responsibility, is to profit, grow, preserve, and control.

To emphasize the bleakness of this system, we see how some of the world's largest corporate entities are interlinked through multiple mergers, and by a strange system of owning each other, they have expanded into amorphous entities larger than most countries[2]. But, regrettably, it does not just end there. With their common *pursuit for global dominance under corporate control,* the relatively small groups of men and women that control these corporations may personally differ in many aspects, but within the corporate structures where they are predominantly selected through relation, affiliation or initiation, *their service to the corporation entity is absolute.*

As a result of this design and structure, these rather surreal entities seek but to exist and to grow, and as such they have created a world that is increasingly complex and volatile. This entity-phenomenon has been able to amplify itself with the onset of artificial intelligence combined with the rise of technology; this, to the point where it may, to some, become quite depressing in that it seems there is nothing we as its observers, can do about it.

I do believe some faith is required though. Indeed, God cannot be conquered, but perhaps this is not an act against God but an act by humanity against its own arrogance. I do not know if it was His aim to allow these developments to occur, or if He ever had such an aim, or for that matter, if He is to be considered separate of the rise and fall of humanity. Perhaps, to find Nirvana, we as humans must accept that the existence of its opposite is equally real, and if humanity fails, or at least this version of civilization, then perhaps its failure will become the foundation of the next round of transcendental beings. Sometimes, it seems, we (as individual but also collective human beings) need to get to the very edge of our demise before true realization and evolution can be possible and can occur (or emerge), and which must then be at the risk of us not making it! Perhaps the overall journey of mankind through billions of lives along countless generations, is one of Emergence as well, and only by us experiencing a certain number of exposures, can the miraculous be found and realized as a Whole.

All that said: Virus or no virus, war or no war, re-engineered people or normal people, UFO's or no UFO's, it does seem that there are many

---

[1] In 2010 the US Supreme Court ruled that certain personal rights are accorded to corporations. Whereas this was primarily to enable political funding, the law has since been broadened to increase these rights.

[2] Some of the largest corporations, such as Black Rock, Vanguard and State Street control 74% of the equity markets, or in excess of US$ 11 Trillion, which is more than any one country has, except the USA and China.

variations of reality that different people see. Although we all eventually realise that whatever path we are on, will be a difficult one, my heart is not overly concerned about any of these paths' prospects. This is because *when they appear to be beyond our influence then their influences in turn are beyond our Higher Divine Selves!* Although the journey of the individual human being exists within the organism we know as humanity, the influence of the higher dimensional or *spiritual* One on the Whole is not the same as that of the *physical* Whole on One. The individual man and woman must therefore learn to exist within chaos, so that he or she can learn that the Light is also found shining indiscriminately here, and consequently, not be drawn into its countless sensory attractive distractions.

Our destiny may therefore not be found 'in the trenches' where once you may have found me in an earlier part of this life; instead, I now feel it is best one simply remains vigilant and patient. Whilst I do my meditations, contemplation and writings, perhaps some direction and some good will come of it, in fact, by the looks of it - something already is !!

With warm regards and best wishes,
John

On Tuesday, June 16, 2020, Swami Vidyananda wrote:

Dear John,
Hari OM.

Thank you for going through so much trouble to explain the details so clearly of the entire setup, which I only had a vague understanding of. I feel bad giving such a brief reply, but I am not knowledgeable on this subject and hence cannot comment; I can only learn.

Thank you also for the many references. Very helpful.

I shall also make some time to read/listen to some of the links you sent[1].

As I said, I don't have any comments, so this may just be a brief reply, but please do not feel that due to the brevity of my reply, your endeavors were in vain. I am very grateful to you.

I am also attaching a scanned image from a page of the scripture called Srimad Bhagavatam[2]. The translation is from Swami Venkatesananda. It appears that what we are witnessing in the world is as if destined; maybe not by a God but by humanity's consciousness becoming more and more materialistic. However, there is mention of a 'messiah'. This 'messiah' may also be the positive movement that you mention. I would be interested to know more about these. Can you share some thoughts on them?

Also, the same scripture gives hope that all of this can be overcome through enlightenment. This seems to be the Eternal Message.

---

[1] This referred to a number of URL's for verification or more informative webpages.
[2] The insert (see overleaf) is from the Śrīmad Bhāgavatam, also known as the Bhāgavata Purāṇa, and is one of the most important and revered scriptures in Hinduism. It is a Sanskrit text belonging to the Purāṇic literature and is celebrated as a masterpiece of Indian spirituality and philosophy.

I am also reminded of a verse from the Bhagavad Gita[1], which states that one has to have knowledge of the world (which includes our body-mind complex) and knowledge of the Transcendent. Then alone is there Wisdom. Knowledge of the world helps us finally to not get caught up in it, knowledge of the Transcendent helps is to remain uncaught and rather be established in Reality. Then we shall be able to live in this world, yet remain free.

You are very much on the Way!

Yours in Prem and Om,
Vidyananda

As quoted from the scripture of Srimad Bhagavatam, translated by Swami Venkatesananda:

"Sage ŚUKA continued:

Kali Yoga commenced when Kṛṣṇa departed from this earth. In this yuga, day after day righteousness will decline, along with the health, strength, and longevity of the people. <u>*Wealth alone will be the criterion for the worth of one's birth, conduct and character. Strength alone will determine who is righteous and just in his dealings. The relationship between husband and wife will depend on mutual liking. Cheating will be common business practice. Masculinity and femininity will be judged by sexual efficiency. Brāhmaṇā will be distinguished only by a thread they may wear.*</u> *Even the administration of justice will be perverted by bribery and corruption. Hairstyles will determine beauty. Vehemence of speech will determine truth! People will do good to society only in order to gain fame. The four stages of life (celibate-student, etc.) will all become one household life!*

During this period the good people will flee the corrupt cities and isolate themselves on mountains and in forests, being content to live on roots, fruits and honey. Elsewhere, people will be overtaken by famine, pestilence, drought and storms. Their wealth drained by taxation and robbery and their energy depleted by their own unrighteous living, they will die young. Even trees will become stunted on account of their own ruthless exploitation by unrighteous men. Cows will become emaciated and will yield very little milk.

At this time <u>*the Lord will incarnate in a brāhmaṇā family in the village known as Saṁbhala, and will be known as Kalki.*</u> *With unequalled splendour he will fly swiftly across the sky, destroying millions of robbers in the disguise of rulers. Then will the next Satya Yuga commence – an age of righteousness and holiness. Satya yuga will commence when the sun, moon and Jupiter rise together in the same house, and the Puṣya constellation is in the ascendant.*

Davāpi, brother of Śantaṇu, and Maru of the Ikṣvāku dynasty will continue to live in the village of Kalāpa. They will be alive when Satya Yuga commences, in order to teach mankind the essence of dharma."

---

[1] The Bhagavad Gita is a classic and probably the most popular text on yoga and Vedanta. It's profundity lies in teaching that spirituality can be lived in every-day life.

On Wednesday 17 June 2020, John wrote:

Good morning my friend,

Thank you for your very thoughtful and clear reply, including the attached translation from Swami Venkatesananda, which I shall study.

I am, indeed, very grateful for your thoughts particularly, especially as many see some of my views as challenging their own personal ways or beliefs; these are often misinterpreted assessments though, as there are, in my view, many doors and windows of varying shapes and sizes for finding and serving the House of the Divine - and perhaps they all are. Either way, my own philosophy on both the physical and spiritual journeys, has not been one where I would stand back to look through the said door or window, but rather one of entering with conscious faith in Divine Guidance, with a readiness to get 'down and dirty' if need be, and then see what comes of it. Granted, there were one or two 'complex pickles' I experienced and that it may seem I could have avoided, but then, only if they are seen as isolated, on their own. As part of the Whole, they simply had to be as well!

I will also try to elaborate on some of the positive movements I am aware of, of which there are as many. To see and understand these, we must enter both strings of the described double-helix[1] - as I believe movements of Light are apparent in both, and when we can observe them in combination, we see them to be capable of the miraculous!

Until then, I only wish to leave you with a quote from an old countryman that crossed my attention once again yesterday:

"I teach you the superman.
Man is something that has to be surmounted.
What have you done to surmount man?
What is the ape to man? A laughingstock or sore disgrace!
And just the same shall man be to superman – a laughingstock or a sore disgrace.
Even the wisest of you is but a discord, and a hybrid of plant and phantom.
Man is a rope over an abyss. A dangerous crossing, a dangerous wayfaring, a dangerous looking back, a dangerous trembling and halting.
What is great in man is that he is a bridge and not a goal;
what is lovable in man is that he is an over-going and a down-going."
(Friedrich Nietzsche)

With high regards and best wishes,
John

On Tuesday 23 June 2020, John wrote:

Dear Vidyananda,
Hari OM.

Thank you for your earlier replies and reviews, perhaps we are beginning to connect our individual strands of the said 'double helix'! Turning to the

---

[1] The double helix refers to the physical and spiritual paths, which are separate but interlinked, very much like DNA. (As without so within!)

spiritual/philosophical strand, it was very good to see it from your perspective; not just as my good and wise friend, but also from your order and your contemplated inner perspectives. Exchanges of this calibre are truly food for the soul, and I am honoured and rewarded with your insight and perspectives.

I agree with your views and would like to respond by, respectfully of course, questioning your teacher's view that some may find themselves 'ultimately being stuck on the same rung of the ladder'[1]. I do not know if this option, of remaining on the same rung, realistically exists. I say this because it seems all things on the physical earth and in the spiritual life-journey of man are in perpetual motion, and even if something seems cyclical and going around and around, then that is likely what a 'birds-eye' view looks like. From a higher dimensional perspective, this motion will likely resemble a spiral (where one goes up or down). Would you agree that if, for example, one does not continue to learn or work towards something, then one's decline begins, instantaneously? It is in my view that one of the reasons the world of humanity is what / the way it is, is because too many egos[2] are trying to avoid change rather than embrace it as part of their spiritual path or journey; this is because, to most, the process of keeping everything unchanged, or expecting that any improvement of living conditions without sacrifice or work, is seen as normal, sustainable and expected.

The same can be contemplated when considering man's perspective on evolution; most people today, especially Westerners, have separated religion/spirituality from their day-to-day lives, are positivist-minded, and as such, will disagree on the view that work is required for the inner-evolution of man, and believe that without work, evolution can still occur. (By this they insinuate that an evolution towards enhancement occurs even whilst one sleeps!)

In fact, I have found the effects of no (inner) work to be quite the contrary to this. In the societal environment of the positivist-minded, the achievements of civilization through combined labour and brain-power, are perceived as human evolution. They marvel at their huge achievements in projects of infrastructure, science, medicine, technology, and of course, war-making capabilities, and consider these as part of the evolution of man. Disregarding whether one chooses to see any of these achievements as good or bad for humanity, they are *seldom* caused by individual achievement and the participants only provide certain (relatively small) aspects of the whole. It may thus be said that civilization as an entity evolves, and this is true if one considers it as such. It seems though, that within this civilization, certain societal entities have evolved to such an extent that they have attained an unnatural but intelligent 'life' of their own and which consequently subjects its participatory units (aka people) to its primary need, which is to exist.

---

[1] See letter in Chapter **2**, dated June 9, 2020, where Swami Vidyananda wrote: "My teacher Sri Gopiji explains it simply. Is the desire taking us up the ladder or down the ladder of spiritual evolution?"

[2] 'Too many egos' refers to both the multiplicity in many individual people, as well as their respective identification with differing views and opinions.

Here we find another link between this line of thought and the parallel one we discussed earlier[1], that one may consider the corporation, political parties, organizations with uniformed order-followers, fundamentalists, etc, as such intelligent entities. The point really is, that achievements by a collective, are often at the expense of individual evolution - in fact, because the individual often only does component tasks, such as, for example, the conveyor-belt assembly-plant worker, he or she has no idea of the concept of the whole and consequently, their independently thinking mind and physical ability, devolves.

Having this understanding of these collective or body-corporate entities, as a matter of interest, my views are as follows:

- I do not consider Singularity[2] as an evolutionary process.
- I do consider a social group forming an orchestra, a choir, a meditation or prayer group, etc, as an evolutionary process.
- Subsequent to these considerations, one could say that I consider a process as truly evolutionary, when:

> (i) a group process aims to serve the individuals' interests, and
> (ii) the individual purpose of participation is the realization of the collective whole as an Emergent Force which, in turn, leads the individual participants' closer to their own personal enhancement.

I read the transcript of Swami Venkatesananda's translation of the Srimad Bhagavatam several times and found it fascinating, especially considering the age of the origin of these writings.

Also, your referral to the 'Messiah' is an interesting view! The positivist-minded will not believe it possible that a normal person could evolve into such a Being, as he does not believe it possible for himself to do so. Consequently, he will either wait for a Messiah until 'Kingdom Come'... or end up taking the Divine's Teachings superficially. The consequent limitations are quite unfortunate as such shallow beliefs may develop a psychic reality of its own, that then disrupts or dissolves certain 'organs of higher vision' which severely reduce the ability to understand the Divine / Divine at Work.

I believe that this is why and how so many hopefuls are easily deceived into following political promises, corporate guarantees, or pharmaceutical miracle pills. These offerings are founded upon the idea that it is okay to harm, subject, or enslave people one does not know, whose history, culture and traditions are not known either, or who are deemed as lesser beings.

Personally, I do believe in a Messiah, but perhaps from a somewhat different perspective. I am quite confident that Messiahs are and have always been among us. We probably encounter them in our day-to-day routines and we may actually have, in part, contributed to their Becoming! Some might find this perspective rather blasphemous, but it is not intended as such, on the contrary; in trying to understand the Divine at work, it makes perfect sense to me! How often do we find that we do things or influence

---

[1] See letter above, dated June 7, 2020.
[2] Singularity refers to the merger of man with artificial intelligence.

others, from a seemingly more conscious self. One may consider that when we are focused and present, we are able to use our analytical thinking mind as a tool, just like our hands, feet, and sensory apparatus, and how, unhindered by thoughts, we can sometimes accomplish things that we have never done before. We sometimes find we know things that we did not study or learn and may even write a complex composition of philosophy or poetry that, when completed, provides us, as much as the reader, with new insights!

Like you, I have over the years observed, read, listened, and learned from many Wise and Enlightened Ones, and even met a few. As such, I understand the path of the Guru or Messiah, and I formed along my journey a theory of such evolving-people, and even found them to be categorized into two types. For lack of a better description, I like to refer to these types as either White Knights or Black Knights. ('Knights' such as those correct and honourable ones who dedicated their crusade to the protection of pilgrims). My description of these is as follows:

- White Knights are the *keepers* of knowledge; when they act they do so passively, assisting ones who are in need when they are asked and able to. Working mostly in harmony with natural energies, they toil unseen and often unbeknownst to those they assist. Although they are already powerful beings, their risk of downfall from that elevated place is still possible. It can occur when they do not act when action is necessary, and they merely stand by passively. By this, they may lose touch with the material / physical world that man must exist in and consequently, they lose their ability to understand man and thus themselves.

- Black Knights are the *defenders* of knowledge and persevere to take the darkness to task. Working alone or with a small following, they will overtly act to address injustice, correcting the imbalances by using their knowledge, skills, and abilities to their full potential. Being occasionally ruthless, they accept the presence of collateral damage. Disregarding social, legal, and even certain moral boundaries in service to the Whole, they will not hesitate to apply force against force, but only if necessary. As equally powerful and elevated as the White Knights, their risk of downfall happens by erring on the side of excessive application of action, or getting caught-up in the action of things, and by which, they may lose touch with their inner being.

The Super-Being (aka Nietzsche's Superman), when in a physical form (like the Brahman?), will likely be embodied as either a White or Black Knight, whose journey it is to serve the Divine by serving humanity. Along this path, he merges the two Knights (and maybe even turns the Black-White Knight into a shade of orange perhaps..?). At the end of his journey, the Emerged Ones disappear without a trace, leaving no sign or legacy - except perhaps some of their teachings. Civilizations are often built on the teachings of such Emerged Ones, but as our civilization has crumbled into an artificial token of these teachings, there are most likely some Messiahs among us!

Perhaps it happens as it does in the comic books, wherein it says that Superman comes when He is needed. This view may lead a lazy man to use this as his excuse to sit back and wait - but would you agree that there may be an element of truth to this? As all things in the physical world, including human life, follow certain cyclic patterns, perhaps the return of the Messiah is one too?

In the end, change comes to us all, in one form or another. Life-changing events will occur, no matter how well one prepared or saved or tip-toed cautiously to prevent the unexpected. Hurricanes, disasters, wars, loss, illness, and death are not things we can avoid, and when they come, they evaporate savings, and flatten all protective boundaries. I believe that by understanding and being aware that such things occur, one may be quicker able to see when it has arrived and, by the timely letting go of that which must be shed, better steer one's journey within the unexpected event, and through it. As such, one may better learn and somehow gain an understanding from any unfortunate event. Consequently, and regardless of the coming or not of a Superman or Messiah, the onset of events is unavoidable, and we can, through Work, the Guru and the Teachings, momentarily transform ourselves into our own mini-Superman (or woman!).

As to your question regarding the positive movements I am aware of[1]. The problems of those human societies that are incorrectly referred to as civilization, will, if one has studied these for some time and without judgement, have yielded a relative understanding of the problems or rather, the causes of their situation. One should therefore be able to see certain positive developments taking place that are as yet unreported, and some of which are merely due to the Law of Unintended Consequences. These are the consequences caused by those who orchestrate the imbalances and who, although being very intellectual, cunning, and with immense resources, are not very wise. They are often stuck to very high opinions of themselves, and consequently are often in battle with peers or others for supremacy.

Today, in the process of 'globalizing' the world into a single order, these cunning ones are united in what they believe is a common cause; however, since these unfortunates are only aware of the one strand of our double helix, the one of physical matter, I believe they have built their considerable global fortress, on ice.

I am indeed aware of certain positive movements or projects, however, which have been in the making for several decades. The architects and orchestrators of these projects are generally people who seek legacy not within their own name, but within the betterment and liberation of the 'Everyman' and by which every man or woman may pursue that which is their birth-right. These designs, when released, will have the potential to act upon the sinister systems that have enslaved the bulk of humankind along with their wealth, life, and liberty. I believe, too, they will have the ability to spread like a wildfire in a strong summer wind, and to convert the "Too Big To Fail"[2] to ashes.

---

[1] See letter above, dated 17 June 2020.
[2] "Too big to fail" is a theory in banking and finance that asserts that certain corporations, particularly financial institutions, are so large and so interconnected that their failure would be disastrous to the greater economic system, and therefore should be supported by government when they face potential failure.

The bizarre conclusion of this view is that I personally know the inner-workings of at least one such a potential and veritable project, and I additionally have had an insight into others. Since I am only one in this world of 8 billion people, that means there must most certainly be more who know of such projects! Ultimately, Truth will prevail as it must, seeing that It is the only thing that that Is!

I look forward to seeing you and discussing this topic further, and others, next week!

Best wishes,
John

On Monday, 29 June 2020, Swami Vidyananda wrote:

Dear John,
Hari OM.

Thank you for your in-depth email.

You are quite right that life is never stagnant. Remaining on the same rung sounds more stagnant than what the expression means. The movement along the ladder, or of the spiral, is always in motion. As you say, some move up and some down.

This idea is also present in the Bhagavad Gita in terms of the three gunas, which are the three basic modes of the mind. Sattva guna refers to a mind that is spiritually orientated, seeking the Truth, and hence is on the upward spiral. Tamas guna refers to the mind which sinks deeper and deeper into the darkness of ignorance and hence gets deluded and is capable of sin, and hence is on the downward spiral. The third guna is Rajas, which is the desire-based and restless mind, which however is capable of both good and bad thought/action, which therefore oscillates between upward and downward movement of the spiral, hence remaining in ignorance but not necessarily sinking deeper, but not rising higher either, hence the 'bird-eye view' same rung of the ladder. Of course, ignorance is ignorance, so even if there is not necessarily a deeper sinking into it, it is still ignorance. Since so many people are in these two gunas, we find that we have the state of affairs we have. Both these gunas seek personal reward and comfort only, hence no endeavour to self-improve or serve society. Incidentally, Chapters 14, 17 and 18 of the Bhagavad Gita give really wonderful and detailed descriptions of the functioning of the gunas.

Re Evolution: Since most people do not give the meaning of life and the meaning of the existence any thought, they themselves cannot be clear on what evolution means. I think most people think of evolution as a biological (Darwinian) process, for which they are not individually responsible, which is the convenient way of continuing their lazy, desire-driven lives. On the other hand (rather contradictory) the so-called progress is of course attributed to themselves as well, making themselves feel good, even if they have not contributed anything. Then there are those individuals who strive for money and power, or maybe scientists who strive for knowledge, who are contributing to so-called progress. If the motives are money and/or power, then they will of course dominate the first group.

However, I don't see technological or scientific progress as a process of evolution. To me evolution means spiritual growth. An enlightened street sweeper has evolved, whereas the bloating scientist is unevolved. Of course, as seeker we should be careful not to think of ourselves as evolved and others unevolved as that leads to a superiority complex, and that is anti-evolution. But on the whole I would regard evolution purely as a maturing in consciousness. And whether that happens as a whole or individually is debatable.

Yes, it is sad that most people do not believe that they can evolve spiritually into the likeness of any of the Messiahs they believe in. The strangest thing is that the Messiahs teach though that it is possible! And really speaking, the Messiah or Guru is really a Divine Principle at work that responds to the seeker, and whose Grace (in whatever form that Grace comes) helps the transformation.

I like your White and Black Knights categorisation. Both are necessary and complement each other, maybe keeping each other in balance, so that there is no likelihood of either of them falling into the traps you mentioned. And yes, the Supermen (which we may call Avatars) would play either role, as is required. The Bhagavatam (from which I had sent you the scan) is full of such descriptions: the Avatars being one of the core themes. However, they seem to only appear when the righteous people have put forth their foremost effort and realise they require some higher intervention. So, definitely the Avatars will not appear without there being effort on our part.

I was hoping to be able to respond to the remainder of your email before we meet but alas, time is against me!

So, I look forward to more discussion, but more importantly, just yours and Terri's company!

Yours in Prem and Om,
Vidyananda

4

Thoughts with a Friend

With the Covid related narrative intensifying, and 'Lockdowns' lifting only to be imposed again, the effects on the crumbling psyche of people under authoritarian measures was becoming more evident. With most people having no way to learn the facts due to the overwhelming amount of state sponsored fiction, John was still attempting to send some factual information to the few who had asked, and this included friends in other countries and territories, such as the US and Europe. He had at that time, stopped sending out informative emails to his growing mailing list, simply because of the potentially negative consequences for him and those on his list. As these potential consequences would not be a factor on person-to person-correspondence, he would write to one person, and then forward it, on an individual basis, to those who he thought it would be of interest and use to. Due to the spiritual meanings within some of his views and findings, he would forward some of these emails to Swami Vidyananda in order to align the swami's spiritually oriented insights with his own more geopolitical, sociological and conspiratorial insights.

On Monday, August 17th, 2020, John wrote:

Dear Vidyananda,
Hari OM.

I am forwarding you an email I sent to a good (and devout Christian) friend of mine in the US, with the purpose of obtaining your thoughts on my views, and especially the last paragraphs.

Where the living-in-a-bubble concept is typical in most versions of contemporary life, I observe that Americans live in a particularly thick bubble[1]; it being one that is cunningly manipulated by their very large corporate-state controlled media. Many Americans are quite oblivious of this and the world outside of their own, and as a result, they are also unaware of how their own trusted ways are gradually being eroded by an increasingly authoritarian system. When, for example, I look at it from the outside, having made quite a few visits to the US over the past twenty or thirty years, I find that the way of life in the "land of the free"[2] is worse than what most Americans believe. Many do not, in the slightest, understand what is happening to

---

[1] John's views are based on regular travels to the US as part of his profession since the early 90's. Having many friends, colleagues and professional relations in the US, he studied its Constitution, its geopolitical sphere as the world's sole superpower, its realpolitik, its social scenes, its financial and corporate structures (and its history).
[2] In reference to the national anthem's lyrics of the United States.

their illusory freedoms, or what goes on inside their heads; they have lazily lost their ability to find out what is happening around them, too or why it matters. It seems to me that most Americans are unable to see through their multiple layers of conditioning, particularly the layer of being an Exceptional American[1] first and foremost, then the layer of political affiliation, a close second, and then their own values on militant dominance in every part of life and which is seen as the American Way. Subsequently, they are entirely unaware of their impending dilemma.

South Africa, in my view, is not far from this descent. This is because there are seemingly ever fewer influential persons in positions of power, who maintain an unbiased understanding of governance and how the world works, and who have truth and care in their hearts. Unfortunately, due to a track-record of decades of injustice, the 'levers of power' are held by authoritarians, who will not allow those intelligent few that do have Truth and Care in their hearts, to hold onto the 'levers of consequence'.

Anyway; following some conversations with my American friend, I wrote the letter below, and am forwarding it to you, in case it is of interest.

The reason for my correspondence to this friend, was because it seemed too few could see the size of the behemoth affecting the Unites States, and through it, influencing most of the world. The point I try to make is that the systems this behemoth employs are actually quite mechanical, predictable, and manipulate-able, and as a result is a very real and very dangerous something in the world of contemporary life. Because I believe I am able to see and understand it for what it is, as well as the world-order it seeks, I also believe I have seen the signs of its nemesis. Regardless of the reality or nature of this 'nemesis' though, the road ahead will still be very bumpy, complex, and bizarre for most. It will at times be beyond anything that is logical, and until or unless man finds his (or her) way out of this confusing darkness, the Sun and Great Nature may become the servants of God, as they have before[2].

As you and I discussed previously, ours is said to be the fifth of seven prophesied civilizations[3], and we may be in a kind-of transition towards the sixth. While that may be so, I still feel we must do whatever work is necessary to overcome the challenges of the transition from the fifth to the sixth era, while still honouring and maintaining a Guiding Light.

Heavy stuff to digest perhaps, but maybe this can be seen as food for thought. Either way, I felt like sharing it as, on this somewhat lonely planet, I do not have many friends like you to share my deepest thoughts with - I can therefore but hope that these do not cause you indigestion or keep you

---

[1] American Exceptionalism is the belief that the United States is distinctive, unique, and exemplary compared to other nations.

[2] In this, John makes reference to cyclic patterns of catastrophic earth changes, such as the end of the Pleistocene (aka the Ice-age) and the Great Flood, both of which likely had solar or cosmic causes.

[3] The concept of seven prophesied civilizations is found in various cultures and traditions, including those of the Yugas in Hindu Cosmology, the Seven Races of Theosophy, the seven civilizations referred to in the Mayan Calendar and other Mesoamerican beliefs, as well as The Seven Ages of Man in Western Esotericism.

up at night!

Best wishes,
John

"Dear Philip,

In follow-up of our discussion, some history and some more words ...

History repeats itself and what happens today has happened before - but more recently (in short):

World Wars 1 & 2 were, like most wars, premeditated, orchestrated and very preventable. That the consequences were known and intended is not just my opinion - these are facts that are well known to bona fide historians[1] and by anyone who is willing to look at facts without judgment, bias, or agenda. The purpose was three-fold:

1. To unite the Western world behind a single type of belief system or dogma, one with political-financial-economic designs designed to enable absolute control by a central and closed (non-democratic) entity.
2. To create the State of Israel (this has <u>nothing</u> to do with the Jewish faith), through which the (Christian and Jewish) Zionists could exert global power.
3. To create a New World Order, seeing that the old one was too stuck in national borders, politics and traditional ways, that were no longer providing impetus for growth.

The new system of belief or dogma (1) was the idea of so-called Democracy (which I see as the 2nd largest cause of the problems of our civilization[2]) and (2), the systematic brainwashing of citizens through the compulsory state-controlled 'Education' (which I consider the 1st largest cause of problems). Media control and manipulation of nation's economies through control of their currencies (FIAT money[3]), were a close second to these, but these were enabled by, and therefore subject to the systems of 'Education' and 'Democracy'.

The old-World Order is that of the British Empire of course, which, from the middle of the 19th century became centralized with the intention to create the Zionist state of Israel (which occurred in 1948). Although this may seem unrealistic to some, consider that it was signed off in 1917, by the Balfour Declaration, and then, consider the absolute power of the AIPAC over the US Senate and Congress[4].

---

[1] Most officially recognised writers of history are those who are inserted in state-subsidized and regulated academia, such as universities and colleges, and where any challenge of the state's narratives has dire financial and career consequences.
[2] See Book II of *The Way of the Pilgrim*, Chapter 9: *The Curse of Civilizations: Education, Religion, Entertainment and Democracy*
[3] FIAT money is a government issued currency that is not backed by a precious metal, such as gold or silver, nor by any other tangible asset or commodity.
[4] The American Israel Public Affairs Committee (AIPAC) is the Israel lobby (or Zionist lobby) in the United States and comprises individuals and groups who seek to influence the U.S. federal government to better serve the interests of (the state of) Israel, which does not always consider what's best for it's people.

The new World Order was largely orchestrated and made manifest by the USA, the UK and the State of Israel (the USA as the muscle or the sword, the UK as the center of finance, and the State of Israel, the brain). Again, these are verifiable facts.

The World Order we grew up in has seemingly served its purpose, and now, like the British Empire before it, it has largely outgrown its usefulness. To replace the present old system, which is limited by countries with borders, their internal politics, and constantly changing regimes, it needs to be destroyed so that the new design, based on a borderless multinational New World Order can arise from the ashes, like the mythical Phoenix.

The USA is a complex entity though; it is very powerful and resilient. Being perfectly located halfway between the East and Europe, with no natural enemies on its borders, the 2nd largest oil reserves in the world, numerous minerals, and an enormous military, its geopolitical and geostrategic power is unprecedented. For a new world order to erase the behemoth known as the United States, it would need to weaken and divide it internally first. This can occur through civil disobedience, instability, and above all, cheap money in the form of credit. The latter will eventually make the currency worthless, and once the currency has been sunk, the economy (which in the US has been artificially hyper-inflated for decades) will also be sunk. Next law and order, together with the military machine will become unable to sustain itself, and when this happens, the consequent public disorder will likely prevent any fast economic recovery.

The worst is that all this would occur outside the general public's awareness, which is distracted by fake-news crises and entertainment.

So, my advice to you my friend, is to stay out of the trenches. Stay away from conflict and avoid angry people. Do NOT think you will find reason and logic among the absurd and insane or those who feel they are politically correct; you will not find it or any friends there.

Inform yourself - but be very careful of the gods of media, including TV, newspapers, social media, and GOSSIP!

Meditate, listen to your heart, and all will be well. Follow Truth, Love, and Acceptance, and weather the hardship; this is especially important when you realize that not everyone will want to follow you on your path of Truth, Love, and Acceptance (as in forgiveness), as they likely only believe in strength, control, sex and substance. This may include some whom you love dearly.

I know you can, and I know you will be fine.

You are in my thoughts and prayers, every day.

Best wishes,
John"

On Thursday, August 20th, 2020, Swami Vidyananda wrote:

Dear John,
Hari OM.

Thank you for sharing the email with me.

I took a while to respond because I wanted to have time to read it carefully again so that I could respond properly.

After reading it again, I realize there is no response necessary. I feel that you have encapsulated the whole thing. Although I am not so clued up about all the power games (I only suspect that they are happening but know no details really), I have also reminded myself of the Wisdom Teachings, that the most important thing is to connect with the Divine within regardless of circumstances. And this requires a constant attempt to keep the mind and heart focused on the Divine. Then, as you said, all will be well because that is the nature of the Divine.

So, I haven't really added anything and hence my reply is 'Thank you for sharing'.

God bless you.

Yours in Prem and Om,
Vidyananda

5

Our Trip

This exchange took place late in 2020, following a brief window when the globally orchestrated 'lock-downs' were lifted for just a few weeks. With a mere few days' notice and on an impulse, John and Terri decided to travel to Europe in an attempt to rendezvous with their two sons.

Although the two boys were in entirely differing circumstances, including careers, countries and even continents, somehow, an almost unexplainable confluence in the midst of extraordinary times occurred. Having exited the southern tip of Africa and traversed different continents, they simultaneously found themselves situated near a favourite family destination, in the vicinity of Split, Croatia, mere few miles apart.

Moreover, John and Terri traversed 5 countries, across many borders that were opening and closing with no particular pattern or notice and then met the boys at that very same spot! What made this even more challenging was that each border crossing was dependent on the unreliable, roll-of-the-dice "PCR Test" that was, oddly enough, being administered by almost every country. The odds, therefore, of them succeeding in this rendezvous, were heavily stacked against them.

On Wednesday, November 25th, 2020, Swami Vidyananda wrote:

Dear John,
Hari OM.

I pray that you and Terri are well.

Are you back in the country? Did you have a good trip?

Someone shared a document named *"UN Agenda 21"* with me. Not sure if you are interested.

Love to all.

Yours in Prem and Om,
Vidyananda

On Thursday, November 26th, 2020, John wrote:

Dear Vidyananda,
Hari OM.

We are very well, and it is always good to hear from you.

We returned a few weeks ago after a most interesting trip: it took us 7 flights, though 6 cities, in 5 countries, needing 4 Covid-tests, across 3 continents to see 2 sons making up 1 event!

Too many interesting things occurred to write about them all, but I have inserted at the end of this letter, a correspondence to a good friend who lives in the US and therein it describes how, with open eyes and understanding, confirmation is found that there is clear, present, and indisputable Guidance in all things that are undertaken in Truth, Love and Acceptance. I believe you will read it with interest but little surprise.

Thank you for that attachment of the UN Agenda 21. To the open-eyed observer who is correctly-informed-through-unbiased-research-and-hardwork, it is extremely toxic. I can imagine that many people will be very excited about this expected unity – this is so because they are unable to see the veritable digital prison – both mental and physical – it represents. Few seem to question or understand the loss of liberty that indirectly follows when the daily challenges are removed, such as choosing between doing the work oneself or having machines do it (laziness). In this one will also lose the lessons that are learned through experience of what is good for one part of oneself, but not the other; that is, the physical part, but not the mental or spiritual part. In this way, one is seen to prefer a finite measurable reward over the invisible infinite one!

Few have the ability to understand the sequence of events that follow when one gives up one's independence in thinking, doing, loving, feeling, etc. Do they consider what people will do if they no longer have a purpose, a necessity? Or how the absence of their physical usefulness leads to a deterioration of their psychic stability. In time, becoming unable to see truth from propaganda, they will not recognise the toxicity of cunningly inserted words such as the following[1]:

"private militarized police", meaning *corporation-controlled,* and

"sustainable development", meaning *population control, aka eugenics,* and

"cancer-fighting technologies", meaning *gene manipulation aka eugenics,* and *"free vaccination for all"*, meaning *enforced inoculation aka eugenics,* and *"New 4th Industrial Revolution enables all to work from home"*, meaning *lack of personal contact, which reduces the divine magic or unity of interconnectedness,*

and *"enabling people to live care-free"*, meaning *as long as we can impose lock-downs unobstructed, i.e. voluntary imprisonment for one's supposed safety.*

---

[1] These are terms and descriptions used by the WHO and the UN, in Agenda 21 and Agenda 30.

This leads to the denial of the individual initiative; by which intuitive and spiritual growth is lost.

My view on this UN Agenda 21 (which was written in 1992), is that it is designed to be a portal through which a series of global legislations can be manipulated. The current Covid-driven 'reset' is only a small part of it. Few can see this though, and even fewer understand this sort of thinking. Part of its design is to take the natural flow processes of Great Nature out of the equation, and many elements behind its look-good-feel-good resolutions will have, as a cost, a level of control on every level of human life. Agenda 2030, which is equally at play, simply spells out an enhanced implementation of Agenda 21.

You know my feelings on this and although these views are easily verified, many will still perceive them as negative, pessimistic, or doomsday-like. However, when people are unwilling to take responsibility for their collective ways (of deferral), then the unavoidable consequences on almost every facet of our observed 'civilization' will be such that they cannot be undone. This in particular, is then exacerbated when those who hold the levers over the ultimate political and financial controls, can no longer be touched by worldly things.

Spirit[1] will prevail though, even though we do not know how or when, and this will likely have a cost of its own. But it is probably what Biblical texts refer to, when they say: "There shall be weeping and gnashing of teeth"[2]. As mentioned previously, there are other forces at work that I know of, but it is still a bit early to go into these – what I can say though is that they are passive by nature. The intention behind the design is to gradually return much of the wealth and ability to exchange back into the hands of the common man.

Regrettably, much of the damage that was done to governance worldwide and the psyche of many during this Covid theatre, is irreversible. One thing that perhaps changed for the better, is how the divide between believers and non-believers of a 'Covid-pandemic' became visibly defined, which led many who were previously in an indecisive no-man's land, to shift to truth.

As for those who moved away from truth, I find that, besides prayer, consideration, and kindness, there is little else one can do for them. This is because most of those who don't know, believe they do, and thus cannot be taught. It also does not help, for example, to argue or even debate the situation – as new religions now guide them, such as those of technology, entertainment, and propaganda flavoured with sensory promises, and fed by mass & social media.

Naturally, truth will persevere, but we may have to wait a decade or two to re-educate the next generation!

Please stay in touch, share your thoughts, and send my love to All,

Best wishes,
John

---

[1] 'Spirit', as in Holy Spirit or Divine Spirit.
[2] The Holy Bible, New Testament: Luke 13:28 and Matthew 13:50

PS. As mentioned above, an insert to my friend Philip, which aimed at offering an insight into the Divine Orchestration of things:

"As you know, in between 'lockdowns', we managed to rendezvous with both our sons in Croatia. The reason I want to mention this to you, is that the odds of this were, in my view, miraculous! But allow me to explain...

Matt was in St Maarten[1] at the beginning of the quarantine (aka the so-called 'lock-down'), and Nick was at home with us - which was a godsend as this made the months without staff on the reserve easier by a HUGE margin.

By April things were closing down fast, and Matt – in order to not get stuck in some little room, had 2 options to leave St Maarten. One was a paid job on a boat headed for the US, and the other was a no-pay position on a world-class racing yacht to Amsterdam. Being the adventurer he is, he chose the latter and after a thrilling ocean crossing, arrived in Amsterdam in May, found a job on another boat & a place to stay. Nick applied for positions as a dive instructor all over the planet and by June was offered a position near the town of Split in Croatia. By that time, Matt had worked on a few boats in Holland, but none that struck him as homecoming, and eventually left a decent job with decent pay on a large boat (doing maintenance work) for a sailing opportunity in La Rochelle, France. This did not work out as expected, and leaving a somewhat complex situation with no money, he put his CV out. He found some interim work helping an English family by teaching them how to sail their boat and made friends for life, and at the end of this period, he received position offers on two boats. One was on a smallish sailboat in Poland, the other on a large mega yacht in the Mediterranean. He chose the latter due to his wanting to learn about hierarchy in organization. Of the hundreds of ports in the Mediterranean, each with dozens of marinas, it so happened that this boat was docked in Split, Croatia.

In the meantime, back in South Africa, a number of things occurred with us simultaneously. Our borders re-opened on Oct 1st, Terri's UK passport, which she'd sent off to London for renewal a few months before arrived in the mail unexpectedly on Oct 3rd, and in addition, we were informed that both our sons would be in the Split region for only another week or so. This led me to buy tickets right away, which was a story with a few incidents of its own, and to do Covid tests on the same day, the 5th, but which would take 48 hours to get the results; we had bought the tickets without knowing what they would say! On the 6th, the day before we flew, I had a chance encounter with the son of a very good friend of mine, who was able to look after the reserve and its business during out time away, and on the 7th, Terri and I flew to Istanbul. On arrival we had to spend the night waiting for the result of yet another Covid test, in preparation for next leg of our journey. We passed that one too, flew to Frankfurt, and from there on the 9th, we flew to Split, Croatia. After all that, on the 10th we managed to organise that both boys and two of us could be together for 1 1/2 hours; a meeting

---

[1] An island in the Caribbean

that coincided with Nick's work, training dive students, and Matt's evening off before having to be back on the yacht for self-isolation before leaving port a few days later.

If you are able to follow this chance upon chance itinerary, you'd note that this rendezvous was either by the skin of our teeth or providence. Had we been delayed anywhere, we would have missed the opportunity... Now, I'm no mathematician, but I do believe that the odds of success for this brief overlap of paths were billions to one![1] Had we known the odds to be this small, for such a small window, Terri & I would likely not have made this risky effort - but which was now turning into quite an interesting trip! In each part of the adventure, there were 2 or 3 chance happenings that could spoil the whole plan, and so we had to think and act fast, and trust fate.

But 'providence' and 'interesting' went further:

On Friday 16 October, both boys left Croatia, within a few hours of each other. Nick went to France, and Matt, out of ten-thousand possible destinations, went to the island of his birth, St Maarten!

Then, en-route, the morning after departure, Matt's boat sailed through the straights of Messina, a channel between the southern tip of Italy and Sicily, and coincidentally, when looking out of a porthole, saw in the distance, the very same sailboat he had sailed to Amsterdam on a few months before. Of the tens of thousands of boats out there, at that moment in time and by him looking out at that porthole in that very direction, he saw it – the likelihood of this being 'luck', is likely one in billions as well..

And so, our experiential journey of the miraculous continues - pure magic my friend, the Divine Pulse!

All this will be called luck or fortune by many, but I know that luck is unlikely. Witnessing the miraculous is, from my perspective, not necessarily something that carries any special meaning, except perhaps to reveal that one is being guided by higher 'oversight'. When we make decisions – even if others consider them irresponsible or reckless – I find that if they are made with a well-intended and trusting heart, then even if the outcome is uncertain or uncomfortable, it is still the path I am meant to be on. Such outrageous (or miraculous) coincidences are then, to me, always very reassuring, as they are akin to seeing the Divine's Footprints accompanying me along my way.

There is to me nothing else to these but That!

In various forms of scripture, it says that 'all is written'[2], and that may be true. However, I do believe that there are differing versions of reality, and that the differences are shaped by our perceptions. There is also the hypothesis of parallel lives. Your dad used to speak of these as well and say that there are (can be) as many as 7 'parallel' lives – which I believe can

---

[1] If one made a casual but calculated guess, it would in fact be somewhere between 1 and 10 Billion to 1, if one considered each step as a decisive one, and being one chance of between 2:1 and 10:1, each step naturally multiplying the preceding one's odds, and in this case, across at least 10 such steps.
[2] Jesus is said to have phrased 'It is written' 17 times across the four gospels.

also be translated as 7 versions. In some of these, we allow ourselves to be herded like sheep, in some our laziness has overcome us and we refuse to leave our comfort zone when we know we have to, in some we try to take shortcuts or avoid a necessary but unpleasant difficulty, in some our courage fails us, and yet in others, we are awakened from our hypnotized state and leave the herd to go on our own.

As a student of history, I observe and study the different manifestations of the psychology and social relationships of people. As such, I have I found that, in the old world of Europe, people will conform with the collective systems of societal rules, even if they make no sense. They will automatically accept law and order as something natural, even if the same systems got them into such destructive trouble a century earlier and then again twenty years later[1]. There are however, many such misguided people in your country as well. They may be correct and truthful people, who remain true to their essential and individual selves, but are unaware of the influences on their psyche by the collective, the crowds, and the media, to which Truth matters little.

The message in this, my good friend Philip, is as follows:

Stay away from crowds, the fanatical masses and the herds of polarity, especially during these times of escalating absurdity and madness; steer clear no matter how right or convincing they may seem about their 'ways', or how much fear they sow for not joining them. Know that these masses of supposedly opposing sides, are often no different from each other, like opposite sides of the same coin, but which are still best avoided. Think things through carefully and independently and meditate before acting - the world is changing fast and it will likely become very difficult for most!"

Saturday, November 28th, 2020, Swami Vidyananda wrote:

Dear John,
Hari OM.

What a countdown! I look forward to hearing about the 'interesting things'!

The human vs machine (or AI) dynamic is most interesting. I was watching the second Zeitgeist movie and to my surprise, they suggested that technology is the answer to all our problems. They believe that the evil we see is due to the monetary system, so it should be replaced by technology, or what they call a resource economy. However, evil does not arise out of a system. Systems are neutral: it is the good or the bad in us that uses or abuses it. When will mankind begin to look within?!

I agree with you that work is important. It is part and parcel of our spiritual unfoldment. And for those of us who are not actively on a spiritual path, it is a way to keep us out of mischief. It is completely idealistic and unrealistic to think that non-working people will be happy. Of course, slaves are also not happy, but non-work leads to sloth and all its cousins.

I also agree with you that the only way through and out of this is the spiritual

---

[1] World War 1 and 2.

way. These powers are very powerful and the ball has been set in motion long ago and is now gaining momentum. I keep reminding myself of what you said right in the beginning: We will have to remain non-attached to what we will witness. Along with that non-attachment, we should endeavour to get established in the Divine more and more. And keep praying for Divine Intervention and guidance.

I feel sorry for the young ones. Already we know of one friend whose 10-year-old son is suffering from depression and anxiety, which was traced by a therapist to the lockdown. While our friend was taking her son to the therapist, she met a mother and classmate of the son at the therapist for the same reasons. One wonders what the long-term effects of this is. Much like post-war trauma I suspect. The saving grace is that we are essentially spiritual beings and therefore the trauma does not touch the inner most being, which is where the true healing happens.

Thank you for giving glimpses of your miraculous journey to meet your sons! I look forward to hearing more.

Please send our love to Terri,

Yours in Prem and Om,
Vidyananda

6

Your Christmas Talk

During the Christmas celebrations in December 2020, Swami Vidyananda published a video of himself on YouTube. On it he expressed his views on the various Covid-related matters, which included the harmful side-effects caused by the wearing of masks and the danger of the untested so-called vaccines. It was naturally offered to a substantially divided audience, wherein the die was already cast in the minds of many; however , Swamiji felt it was important to be truthful as well as to be clear without offending, or causing fear, or concern. It was the guided beauty and perfection in this presentation that John observed, and which led him to write what follows.

On Wednesday, December 30th, 2020, John wrote:

My dear friend Vidyananda,
Hari OM.

I very much enjoyed your talk, and naturally took note of the considerable skill, knowing the complexity of the subject and audience you chose to address!

For one, I saw you 'bobbing and weaving' (like an experienced boxer), around the new laws and regulations, many of which are in constant flux. For two, I noted the considered way you were 'dodging' many a devotees' sensitivities, that were rooted in a fearful state of mind. From this perspective (as a judge), I will rule the bout's outcome as an undisputed knock-out ... naturally with you still standing!

It was indeed, a very good, well-compiled and interconnected talk, that was well presented.

Here all is well. We are very busy, and although this is a blessing for us, we look forward to the slower post-holiday routines. My personal work continues, but I have not spent much time following the 'news'. I find it simply too complex to find any semblance of unbiased truth among most (if not all) main-stream media channels. I have also not sent out any updates[1] to advise on whether what is out there is factual or not; I feel, by now, most will have chosen the narrative they wish to stand behind. Regrettably, I find most have chosen to ignore bona fide research and testimony, and have for reasons of their own, chosen to follow the pharma and state sponsored narratives.

---

[1] John had been sending out more bona fide news updates to a private mailing list.

We note how the forces that stand <u>against Truth</u> continue to grow in mass and power. Every time some fact and truth revealing project hits the surface, it is either quickly censored, or it is drowned out by the main-stream media's globally orchestrated compliance and guilt-enhancing 'tsunami'. Now, while some of this may then contain tokens of truth, the larger volume usually contains a combination of confusing and chaotic propaganda, with incomprehensible and often sinister agendas.

There are of course many good and powerful; entities and persons hard at work to bring the ship of humanity back on course:

but this is a large ship,
and it is a ship that has been off-course for decades,
and it is a ship that has a very small rudder,
and it is subject to the winds and currents that are strong, and severely against the attempts of correcting it!

With best wishes to you and all at the Ashram for 2021,
John

On Saturday, January 2nd, 2021, Swami Vidyananda wrote:

Dear John,
Hari OM.

I feel honoured that you listened to my talk. Thank you for your kind words. I am glad that you are having business, and I guess many need to get out into the country.

Thank you for the links. Quite something!

It is truly sad to see that scientists are succumbing to power and wealth, and are willing to be unrighteous, which is a severe blow to science and of course humanity. My repeated prayer is that these scientists wake up from the errors and make the necessary amendments. Furthermore, my repeated prayer is that other scientists speak up more and challenge the entire thing in a united voice, taking legal routes, even through the international courts, if necessary. Since the whole thing is based on "science", it requires scientists to challenge the "science", and it is the duty of scientists to stand up. It is of course not in their nature, generally, but I feel this could be the way out. And also I repeatedly pray that righteousness should prevail. May our prayers fructify.

Much Love to you and Terri,

Yours in Prem and Om,
Vidyananda

On Sunday, January 3rd, 2021, John wrote:

Dear Vidyananda,
Hari OM & Happy New Year to you and all!

Thank you for your response.

Rest assured, the number of scientists and academics representing the truth is great, but many are under severe threat for coming out in the open. There are almost daily examples of specialists in differing fields, who have lost their jobs and stature as a consequence of sharing the truth, and there are many others who have simply had their postings deleted or censored and their voices drowned out.

Besides looking after one's own mind and the minds of those in one's care, there is very little the contemporary man can do about the current situation. One may consider how little of the officially declared causes for the various 20th-century wars is true, or for that matter, who was truly behind the high-profile assassinations of the 1960s and 1970s. In the same token one will find little that was unavoidable in the causes of the various more recent wars and military conflicts in far-off countries. The same will be found if one were to make independent studies of the various economy failures that ruined the savings of millions across the decades; these too were often intentional or at least avoidable, and without consequence to their architects.

Peaceful protesting, for example, can be considered as equally futile, especially when they are not in favour of the state narrative, when they are easily and often purposely made violent[1]. A peaceful protest or rally that then turns violent, regardless of how the violence started, is even worse; as violence only begets and enables more violence, this then enables the implementation of more laws, often backed by militarised police.

We will regrettably see many examples of such 'state-organized-or-initiated' civil unrest over the coming months - the first, likely to occur on January 6th, in 3 days' time, in the US...[2]

It seems to me the only solution lies within the heart of the individual. Although this too is easily corrupted by external forces, the onus to protect and sustain the light and the truth within it, rests with the individual. If the heart (and mind) are not observed and guarded, one automatically adopts the external or collective-ego. This entity will then drown out the voices of truth with an orchestrated cacophony of narratives; often written by a number of trained, well-funded, and organized 'narrative script' writers!

All that aside, 2020 has been a most revelation-filled year for me; one with some very complex questions and contemplations, but also one with many good and interesting experiences! My heart did experience regular moments of negativity and intense darkness though. This, I noticed, was mostly due to seeing so very, very many people irretrievably stuck within the mass-psychosis[3] which was caused by their attention being

---

[1] See *From Rallies to Riots*, by Brandon Ives and Jacob S. Lewis in *The Journal of Conflict Resolution*

[2] John's prediction was spot on. On January 6, 2021, the Capitol Building in Washington, D.C. was (supposedly) 'attacked' by supporters of U.S. president Trump, which was publicised as an attempted coup after his defeat in the 2020 presidential election. This report was fraudulent, as there is sufficient evidence to indicate that the rally began as a peaceful march, and the violence that ensued was instigated by non-partisan actors

[3] Mass psychosis is the phenomenon whereby large groups of people experience shared delusions or irrational behaviours, that are often triggered by social or

mesmerized by screens that contained falsified narratives and thus created false realities. Seeing the impact of this agenda on both the psychic and physical wellbeing of people, I noted that, unless these ones were able to come to this realization and extract themselves before it was too late, they would likely remain stuck there for the rest of their days.

You see, much of this Covid program follows a pattern whose design began shortly after World War 2, or perhaps even earlier, as the dark energy that drives this pattern, is one that has always been part of humanity. In the same way, I continue to see certain movements with great and beautiful people in them, that indicate that the tide will eventually turn, and still within our lifetimes (Inshallah!). I read some work by Maurice Nicoll[1] recently; having lived through WW1 & WW2, he wrote that war was the one thing that could shake many people out of their spell-bound, mesmerized states of sleep. In confirmation of this, the Carnegie Foundation[2] had conducted certain studies between 1907 and 1909, and concluded similarly that nothing shaped the public's opinion and mind-set more than war. Naturally this kind of thinking substantially aided the geostrategic plans that were being put in place for the wars of 1914 and 1939. Considering the collateral damage of these wars, perhaps one can consider that the present actions may be a less barbaric alternative.

Either way - 2021 is going to be a very bumpy one for many, and likely bumpier than 2020. Economically it will get worse, and there will likely be additional lockdowns and restrictive regulations, riding upon purposely created and amplified civil unrest to motivate these.

This knowledge is not hidden and is openly applied in the shaping of societies everywhere. And yet, the average individual remains oblivious. Subsequently, I do not believe it is possible to awaken the sleeping ones gently. One may suggest they switch off their TV, Social Media, and all other forms of sponsored news, and not listen to all the so-called experts that pervert the public's reality, but such efforts are usually wasted. As you explained so very well in your talk: "This is not reality". The TRUE reality is what we see through our eyes when we go for a walk or drive, and meet, socialize, and speak to our family and friends using all our senses, and not anything that is filtered through limited and processed 2-dimensional electronic screens. But this is complex as most are afraid to switch the screen off.

Did you know that sugar is supposedly more addictive than tobacco and drugs? Well, I honestly believe that the contemporary desire to keep up with one's artificial TV-reality, is more addictive than sugar, tobacco, and drugs combined! This (to me) is the real problem because a sudden change of one's artificial perspective on reality could lead to severe trauma, and serious issues for one's mental stability – especially if, under such a false perspective, one did things that were harmful to others! As we

---

environmental factors, as well as 5th Generational Warfare (i.e. mind control).
[1] Maurice Nicoll (1884-1953), a student of G.I. Gurdjieff, friend of P.D. Ouspensky and C.G. Jung, and a neurologist, psychiatrist, author and Fourth Way teacher.
[2] The **Carnegie Foundation** funded in 1905 is a U.S.-based education policy, research and government advisory center.

can see in history, economies can be restored and cities rebuilt with relative ease, but the damage that is done is to the collective psyche of people, can last for generations.

As for these 'lockdowns', the lack of physical contact and interaction is probably more damaging than the sensationalism and fear-mongering in the news. Perhaps we must suggest to people that they bend their cherished rules just a little, and sneak out to go see, hug and talk to a friend and to sit close and look each other in the eyes, at least once a day! And then, instead of TV & Netflix, advise them to take some of that extra time to read a good book, listen to music, plan to drive somewhere nice and then just go there, or study something novel, like a language or the name of stars!

Best wishes,
John

On Tuesday, January 5th, 2021, Swami Vidyananda wrote:

Dear John,
Hari OM.

Thank you for your sharing.

I think you are quite right that the ordinary person is quite helpless unless there are some strong characters like Gandhi, which God seems to supply very little of.

Although it is from one point of view unfortunate that one cannot penetrate the heart of another to help them; on the other hand that is also the safeguard from being irreversibly polluted by ill-meaning individuals. The saving grace in all this is that the Self is ultimately untouched by all this. Whoever discovers that Self lives in Truth and Divine Power, which Gandhi called 'Satyagraha'.

I share your sentiments that it is sad to see that people are stuck in their view of reality and hence caught up in suffering. I must say I also feel sad at the thought of how many people have been simply thrown into poverty. We see it here in the streets. Also, I feel helpless at times as to how to get the ashrama going, when people are locked into that COVID (non)reality and unable to come out of it. Often I feel that if we were a private enterprise we could do as we deemed fit. Alas, that is not possible. So, we have to see how everything unfolds.

I am rather skeptical about the awakening of humanity. There was so much talk of that in the first lockdown. Lots of WhatsApp videos floating around of feel-good awakening: time to one's self, reflection, etc. But, still, everyone continues in the same way. And now the fear is even greater than before. We see it in the eyes of people. The other day was the first time that someone scolded me for not wearing a mask on the mountain! If there is any awakening from calamities, it seems to be short-lived. How quickly we fall asleep again. There is a saying in one of the Upanishads[1]: Wake

---

[1] The Upanishads are ancient texts that describe the Absolute reality. Each

Up! STAY ALERT! Having a wake-up call is one thing, but to remain awake is quite another.

I also feel, as you do, that 2021 will have a lot more in store for us. If people think and hope that we will get normality soon, they might be in for a surprise, and maybe regret.

Yes, we have to hug etc. What a wonderful moment we had on the mountain when a friend of Vani's greeted us with an unmasked hug! For many this means having to overcome fear. Maybe they'll get to that place when the isolation begins to be worse than the fear of death. Our quality of life has to be more important to us than the fear of death; maybe then there will be change.

In the meantime, I realised also that I can get swept up in all this, albeit from the other point of view. Important to keep the mind focused on what is most important: the Self. There alone is Freedom.

Wonderful to write to you, speak to you, and be with you. We get a taste of that Freedom.

With Prem and Om,
Vidyananda

Upanishad is an independent text leading the seeker to enlightenment.

7

An Interesting Development

The following exchange was based on the discovery of a variety of activist incidents, of a non-violent nature, that were underway. This action, by brave people with veritable qualifications and reputations, was often met with violent force from a now militarized global order.

One such action was that taken by Reiner Fuellmich, a German lawyer and spokesman for the Corona Investigative Committee, a non-governmental investigative committee based in Germany. Using his legal expertise and an international panel of colleagues, which included a judge, Fuellmich set up an on-line international court, took the state to trial and determined that the actions by the state to the people, were illegal, immoral and harmful.

Tuesday, February 8th, Swami Vidyananda wrote:

Dear John,
Hari OM.

I pray that you are well.

This is the website of an initiative by Reiner Fuellmich, called the Grand Jury: https://grand-jury.net

What is happening on your side?

Yours in Prem and OM,
Vidyananda

Wednesday, February 9th, 2022, John wrote:

Dear Vidyananda,
Hari OM.

It is good to hear from you and thank you for this link. The forces against this darkness are phenomenal, especially if we consider the writing of Fuellmich. However, having been unable to find a court within the current system to hear their plea and study the evidence, Fuellmich's side is but a handful of Davids against untold legions of Goliaths. They (the Goliaths) are unwaveringly moving forward and their programs of Active Measure against all who resist, are brutal. From the popular podcaster Joe Rogan to the very persons who invented and patented these 'Covid-technologies' that have now literally been weaponized – all are targets. There are executive officers of corporations and Nobel laureates, 50,000 truckers in Canada and (at last count) 130,000 truckers in the US, and other similar programs and protests in every major city in the world, (including dozens of cities in Germany this past week); and yet, no court will hear their plea!

This fascinating situation is one that can likely only be resolved by enabling the darkness to be investigated, and to step into the light, so to speak. There is no other way, and it will require compassion, acceptance, and forgiveness, but when the dust settles, such forgiveness will be hard to find. This is because new factions will form on the remains of the preceding one's ruin, and most contemporary people will go back to sleep, and not notice that the old factions have simply been supplanted. It thus requires a miracle, and if I must try and imagine the sort of miracle this would have to be, I get more fascinated and I get goose bumps!

Terri and I are well, and we are days away from the final documentation[1]. Patience is key now, but once that is done, we will likely leave Welbedacht within a day or two, and then spend a few days near the city finalizing our administrative affairs before leaving the country. We will naturally persevere to see you and Vani for tea before we do though and will let you know when we do.

Best wishes,
John

Wednesday, February 9th, 2022, Swami Vidyananda wrote:

Dear John,
Hari OM.

Yes, it is quite something that courts won't hear them. It shows that Divine Justice is the only true form of justice.

And the onslaught on the protestors and truckers is quite something; one must wonder how this is all going to pan out.

Yes, if you can, please visit us, or we can visit you before you leave.

Yours in Prem and Om,
Vidyananda

---

[1] John and Terri had decided to sell their property in SA and relocate to Europe.

8

Reply

In a continuation of the previous exchange, Swami Vidyananda and John exchange views on the reality distortions and concerns to do with the controversial Covid-19 testing mechanism, known as the "PCR test". At the same time, they discuss the convenient confluence of the Covid related measures with the measures prescribed in the United Nations Agenda 21 and 30. They also observe the continued complexity of alerting others to the distortions of their perceived truth and reality.

On Saturday, July 24, 2021, Swami Vidyananda wrote:

Dear John,
Hari OM.

I pray that you and Terri are well.

Here is an interesting interview:

https://thehighwire.com/videos/w-h-o-whistleblower-connects-the-dots/

(Note: This link is of the former ethics researcher at the World Health Organisation (WHO), Astrid Stuckelburger, PhD, shedding light on the behind-the-scenes at the top world health agency, their conflicts of interests, alternate agendas, and who's really been pulling the strings in the #Covid19 pandemic response. Posted: July 20, 2021)

We look forward to seeing you soon.

Yours in Prem and Om,
Vidyananda

On Saturday, July 24, 2021, John wrote:

Dear Vidyananda,
Hari OM.

Good to hear from you and thank you for this clip.

Indeed, I followed Astrid Stuckelburger's bona fide reports some time ago and forwarded them on to a few others, too. However, it seems quite pointless to do so, as no matter how much one tells people about what is actually happening, they none-the-less continue to stare at the TV, mainstream news and social media, all which repeat the same narrative over and over. It seems most prefer to follow the herd.

As mentioned before, I have stopped forwarding reports. One of the reasons was that I found, if one informs people of these agendas, and they decide to go ahead with *the irreversible act of vaccination* in anyway, doing so then makes them feel uncomfortable and scared, which only makes things worse. One cannot easily awaken another to such multi-facetted deceit; especially, as I'm sure you know, this realization ultimately comes from within. Some whom I thought had awakened to this scheme, and who I thought were now aware, are regrettably no longer. Perhaps the uncovering of a conspiracy is unpleasant enough, and if it becomes evident that, when one removes one layer one is likely to see the next layers that also need to be removed, then the very prospect of looking too deeply becomes problematic in itself. The belief that then sets in, is that it's probably better (or easier) to not question the narrative and accept it, even when it an obvious fabrication, as truth. This type of reality perversion is, to me, a type of black or dark magic and similar to the practice of Voodoo; it works on changing people's reality by reversing their beliefs.

The agenda behind these measures is primarily about population control, whereby they implement forms of compliance that enable the state (and corporations) to steer, and if need be, manipulate, every segment of human existence. This includes certain aspects of movement, wealth distribution, and the use of resources, but also demographic and life-expectancy manipulation. This is all in line with UN Agendas 21 and 30, but the vaccination scheme is the beginning of much a larger objective. The entities behind it are very serious and very powerful; even though malpractice and legal suits and protests are cropping up everywhere, they still barge ahead. With state granted immunity, they believe they can reach a point where they will have the majority of people compliant and thus enable these programs to become mandatory.

This dark magic works well on all who are deeply immersed in the state propaganda. Some people and dear friends, whom I know well and who I advised in great detail, and who were adamant about not having the vaccination, have, within weeks turned 180 degrees, now claiming the vaccination was the right thing to do and that they never thought otherwise. Subsequently, they got their jabs and are in the program.

Those who are conscious to these schemes, do not succumb to them. However, since this has been known to the engineers and architects of these schemes, various dumbing-down programs[1] over the past decades have been used to support their implementation; so well in fact, that I am convinced that they are linked. In reality, these untested gene-based vaccines, are of considerable concern. This is because, when something is untested, it means that it could be helpful or harmful – but no one actually knows. But this is not disclosed, on the contrary, the dangers are purposely suppressed, whist the flu-like symptoms (and deaths) are grotesquely exaggerated.

One of the objectives of the vaccinations (there are many), is to suppress

---

[1] Dumbing down is the deliberate oversimplification of intellectual content in education, literature, cinema, news, video games, and culture. Originated in 1933, the term "dumbing down" was movie-business slang, used by screenplay writers, meaning: "to revise so as to appeal to those of little education or intelligence"

and alter consciousness[1]. It should come as no surprise since eugenics programs date far back, and yet, are still quite common today[2].

On the topic of eugenics, as a side note: I undertook some research on the genetic structure of man and with that have reason to believe that man may have been genetically altered around 40 000 years ago.[3] Consequent to these findings, I considered how 'genetically imperfect' the modern man seems to be, especially when compared to the plant and animal kingdoms, and why mankind often (subconsciously perhaps) considers itself separate of nature. If we consider how, prior to that time, very little creativity or advancement was present[4], then it could be feasible that genetic alteration by higher evolved beings is also what made man able to become God Conscious. The point is that if this is considered as such, then it must also be possible to reverse this process - and that this process of reversal is subconsciously occurring in many programs, including those of entertainment. These considerations represented a strange journey of research, but did lead me to dedicate a few chapters to this in my books; largely because I found it important to my understanding of what exactly man is, and how the overall workings (and purpose) of the mechanisms of Life function.

I would welcome your views on these thoughts. Either way, God willing we'll see each other soon.

Best wishes,
John

On Monday, July 26th, 2021, Swami Vidyananda wrote:

Dear John,
Hari OM.

I also found that it is nigh impossible to even warn people. Some people had quite strong reactions to some of the emails I have sent. The strange thing is that my emails only contained links to the official adverse effects reporting sites and to one open letter that was written by scientists to the European Medicine Agency. And yet some thought that I was being influenced by algorithms on the internet. Since they were watching 'trusted' media such as BBC and also watching various other news channels (who of course all say the same things), they thought that they knew what was going on. But also the tone of some emails was a little concerning.

---

[1] The CIA conducted experiments involving drugs that could influence consciousness, most notably through its secret program, MK Ultra.
[2] Consider that Sweden ran a eugenics program up to the 1970s that included forced sterilizations of people considered "genetically inferior". This included prostitutes, women with "immoral" behaviour, or women deemed to be "promiscuous" or "unfit" for motherhood.
[3] The potential source of these genetic alterations corroborates with the translated descriptions from ancient Sumerian clay tablets.
[4] Based on some of the oldest known evidence of advanced human creativity, such as those cave paintings in Sulawesi in Indonesia, as well as Chauvet and in France, dating between 25,000 and 40,000 years ago)

We also posted the attached diagram in one of our e-newsletters[1]. As you can read in the document, it is merely an attempt to depict the numbers in the form of a diagram. Yet, we have been accused of coercing people not to take the vaccine. It is remarkable how emotional and irrational the reactions have been. They simply assume things that are not in the emails. I think this is due to the intense brain-washing (or brain-polluting as Swami Venkatesananda would call it) that the media has been very successful at. It is quite astounding. I never really believed in brain-polluting as a possible thing, but now I am seeing it first-hand. There is an unwillingness to even look at other points of view, clearly because they have been labelled as 'dangerous'.

There are only about 20 people who have expressed the wish to receive more info from me regarding vaccines. So, I keep sending them relevant info.

I would be interested in the views that the homeopath expressed. Could you please share some of those with me?

Yours in Prem and Om,
Vidyananda

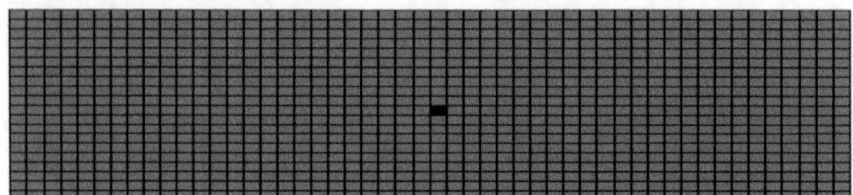

The entire rectangle ABOVE represents South Africa's population of about 59 million people. Each block represents 59 000 people. The dark square are (supposed) fatalities of COVID-19. (As per SA Gov. website: https://sacoronavirus.co.za/covid-19-daily-cases/).

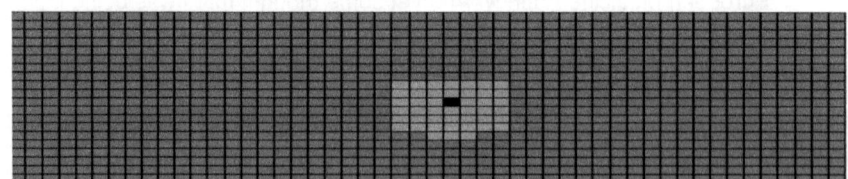

The entire rectangle ABOVE represents South Africa's population of about 59 million people. Each block represents 59 000 people. The grey squares are the population that (supposedly) tested COVID-19 positive. The dark square is the population that are said to have died of COVID. (As per the SA Gov site: https://sacoronavirus.co.za/covid-19-daily-cases/)

---

[1] See diagrams inserted above and below.

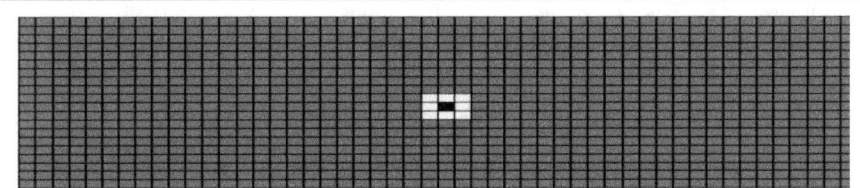

The entire rectangle ABOVE represents South Africa's population, each block represents 59 000 people. The dark square is the population that (supposedly) died of COVID-19. The light squares are all other deaths (based on the average of 450 000 deaths per year in South Africa).

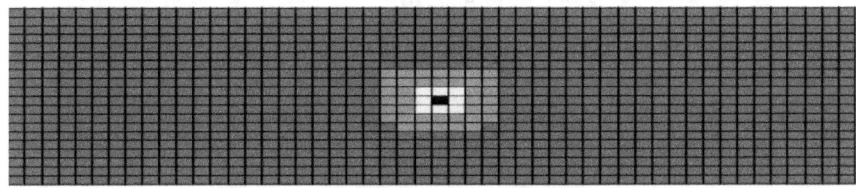

The rectangle ABOVE combines the above three

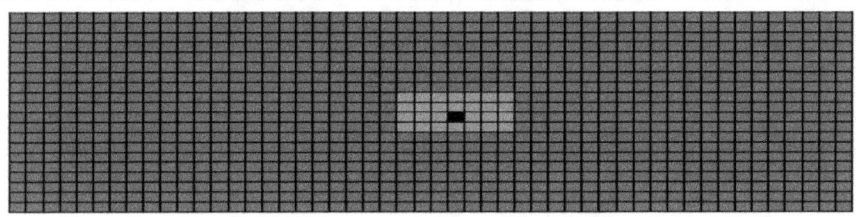

The entire rectangle ABOVE represents the world's population of about 8 Billion.
Each block represents 8 million people. The grey squares are the population that was allegedly tested COVID-19 positive. The dark square is the (supposed) population that died of COVID-19.
(Based on https://www.worldometers.info/).

On Tuesday, July 27th, 2021, John wrote:

Dear Vidyananda,
Hari OM.

Thank you for sharing these views. Yes, I share your concerns and have grave feelings about the outcome of things - not so much for me, but for those close to me, as well as the greater percentage of humanity; our friend the homeopath expressed the same feelings.

FYI, I had an interesting experience recently. I began to notice some symptoms that indicated an immunity disorder. This was no surprise to me, as my past activities included all sorts of tasks that led to various maladies, most of which I wrote off to stress, working in dirty environments, bad nutrition, and other 'unsavoury' habits.

This time however, I was forced to treat the symptoms in several ways including use of a cortisone cream and arrangement of a dental appointment (the former was following my academic mind, the latter following my intuitive one). The cream helped and the dentist found one bad tooth and another suspect one - even though I experienced no pain or symptoms, he nevertheless pulled both out. The skin disorder began to go away almost immediately but I intuitively felt that the two bad teeth were not the cause, and I had to investigate deeper - which I did. To make a long story short - during my (7 year) sojourn in the military during the 1980's, I was vaccinated against pretty much everything and then some, and sometimes twice!! Now, when I think back to the various immune-related disorders I experienced, I note that these started within a year or two of those vaccinations, and ranged from Psoriasis to Scleroderma, to Vitiligo, and Sepsis. Thanks to some nutritional and lifestyle changes, and the embracing of 'a more sincere path with awareness', I have overcome most of these. Only the psoriasis crops up every now and then, but I believe I am mastering that one as well.

The point of this is, that I can now motivate the request of a letter from a qualified MD that says I react adversely and must not be vaccinated anymore. This is true of course, but the other reason is to not be expected to be vaccinated for my impending travel plans and global interactions. I also prefer not to be labelled "vaccine hesitant". Such a label may defeat my ability to interact with those who were vaccinated, and who may look upon the "vaccine hesitant" as irresponsible and therefore, best censored, isolated or even criminalized and potentially imprisoned (as that is what is occurring already).

My discussion with the homeopath on this was open and clear and in fact, there was little we did not agree on. Where normally a consult is 20 or 30 minutes, mine was at the end of the day and hence, we sat and talked about these things for almost 2 hours... You would have joined in happily on every aspect!

At one point he said to me that perhaps most people simply did not want to wake up, to which I replied that perhaps that was so, but perhaps we needed to approach these things differently. One cannot awaken another but one can arrange the environment in such a way that the seeds for their awakening can germinate. The answer to this does not lie in intellectual or academic noise, or even religious or spiritual persuasion, as many of these sleepy ones are what I would call pseudo-spiritualist, because they are fixated on what they believe is real – even though their theories are easily disputed. To these, any revelation is like painting on top of a greasy surface, to which nothing sticks. People have been *naturally* prone to such 'mental contaminants' for centuries, and today's Public Relations agenda (which is simply a nice word for brainwashing), reveals the contaminants as having been irreversibly immersed in grease for decades!

One may of course consider it possible to try and impose or re-establish sincerity and purpose in people. If they can then re-establish such by helping others in need, and if they can become sincere in this, within such service they can find themselves. The trouble with this 'solution' is that 'the need' cannot be faked or pretended, it requires 'real need'; the need must precede the purpose in other words. Further, the conditions of those who are unawakened as yet and who must then be able to help those in need, must also be 'real', as it were. This is complex to accept. It does stress me considerably, as at times it feels that the forces that resist the awakening of the many are insurmountable, and ever increasing.

If it is of interest to you, my view on the depth and strength of this 'Assault on Consciousness' is based upon findings from the 17th century. During this period, a philosophy was initiated by Sabbatai Zevi and then carried forth by his successor Jacob Frank into the 18th and 19th centuries called Frankism. It is a philosophy of 'Redemption through Sin', that spells out a dark path to salvation to speed up the return of the Saviour / Messiah, or The Rapture. Despite the absence of mass-media during those earlier times, these practitioners none-the-less had a following of over a million. In the 18th century they allied with Adam Weishaupt (the founder of the Illuminati), and the banker family of Amschel Mayer (later Rothschild).[1]

The point of this is that these persons represented an interesting collection of characters - whose fingerprints, in my view, are quite evident in many of the 'causes' of things today ...

Best wishes,
John

On Wednesday, July 28th, 2021, Swami Vidyananda wrote:

Hari OM John.

I too noticed the bull-dozing. And very often they 'steal' the rhetoric of the opposition and twist it to their means, e.g. herd immunity was first spoken of by the dissenters. Then suddenly the authorities also speak of herd immunity but twist it to imply that herd immunity can only be achieved through vaccination.
Yes, this criminalization thing is mentioned over and over again.

Yours in Prem and Om,
Vidyananda

---

[1] *1666, Redemption through Sin*, by Robert Sepehr

9

Life for the Unvaccinated

As the media propagated development around societal acceptance at an increasing rate, so too the non-acceptance of the supposed 'vaccinations' also gained support. The latter, occurred through an ever-growing number of verified circles, that included scientists, academics, and whistle-blowers. Even in our daily interactions, it was clear that a schism between the two sides - those who were pro-vaccination and those who were anti-vaccination - was forming. The following exchange reflects the complexities of remaining conscious of the good in people on both sides of this divide, without taking a side. For the ashram and Swami Vidyananda, the need for focus and vigilance during this complex time was amplified due to Mother Yogeshwari experiencing her last days before transcending to meet her Guru and God.

On Wednesday, November 3rd, 2021, Swami Vidyananda wrote:

Dear John and Terri,
Hari OM.

I pray that you are well.

You may wish to read the email below.

Yours in Prem and Om,
Vidyananda

"On Monday 1 November 2021, Swami Vidyananda wrote:

Dear Friends,
Hari Om.

I write this email not with any criticism to anyone who is vaccinated, and also not with the view of causing division or antagonism.

However, the situation seems to emerge due to vaccine certificates/passports that those who have chosen to remain unvaccinated may face circumstances that make it difficult to have employment, have access to certain facilities, etc. Besides these certificates or passports, other concerns seem to be related.

It is merely with the view of providing some kind of support system that a few friends met to discuss the pathway ahead.

We envision a network in which anyone (regardless of vaccine status) could participate and be able to live a basic life. We also envision the possibility of an alternative form of living, such as a rural self-sustaining community.

If you wish to be part of such an endeavour, please contact me for further information.

I wish to reiterate that we do not wish to alienate anyone. This is merely looking at meeting our day-to-day needs.

May God guide our hearts so that we ever remain in the Spirit of Unity.

Yours in Prem and Om,
Vidyananda"

On Monday 8 November 2021, John wrote:

Dear Vidyananda,
Hari OM.

We trust you and all are well.

Terri and I would like to pay a visit to you and the Mothers this coming Sunday afternoon for tea and a chat; would this be OK with you? We have one earlier stop to make that day and plan to be there with you between 13h00 and 15h00. Let me know if this is convenient, please.

The above aside - thank you for the email (of Nov 3rd). I note similar moves towards forced vaccination. Further, the propaganda in the electronic aether of many countries, does not always seem to synchronize with what is taking place on the ground. The reason for this is probably easier to understand if one can see that there are four centers of Truth in play (besides that of Divine Truth of course!):

1. The first center of Truth is that of the working- class people - through Mainstream and Social Media channels; they receive mostly (90%+) propaganda that is coated with a thin sugar layer of truth.

2. The second center of Truth is that professed by the middle class - through infiltrated, often biased, and not always correctly informed Alternative Media channels; they receive mostly factual information that carries within it subtle but very real elements that are equally infectious and toxic to the psyche.

3. The third center of Truth is that which adheres to the higher echelons of people and big business of the world, wherein global impacts are seen within the greater strategic context and thus, in terms of profit and influence only. Here, there is usually an awareness that the trajectory of the currently unsustainable economy is perpetuated by their systems. Yet, due to their primary concern for loss of profit or influence, they are supportive of whatever social measures and actions are taken – these are then deemed unpleasant but necessary.

4. The fourth center of Truth is that which serves the Elites. Groups one and two, above, seldom, if ever know of this group, whereas group three,

pays homage to it. 'Mr Global' as the elites are referred to by some, is not 'a Mister' though, but a few small but immensely powerful cooperative groups that directly or indirectly pretty much own and control everything.

I look forward to hearing your thoughts on this!

Best wishes,
John

On Monday, November 8th, 2021, Swami Vidyananda wrote:

Dear John and Terri,
Hari OM.

Thank you, John, for your insights regarding the 'truths'.

You are welcome to visit. Please confirm. I would love to see you.
Mother Yogeshwari will most likely not be available for a visit. She is on her way to meet her Guru and God. We are keeping her comfortable as best as we can. Right now we are not allowing any visitors other than her family.

Please pray for her.

Yours in Prem and Om,
Vidyananda

On Wednesday, November 10th, John wrote:

Dear Vidyananda,
Hari OM.

Thank you for your reply - we understand that we cannot see Mother Yogesh, but this is not necessary as her presence already shines so brightly in our hearts - and will continue to do so after she transcends to her Guru and God.

God-willing, we will see you on Sunday around 13h00.

Best wishes,
John

10

On Censorship

During the ongoing changes in the social, political and geopolitical spheres, John would often share informative details with Swami Vidyananda; the emails contained links, insights, and his correspondence with others on these topics.

This exchange enabled Swami Vidyananda to remove the clouds of uncertainty created by the external influences upon the ashram life; influences such as those which affected the devotee's ability to attend or gather and practice together.

John's wish to keep Swami Vidyananda abreast of the actual and more logical causes behind the various developments which were often in contrast to those propagated by the biased media, carried within it the knowing that, if his research into the darker elements of humanity came to a point of compromise, then his friend the Swami would likely advise him. It felt comfortable for John to share his findings with the deeply devoted and spiritual Swami, knowing that by doing so, he had a kind and watchful companion along his journey.

The following is one of such.

On Tuesday, March 1st, 2022, John wrote:

Dear Vidyananda,
Hari OM.

FYI. Below is a multi-faceted collection of exchanges between myself and a fellow-thinker, who was a senior analyst in the Dutch government. On Monday, February 28th, 2022, I wrote:

"Thank you for your detailed response to my inquiry on the Dutch political scene - I value your opinion. My inquiry was not so much about the nature of the parties, be it those of Rutte[1], Gideon, Goofy or Gandhi, because when it comes to such positions of absolute authority, or absolute power, then the same corruption that infects one, will inevitably infect all. (This is why Ghandi wanted nothing to do with the political processes themselves, as he knew how this would infect and stain his soul).

---

[1] The at that time, Dutch Prime Minister.

My enquiry was to see if the Dutch public was now at last able to see fact from fiction, and truth from obvious and blatant lies, as was pointed out by Gideon Meijer[1]. It is a pity to see that this is not the case and that, between attention now fixated on Ukraine and various other distractions, their two-year Covid 19 campaign has already been forgotten.

It goes to show how futile and corruptible the system of 'democracy' really is, and how its system of politics and central government is very old and based on control for (and by) a certain selected powerful few, against whom one cannot fight. It seems the system has a metaphysical design intended to incite resistance that then causes this 'left-and-right' swing to become like a pulse that further fuels this system into its own unnatural form of life. In addition, it feeds off the residual hate and vengefulness, and thus, regardless of who wins or loses, it always wins.

That said, the non-partisan path is, in my view, the only sensible and effective way to deal with this. Anything else will eventually turn and become polar, as all things in the physical material world must (and do). It is here where the light and natural magic is found, by all who but seek and ask!"

On another spectrum: I wrote this to another friend in the USA just a few days ago:

"Having left South Africa, we are currently traversing through North Macedonia. Yesterday, driving through the remote frosty forest-covered mountains of its countryside, I had to stop my vehicle for an old grandmother who, accompanied by three very large dogs, appeared on foot, out from the forest, to cross the road with her herd of goats. She gently encouraged each goat in her herd to cross rapidly, and after the last hesitant old billy-goat had crossed, she offered an appreciation for our patience, with a wave and beautiful smile. We waved and smiled back, and spontaneously began the most wonderful conversation. Although we did not understand a single word she spoke, and neither did she understand us, this mattered none - there was a simple but immensely powerful and magical exchange of warmth and an appreciation of the miracle of life. After many smiles, handshakes, and hand kisses, we parted.

Although this country has a history of oppression and violence, I find the people at heart to be warm and hospitable. In fact, a few days before this encounter with the grandmother, we had stopped in a remote little village, where we entered what we thought was a cafe. Ordering some coffee and water, we conversed with the men there in a combination of German, English, and other. They offered us salami sandwiches and cigarettes as well, but as we neither smoke nor eat pork, we politely declined these, hoping that we did not offend! When we left however, they refused to take our money, and we realized that it was, in fact, a community hall of sorts, and that they were poor but happy and proud to be able to give. We realized that it would be inappropriate for us to insist on paying. Here too, we parted with sincere smiles and handshakes.

---

[1] An outspoken Dutch politician who expressed concern against the prime minister's handling of the Covid situation and his personal relationship with Klaus Schwab, director of the private entity known as the World Economic Forum (WEF).

Then this morning we woke up in the city of Ohrid, which lies by a lake of the same name. Here, like in all cities, families and small children are equally glued to their phones and TVs, mesmerized by the attention and consciousness devouring forces that I suppose must also exist. In this I recognized that my travels enabled me to better see the Whole for what it is, which reminded me to continue our journey, without opinion or judgment."

Then, you asked me about the war in Ukraine:

From the perspective of a former soldier: I do not have much to say except perhaps that war is an environment within which one finds, besides violence, a lot of brutality and cruelty, that many men lose themselves. It is however also an environment within which the seeds of the opposite can be germinated. In fact, many philosophers and deep thinkers became enlightened during their time in some or other war. One may think, for example, of those giants like Marcus Aurelius[1] and Rene Descartes[2]. The physical war, regardless of how destructive it is, actually means very little except to the civilians or non-combatants, who suffer the most and who have no choice, and who are left to mourn, repair, and rebuild. (They never see that the war's sole purpose is, ultimately, to steer their opinion/psyche).

From a political perspective: Almost all wars and their outcomes are known and predetermined, long before the political spinners of truth commence with their political debates.

From a geo-political perspective:

1. Ukraine is seen as a necessary wedge between Germany and Russia, and which ensures Germany remains aligned with the US / NATO and not Russia (Germany, if combined with Russia could form the next Superpower, which Iran, and likely Turkey would join);
2. This is a part of the Great Chess Game[3] for global power by the New World Order, and the predicted conflict we foresaw in 2020.
3. This is (according to this New World Order) a necessary war, as it will act as a public distraction after the two-year Covid 19 circus and whilst the stage is prepared by them, for the next move.
4. It is the potential vessel by which the NWO will motivate the restructuring of the terminal, global financial system.

*Therefore, regardless of who the losers and who the winners of this 'war' may 'appear' to be, **all** the players ultimately are agents of the same Central Powers (Banks and Globalists)".*

To conclude: Although, from a geopolitical perspective, Ukraine differs from other theatres. From a geostrategic perspective it is the same story as Afghanistan, destabilised to justify military enforced control over

---

[1] Aurelius was a Roman emperor from 161 to 180, a Stoic philosopher, and the last emperor of the Pax Romana, an age of relative peace, calm, and stability for the Roman Empire.
[2] Descartes was a French philosopher, scientist, and mathematician, widely considered a seminal figure in the emergence of modern philosophy and science.
[3] A term used by Zbigniew Brezinski, a former adviser to 4 US Presidents.

Trillions worth of Rare Earth metals[1], or Libya and Iraq, which were largely destabilised for challenging the Petrodollar[2]. The only victims are the contemporary people **on both sides,** who must live through and pay for these wars, and as long as technology and a centralized financial control enables this global agenda to remain in place, it is an unstoppable force.

Ultimately, in this deceptive and complex game of cat and mouse, where they look the same and keep changing places, the only true winners here can be those who remain conscious of Truth to themselves, conscious and independent in their personal needs (debt free), and physically out of the fray.

Best wishes,
John

On Wednesday, March 2nd, 2022, Swami Vidyananda wrote:

Dear John
Hari OM.

Yes, we are well. We had an all-night vigil last night for Maha Shivaratri: 12 hours of singing and worship. Wonderful!

Thank you for sharing some news about your trip, as well as the ongoing saga (I guess it shall keep going on because it is simply just that).

Amazing, how all this lying is happening.

It is quite true what you say, we need to remain outside of it and most importantly, focused on our spiritual path.

Prem,
Vidyananda

---

[1] Rare-earth metals are heavy metals with diverse applications in electrical and electronic components, lasers, glass, magnetic materials, military and industrial processes.
[2] The petrodollar is a currency imposed by the U.S. used to pay oil-exporting countries for crude oil sales.

11

Truth vs Hydra

On Monday, April 4th, 2022, Swami Vidyananda wrote:

Dear John,
Hari OM.

Yes, we are all well.

Thank you for the link to the RT (Russia Today) interview. Although some of it I don't understand due to my lack of political knowledge, I hope to have gained the gist, which is that the Ukraine is not just an innocent victim, Russia is not just a big ogre, and this war is just the outcome of decades of political battles between powerful nations (and of course those who 'govern' them).

I can see more and more why the scriptures mention that the good people flee into remote places to flee the cancer and be able to focus their minds on God. However, I have my doubts about whether the countryside is as divorced from these things as may have been in past centuries due to 5G and other technologies, which are almost omnipresent.

The real retreat I guess is inwardness and keeping the mind in higher states of consciousness despite all the mayhem.

Sending you and Terri much Love.

Yours in Prem and Om,
Vidyananda

On Tuesday, April 5th, 2022, John wrote:

Dear Vidyananda,
Hari OM.

Indeed, the battles people see on TV are not the real battles - these are mere distractions of the actual ones, which are fought in 'other' dimensions. My view on these 'other' dimensions, however, is not that they are Higher Dimensions, on the contrary, and these 'battles' are not between light and dark or good and evil either, but instead they are between different forms of darkness that seek to overpower each other.

It is my understanding that these 'other' dimensions are a kind of twilight zone, that operates on lower but differing frequencies if you will. As such I see them as meta-physically and psychically powered, by which I mean that they are energized by the powerful psyches of *living* people.

This psychic energy originates from the emotions of *fear and desire,* and some of the demonic entities this dark but rather abundant energy has manifested, and which has gradually accumulated power across centuries, maybe even millennia. The onset of globalization and its 20th and 21st-century interconnected technology enabled humanity to become more informed and connected, but to these entities, this has had an effect such as spraying gasoline on a smouldering fire. Now, as a veritable Frankenstein Monster[1], the entity is intelligent, resourceful, and aware of itself and it has also enabled itself to rule the physical world of people by any means at hand.

Its nature is very much like the average inflated human ego, except, like the mythical Hydra[2] with its nine heads, all of which are psychopathic, its power is amplified by the countless fearful and desirous people. At present it desperately seeks what it cannot ever obtain: changelessness and immortality.

This entity aims to drive the masses of unaware and increasingly fearful and desirous people, into systems of permanent subjugation. The vaccination programs and your observations of 5G (that will be followed up by 6G, 7G etc) are part of this. I do however believe that the effects of vaccines and 5G, although very unhealthy and detrimental to the state of well-being, cannot override the sincere and disciplined conscious mind.

But this 'mind' must be free of desire and liberated from fear, and this is no simple task. To do this *sincerely, without pretension,* we have to let go of the things of attachment, toxic relations, and social principles that are so valued. We have to face our fears, especially those of loss and death.

This is a bit of a paradox, as unless one is born in this state, one has to let go of that which one has spent much of one's life gathering. It requires many years for most people, or the remainder of their life, and the older one is, the higher this proverbial mountain will seem, and naturally, the more complex the work becomes.

The one side and biggest part of this 'paradox', is the complexity of Time[3]. The remaining lifetime we have against the duration we have spent, becomes engrained in the false reality that we see as 'ourselves' and 'the world'.

The other side of this 'paradox' entails the natural cycles of the individual human (biological and inner) evolution: People typically only become aware of these cycles which are encoded in our DNA, from the age of around 40 - 42 years, and most are, as we know, by then deeply buried in the system of social acceptance through qualifications, possessions, and relations. Thus, it is likely going to be up to the younger generations to resurrect this, but most don't seem to have a fighting chance, particularly when parents are seen putting their toddlers in front of these toxic and addictive screens from the age of two or three.

---

[1] Based on the fictional creature of Mary Shelley, the monster is the creation of Dr Victor Frankenstein, once assembled from parts of a number of victims and strange chemicals, it is animated by a mysterious spark.
[2] Hydra is a Greek myth of a gigantic water-snake-like monster with nine heads.
[3] J capitalises Time, when using it as a name, with a Divine or higher dimensional connotation.

Hence, the few who see this can but stand by and watch because, as much as it pains them, one cannot force another to wake up. Even if another were to come forward and say "Please wake me up"; this would be a start, but then they'd still have to do the work. It is like having to leave the protected and sacred space, or the temple, ashram, or helpful guide; they must now, individually, go back to make peace with their bodies, their lives, their homes, and their problems.

In an excerpt from "The Outer World of Man"[1], a book that I am currently editing, yesterday I came across this paragraph:

"To complete the Cosmic Dance within the Law-of-Opposites, where there is an Overman, there must also be an Underman. The cyclic nature of all things is also reflected in the ordeal of man, and completing the dance depends on this. The Overman seeks to be at One with the Infinite All, and which he shall eventually find. The Underman seeks to be his immortal own, by persevering to improve man and the world; but this is finite and not possible. Hence, fall he eventually must."

Hence, there is perhaps little we can do but 'arm' ourselves through knowledge, inner work, service, and exchanges with other Seekers. Other than that, we must but wait patiently. In the interim, I rest assured that there are many awakened and awakening ones: about 375 million by my last estimate![2]. These will likely also be interconnected, and not by electronic means. When the time comes, I believe the Divine will put his awakened ones to good use to gather the lost ones, and I cannot but also feel that somehow, even this process is still part of a Divine Design in a greater and natural cycle.

Perhaps another 'Fall of Atlantis' or 'Sodom and Gomorrah' type of event is what lies on the horizon. My own research shows that this has occurred twice in the past 12,000 years[3], and judging by the confluence of many things, over and above my daily geopolitical observations, another version of such a cyclic 'turn-around' is possible. This one I believe will be referred to as something like the 'battles between forms of darkness', which insinuates (to me) that, once a parasitic organism has devoured its host, and begins to feed on itself, its demise is not far off.

Only upon the arrival of Heracles, the mythological Greek hero, is Hydra slayed, and the demon 'switched off'. Then, there will be important work; work upon which the ages that follow will depend - but until then, no pressure! 😊

Best wishes,
John

---

[1] *The Outer World of Man* was published as part of a trilogy in August 2022.
[2] If taking the somewhat naïve and hypothetical opposite of 4.5% of the world's population having psychopathic tendencies, then this must be balanced by at least the same amount of the population being enlightened!
[3] One of these being the end of the Pleistocene or Ice Age, leading to the Deluge or Great Flood.

On Wednesday, April 6th, 2022, Swami Vidyananda wrote:

Dear John,
Hari OM.

Thank you for your wonderful insights.

It is interesting to me that the 'way' that you describe to 'survive' all these are the basic principles of Yoga: to be desireless, fearless, to raise one's consciousness, and ultimately be one with God. It reminds me that regardless of what the outer circumstances and challenges are, the same eternal truths are not only relevant but are the way out. That the ongoing conflicts are kept alive by fuelling desire and fear is also recognized by the Yoga Scriptures as the fundamental aspects of ignorance. i.e. ignorance is maintained and deepened by desire, fear, and anger. Perhaps we could reduce it to desire because fear and anger are born of desire.

So, these insights show that these are fundamental universal truths.

Swami Venkatesananda also repeatedly taught that you cannot fight evil without being tainted by it. Just keep to your spiritual journey. Delusion cannot last: it is always self-destructive.

Your point that one cannot help others to get out of the delusion is quite true. You said it long ago, yet I gave it a try; and failed. I realized that those who are receptive are already skeptical or know; the others won't listen. So, I guess there is no alternative to watching the possible carnage.

Here in SA the State of Disaster has ended but we are in a 30-day transition period, in which the same rules still apply. Then the government introduced the Disaster Regulations into the Health Act. So, in reality, it appears nothing has changed, the same saga continues. We simply need to get on with our lives and ignore the regulations as much as possible.

I also realized that I need to be careful for the mind not to get preoccupied with all this, and keep it focused on the spiritual path, keeping my heart and mind focused on the Divine.

I often pray for God's intervention. It seems that this alone will help. The corruption and evil are so pervasive, that it seems that only a Mighty Power can change that.

I pray that you and Terri keep well.

Yours in Prem and Om,
Vidyananda

12

Imminent Visit

On Tuesday, July 7th, 2022, John wrote:

Dear Vidyananda,
Hari OM.

I trust this finds you, Vani, and all at the ashram happy and in good health!

It's been a while since we corresponded or shared information. Much has happened and is happening in the world at large, but there is little chance of finding anything truthful, or of substance in the news. In addition, it seems as if simply occupying people's attention is now the media's only purpose.

However, I do believe we have realized that, when we are within the conceptual space of our present reality, which is controlled, we are under the spell of society's one- and two-dimensionally oriented collectives. Subsequently, we are subject to illusory forces that we are not part of, but which the physical or three-dimensional world is subject to, and about which we cannot do much.[1]

As you and I already determined (in some of our past discourses and as verified in the discussion between Swami Venkatesananda and J. Krishnamurti[2]), the unawakened go through life wishing only to be entertained. As a result, in the absence of attention to their reality which has deceptively blinded them, they have become subject to its dark influential forces. As such, they are akin to leaves in the wind, or mere pawns on a greater chessboard; doing whatever the symbol-bearing[3] authorities tell them to do.

This is a complex matter as it affects people's state of mind (or identification), and leads to volatile emotions as well as challenges to everyday life.

---

[1] John refers to his hypothesis that all people are divided not by race, religion, education, or other, but by the dimensional level of their perceived reality. In this, a one-dimensional person is one who believes everything is either one or the other and lives by a one-sided belief in how things are supposed to be; a two-dimensional person sees reality in pictures that have no depth, and thus lives in a world in flux, and by how things appear; a three-dimensional person sees reality as the physical realm the senses detect, but does not acknowledge the invisible or meta-physical influences as anything 'realistic'; the four- and higher dimensional ones access the intuitive and spiritual influences and enter a reality that the first three realities consider as non-existent and imaginary. This view is expanded on in later correspondence – see Chapter 15 dd 14 Oct 2022; *The Reality of Dimensions*.
[2] Jiddu Krishnamurti (https://www.jkrishnamurti.org/) was an Indian philosopher, speaker, writer, and spiritual teacher who emphasised introspection and freedom https://en.wikipedia.org/wiki/Jiddu_Krishnamurti
[3] Symbols like national flags, emblems and currency denominators ($, €, £, etc).

Regrettably, there is little we can do but be ready to offer some comfort and a place or space where help can be found, when it is sought.

As sad as this may appear, I can see how this fits in as part of our Creator's design, particularly when I see how it aligns with the consequences of complacency and the deferral of responsibility. Perhaps the discovery of beauty and perfection is made manifest within cycles of Chaos, on top of what we see as a bed of suffering. The learning in this is in finding that suffering ceases to be so, when it is accepted as such.

What a trip! Not that I take any joy in any of these affairs, but I do feel awed and blessed to be alive during these revelatory times, and to be able to see this. As long as we do not get caught up (or down) in it, it is a veritable spectacle.

To me, it's like we are afloat, bobbing along downstream in an ever-changing and ever-widening river. Our arms and legs are free and made strong enough to swim, and our minds are focused and awake; but we know logically that to try and swim back up or even across the stream is foolishness. Unlike the path that so many prefer to follow, perhaps our current destiny does not reside in making it to shore and settling there. Rather, we opt to not struggle and to just use our God-given intuitive abilities to steer ourselves within the stream. All we must do is avoid those parts that have eddies[1] - where one gets cyclically stuck; and dead zones - where the water is trapped and becomes stale and toxic. Along the flow, the stream may flood its banks and deposit us for settlement, or we may create ways to assist others who are stuck in eddies and dead zones... Who knows? Perhaps the whole river will dry up because someone decided to build a dam way back, and we find ourselves waiting for the next Deluge![2]

Returning to our acting roles in this play, and a more practical note: Terri and I will be visiting SA for a few weeks next month. If it is convenient, we would like to come and see our good friends at the Ashram for a quick tea and a chat. If this can work, would Thursday the 18th of August perhaps work for you?

Best wishes,
John

On Friday, July 8th, 2022, Swami Vidyananda wrote:

Dear John,
Hari OM.

Wonderful to get your email. We were talking about you and Terri, and I had been thinking of writing to you, and Voila, the same day I received your email!

Yes, we are all well. And by the sounds of it, you and Terri are also well?

---

[1] Sometimes the flow of currents can pinch off sections and create a circular current of water called an eddy.
[2] In reference to the Deluge, also known as the Great Flood.

Thank you for sharing your thoughts. Indeed, your comments early in the pandemic, that we cannot help anyone are quite true. I realize that despite my efforts, maybe one or two people have listened, who otherwise may have gone with the narratives. The others did not need me to say anything as they already saw through this, so there is just mutual support. And those who refuse to even listen a little to what one has to say, well.... One can even be regarded as a troublemaker!

Hence I have decided to keep myself a little bit informed, maybe learn a bit more about this phenomenon, but otherwise continue with my life at the ashrama.

But more is to come, especially with this Pandemic Treaty, which seems to be key in getting many other things implemented. I try to keep myself open for Divine Guidance.

We look forward to seeing you and Terri again! Yes, we can meet on 18 August. Swami Parvathiananda is leaving for Australia for a few months that day, but her flight is in the morning. So, we would love for you to join us for lunch (12h00) and tea and....

With much Love to both of you from Vani and myself,
Vidyananda

On Sunday, July 10th, 2022, John wrote:

Dear Vidyananda,
Hari OM.

It was great to receive your reply and to hear you and Vani and all are well; we think and speak of you often!

These are such strange times; the psychosis is very visible but mostly, so it seems, within the Americanized Western countries - and the fear-based frenzy and greed are some of the dominant side effects theretofore.

In the interim, we must all do what we can, but yes, I agree, it serves little to be branded a 'troublemaker' or such. Where today this may not mean much, tomorrow it may cause consequences which, when one has dependents, may have an unnecessary knock-on effect. This is a matter of choice though; if one can make a difference to just one in one-thousand, then maybe it is still important that one does what is necessary. We must just be conscious of the Why and How we undertake to do this.

Divine Guidance knows all this though and, while prayer helps, in the current environment I believe that Guidance is here and everywhere already. It is visible to all those who wish to see and hear - but not to those whose eyes and ears are shut.

I believe we can see this Guidance daily, and in a great many things. However, to do so, I maintain that it is best that one remains out of the confusing fray, the treacherous trenches, and the endless debates. One does not have to look far to see numerous "smoking guns"[1]. This debacle began at

---

[1] Something that serves as strong evidence or irrefutable proof.

the turn of the century with 9.11 and the controlled demolition of the three World Trade Center towers on September 11, 2001, followed by the predictable financial crisis of 2008, the COVID 'plandemic', the premeditated and predicted Ukraine situation, and now the illusory food and health scares, and regulations. Every observer of these events has kind of chosen their version of truth for each of these.

For some, however, the truth is simply too uncomfortable, as there are too many painful-to-remove 'layers' that cover their hearts. It is a bit like the relative of a friend that I heard of, a lady who is just 73 and not terminal or depressed or such, but who just doesn't see the point of sticking around anymore, who has scheduled to be officially euthanized[1] and is currently going through the administrative process to do so...

We look forward to seeing you on the 18th at 12h00 for tea.

With much love and best wishes,
John and Terri

On Monday, July 11th, 2022, Swami Vidyananda wrote:

Dear John,
Hari OM.

Confirmed for 18th! Great!

Yes, prayer is essential.

I read recently that assisted suicide is becoming legal in some countries. Wow! It makes the job of the depopulation agenda much easier!

However, people do not realize that suicide is not the answer either. Where are they going after the body is shed? Will the mind be at peace after suicide, or is it the same mind that continues? Will we not end up in similar situations, if not a hell on earth, then a hell somewhere else?

Even within the horror show, we need to learn to attain equanimity; even when we are the immediate victims. Not easy to do, but that is part of the spiritual journey.

It is astounding to see what is happening in the name of ethics: certainly, a radical change is happening. It seems that more and more of what was considered unethical is now considered ethical because the intellect of the academic has decided it to be so. However, there is a Divine 'Law'; and that of course finally determines ethics. But I see that the Divine is not part of the thinking of the elite. We need to stay firm in our understanding of the Divine.

God bless us!

With Love,
Vidyananda

---

[1] Euthanasia is the practice of intentionally ending life, usually to eliminate pain and suffering, and officially supported in many western countries and states.

13

On Possessions

On Saturday, July 31st, 2021, Swami Vidyananda wrote:

Dear John,
Hari OM.

In my spiritual studies, I came across a few statements that are making me look at the Plandemic[1] (and the possible Genocide) in a different light. This is not a conclusive argument I am putting forth but rather an ongoing contemplation.

I thought I'd share the statements (as understood by me) and how they may pertain to the Plandemic.

First of all, there is Jesus Christ's statement that not even a sparrow shall fall (i.e. die) without the will of God. This seems to indicate that nothing (including the Plandemic) can take place without the cosmic energy, which is one with God. So, there is always a higher impulse to all action. That higher impulse is the law of karma.

Then there is a statement in the *'Yoga Vasistha'* (The Supreme Yoga) that when there is overpopulation, then Lord Vishnu incarnates to destroy human beings. Lord Vishnu is the Protector. So, the destruction of beings can also be an action of Protection of the Cosmos, or in a limited sense, the Earth. So the depopulation agenda may have its roots (unconsciously) in the law of karma.

Swami Venkatesananda in his Introduction to his translation of the text *'Valmiki Ramayana'* postulates the possibility that those who are the victims of genocide may be doing so 'voluntarily' (possibly subconsciously) as part of their spiritual evolution. Maybe that is why so many are almost eager to take the vaccine, even if they know of the possible harms and have been anti-vaxx themselves.

Paramahamsa Yogananda[2] in his book *'The Second Coming of Christ'* explains that Judas was chosen to commit treason so that Jesus could be crucified, as the crucifixion was part of the karmic dispensation. However, for any karmic act to be committed an instrument is required. And even though the treason was necessary, it was still sinful, and only that type of instrument can be used, that has the potential of sin in it. Hence a Judas

---

[1] The term Plandemic refers to a Planned Pandemic, used because of the testimony of many expert witnesses. See https://plandemic.com/
[2] Paramahamsa Yogananda was a great yoga master who was one of the pioneers of bringing the authentic yoga teaching to the West in the early 20th century. https://en.wikipedia.org/wiki/Paramahansa_Yogananda

is chosen and not a John, since Judas had those weaknesses. Yogananda also points out that the 'instrument' does have the choice not to be an instrument, if they choose to walk the path of light. And since they choose the sinful action, they have to experience the karmic consequences of that sinful act.

So, is it possible that this Plandemic/Genocide is an act of the karmic law, in which depopulation is required? Is it possible that the instruments used are the corrupt elite, who are the 'ideal' instruments, but who due to their weaknesses will still have to pay the karmic debt? And is it possible that all the lambs to the slaughter are unconsciously sacrificing themselves as part of the spiritual evolution?

Food for contemplation?

Yours in Prem and Om,
Vidyananda

On Friday, Aug 19th, 2022, John wrote:

Dear Vidyananda,

It was like a breath of fresh air and a clear ray of sunlight to see you and Vani yesterday; thank you again for your love and friendship and, naturally, the great lunch and copious amounts of Dutch coffee!

As we mentioned before: Ours are exceptional but immensely complex times, and it seems the Divine has brought us into a surreal dimension, like nothing we have experienced or, for that matter, that has been seen within our known or recorded history. Perhaps not even our various teachers had an inkling of a challenge of this nature: The challenge to maintain one's psychic and spiritual awareness within the subtle, innocent, and attractive-looking, but deadly toxic and 'infectious' environment and especially so, as this is an invisible infection that transmits itself through our highest senses - our impressions!

It also appears as if this 'infection' was customized using our surrounding technologies of entertainment, Artificial Intelligence, as well as other false prophets and gods. If only we could switch these off, or get rid of 'them', then most would be OK!

But this too is illusory, as this infection is not an infection as such, but rather a possession, and one that can mutate and jump from one 'host' or 'person' onto the next. One need but see the nature of the vast bulk of a complacent contemporary humanity to notice how, with ever increasing technological advancement, this inevitably occurred. It was as inevitable as the famine that follows the drought, and the pestilence that follows the famine, and the authoritarianism that follows the pestilence, the suppression that follows authoritarianism, the revolution that follows the suppression, and finally, the renaissance or rebirth that eventually follows these. If one then reverses this example (of drought), science may say that the drought would be simply traced back to Solar activity - that much is true, but what the Sun is or how it functions, science can still not explain. In my view the Sun is more of a portal, a Higher Dimensional window for manifestation of the duality we see as our three-dimensional reality; as such, it created both light and the shadow. Hence, what occurs today as vast darkness, implies that there is much light as well! I see this all the time when I speak to people directly, from all walks of life, and it warms me when I see it shine so brightly in you and in Vani.

The higher path, also known as the journey inward, is indeed the only path, but either way, we evidently must continue to exist in the outer and lower dimensional world as well. Today it seems that this is a world where we may easily wander off and lose track of the reality of ourselves, simply due to the ease with which our attention is captured and how this then effects our perception and our state of consciousness. Hence I would like it very much if we were to remain in contact with updates, comments suggestions, and even trivial exchanges - as I believe all these to be essential!

As such I wish you both well.

With fond regards and best wishes,
John

On Saturday, August 20th, 2022, Swami Vidyananda wrote:

Dear John,
Hari Om.

We too are delighted to have had your loving visit. Friendship as yours and Terri's is rare and a precious gift.

Krishnamurti seems to have foreseen this as he warned that the technological advances and the development of AI would lead to tyranny. In some of Swami Venkatesananda's writings I now also recognize the warnings although he did not emphasize these much.

As you say, the mechanisms are not that important, it is what you call possession, although they may facilitate the possession well. I would like you to please explain more about what you mean by possession.

Have a blessed weekend and send my love to Terri.

Yours in Prem and Om,
Vidyananda

On Sunday, August 21, 2022, John wrote:

Dear Vidyananda,
Hari Om.

We will plan our movements tomorrow to meet you at the airport, please text me when you land as I do not know how smoothly our check-in arrangements will flow before departure, and we cannot discount the presence of the occasional jinn in the works![1]

---

[1] In yet another 'coincidence', Swami Vidyananda passed through Cape Town airport at the same time that John and Terri were leaving South Africa.

As to your question about my view on 'possession'. This is a considerable subject that is difficult to explain as the contemporary world has so many innocently misunderstood words; these range from schizophrenia to depression and other fear-based states, to dozens of other psychological terms that Big Pharma is happily selling their easy-to-get drugs for. The subject of 'possession', or at least my view on it, is one that I can offer either a lengthy response or a shortened version to – and you will likely be very pleased that (for now), I have opted to offer the shortened one!

In the Creator's Divine Duality that we perceive, the Possession is a side-effect that is made manifest by the psyche of man (as in human beings). It is the psychic energy that is generated by the ego and which forms into an entity of its own. It is connected to the physical body, and therefore, ultimately, it belongs to the reality of the living Earth. It is therefore finite and a mirror-like, carbon-copy of the opposite of that which we refer to as Spirit. Spirit is made manifest by Consciousness, which is an eternal phenomenon, not of the Earth and as such infinite.

To describe this meta-physical entity called Possession as an infection would be incorrect, as an infection is bacterial, which is treatable with care and basic intervention. It is then better described as a virus that penetrates deep in the psyche of the unaware Ego, and once it has done so, it spreads itself out and, without some small miracle, becomes almost incurable due to its ability to mutate at will. Incurable, here, refers to the use of mechanical, psychological or *external* means.

The Possession however, unlike the bacteria or the common virus, is worse due to its method of spread; it spreads via that highest, most sensitive, and least acknowledged part of our being, our 'impressions'[1]. *(Imagine, as an example, a person entering a large crowd of football supporters. The psychic energy of the crowd rapidly overcomes him, and soon he sings, cheers and cries with the others, as if he is a single being with them. People may leave the stadium and others come back in, but the mind-possessing 'spirit' remains).* The same possessing entity can mutate along one form of impression to another, from cheer, to upset, to anger - there are hundreds - and it can transmit itself from one 'idolized' host to another, often via, or at the expense of, many of the subjects.

Consequently, like nations, religions, affiliations and certain trades or traditions, some Possessions are able to exist for very long periods, perhaps even millennia; patient and unobserved, they await the next cycle.

Some unite with other entities that are alike, and form collectives that have a common identity that then grows in power and influence. Enabled and enhanced by technology, it finds paths to attain a measure of immortality, to the extent that it believes it can exist outside its living, psyche-emitting human host. In this it has deceived itself though as ultimately it is still a side-effect of the human psyche. In fact, in contrast to Spirit, the Possession is finite: without psychic life, it will cease to exist, in the same way that darkness without light, is not darkness but a no-thing.

---

[1] Impressions here refer to the effects of stimulation upon the psyche, caused by environmental and circumstantial influences, as well as that of people.

Where this will go is complex to predict, but it is in my view hazardous to ignore this phenomenon, or to simply see it as a side-effect of the mind. To be able to recognise the effects and influences of the possession, is not to see it as a human psychological something, but to see it as a non-human but conscious and aware organism, that is invisible and only detectable by its effects.

This may seem eerie or scary to some, but (to me) the Possession is simply another feature of Great Nature. In this we see how the pendulum of a Divine Mechanism continues to swing from one pole to another, as it does in all things. The same 'swing' is seen in the changes in the functioning of man, with which I do not mean a type of evolution, but the swing from one form of functioning to another. For example, it used to be that the physical man was valued - even though his physical state was vulnerable to illness and injury which would affect his ability to work - and the errors of the sentient-man, as a sentimental and thinking man, were easily forgiven and overcome. This has now completely reversed. The physical state of man is no longer valued as essential and the sentimental and psychically sensitive sentient man is valued as more important. While the physically hampered man was relatively easy to heal or replace, the sentimental man who turns to chaos, is virtually impossible to heal or replace. As it is often in this chaos that a Possession can thrive, it happily fans the flames of chaos – and even more so now that it believes it can exist in A.I.

I believe that this is not going to end well for many; by the time this Divine Pendulum has stopped its current swing, the world of man will look considerably different and – from civilization's perspective - unlikely to be for the better.

Much work will then lie ahead...

I hope your trip to KZN goes well, and that we will be able to have a cup of tea or other tomorrow.

Best wishes,
John

On Wednesday, August 24th, 2022, Swami Vidyananda wrote:

Dear John,
Hari Om.

Thank you again for seeing us for lunch at the airport.

Does Possession refer to an entity or to a thought structure?

Yours in Prem and Om,
Vidyananda

On Thursday, August 25th, 2022, John wrote:

Dear Vidyananda,
Hari Om.

I believe our meeting at the airport , where we met up with both you and

Uma, was another one of those Divine Crossroads. It was a pity Vani could not be there as well; I hope she is feeling better. We are back in Dubrovnik where Nick has joined us for a few days before returning to the Netherlands, and all is well.

Given your question - the following is simply my perspective and understanding of this:

In short: One could say that the Possession is an 'entity' that consists of 'thought structures', but not ordinary thinking patterns that we are conscious of. To analyse this view, one would need to go deeper and to the beginning of things.

Unlike contemporary belief, the conscious and thinking man did not evolve from a worm or ape; there may have been a lesser organism, but a lower and lesser thing or being cannot create a higher one - it always requires a higher 'Force' or 'Influence' to do so. One may thus observe that the body was made manifest through the Divine's (higher dimensional) 'wish' to be able to feel and interact with things of form, 'things' that were before, only 'sensed' (Please note that I am using this type of analogy only to clarify the point). One could therefore say that a finger grows, because it was stimulated by thought, like a tentacle or vine, with a need or wish to be able to touch or grab.

The quality or nature of the thought (or psyche) will therefore determine the quality and nature of that which is made manifest. This is obvious when one sees how thought quality affects not only rudimentary things like our work but also the more refined things like our interactions with others.

One could therefore say that all things originate from the psyche's forms of thought. Some of these thoughts are attentive and Conscious or Intuitive Thoughts, but mostly, they are mechanical-reactive and unconscious. Hence:

- Along our journey, in service of the Divine, our Individual Spirit (that some would categorize as the Soul), arises from Conscious or Divine Thought; the unconscious or unobserved and mechanical-reactive thought is what grows the Ego.

- Whereas the Individual Spirit (or Soul) is embedded in a *Single* and Universal Truth, the 'All and Everything'; the Ego is *dual* and embedded in an illusory impression of itself. As such, the Ego will seek others who are like it or similar, for physical and emotional identification and strength, regardless of Truth[1].

- Whereas the Individual Spirit merges, through the 'guru', 'way' or 'path' through life within, to 'All that is' or Truth, and which as such is of an Infinite and Higher Dimensional nature; the Ego seeks to mirror this process of 'artificial infinity' in its three-dimensional physical and finite realm, using one- and two-dimensional methodology.

Thus, the unconscious and mechanical-reactive thoughts on the Earth can

---

[1] Consider the powerful effects of the old Dutch and South African state motto "Eendracht maakt macht" (unity makes strength), used to militarize its masses.

become like the pack, as in a pack of hungry or even rabid wolves; an entity of its own. In this example, one could say that one could just shoot or contain the pack of wolves, and this would be true in the case of an 'entity', but the phenomenon of the Possession is such that it has no defined boundaries and cunningly merges into its surrounds. In fact, on the fringes, it would look harmless and even useful or important.

One could therefore say that the Possession is an atom-less entity, that is fed by the psyche of the living individual and/or collective humanity, but as it is connected to living beings, it is still vibratory in its nature. Its reality can be positively motivated as critical to human survival and existence - but as it has the power to coerce others who are unaware and asleep (from a consciousness perspective), and it can make them blindly trust it, follow it, defend it, and die for it.

I always felt that the story of the Pied Piper of Hamelin was a reference to this phenomenon. In this fable, although the Piper or his magical flute were seen by most as the cause, I felt this was incorrect; it was the existence of a particular vibratory sound that he and his flute were able to create, that mesmerized the rats (and the children) of Hamelin...

I would be very keen to know how your teachings explain the nature of this phenomenon.

Best wishes,
John

On Monday, August 29th, 2022, Swami Vidyananda wrote:

Dear John,
Hari OM.

My apologies for the late reply but I sought some quiet time for reflecting on the concept of 'Possession' as you described it, and as I am endeavoring to understand it.

I don't think that there is such a concept as such in Yoga or Vedanta, although, if my understanding of your description is correct, then there may be some similarity.

From the Yoga/Vedanta point of view, the Soul is the indwelling Presence of the Divine appearing as if individualized consciousness. On this dimension, there is the experience of Oneness with the Divine, as well as Oneness with the Creation, as these are essentially undivided[1].

Since the Soul is embodied, an identification with the body (which includes the mind, etc.) arises, and this is what Yoga/Vedanta refers to as ego: a subtle thought of 'I' that arises with every experience and/or action. Simultaneously ignorance of our true nature arises. Ego and ignorance are together.

---

[1] In Yoga and Vedanta the word Soul refers to the essential being that we are. It is of the nature of consciousness-existence-bliss and is one with Universal Consciousness (or God).

The ego then begins to erect a structure of thought based on experiences, what it learns from society, and its actions to perpetuate itself. It will hold onto anything to perpetuate itself, even if that means holding onto suffering. Maybe this we would call possession, in the sense that the ego 'possesses' its thought structure(s) and is then possessed by them, as these will determine the ego's way of thinking and acting. It becomes a self-perpetuating vicious cycle of ego reinforcing the thought structure, and the thought structure in turn reinforcing the ego. Hence the person is 'possessed' by this.

The spiritual path, as you mentioned, is to surrender the ego to the Divine. As long as there is a body-mind complex, there is ego, but now it is surrendered, hence purified, and becomes a tool of the Soul. The Soul remains in Oneness with the Divine, and hence all thoughts and actions are now based on the Divine.

I pray that this may make some sense when relating to what you call 'Possession'.

Yours in Prem and Om,
Vidyananda

On Wednesday, August 31st, 2022, John wrote:

Dear Vidyananda,
Hari Om.

I understand; Thank you for your thoughts - your explanation makes much sense.

All is well here; Nick left Dubrovnik and arrived in Florence yesterday and Matt let us know that he had arrived in Portland (Maine) from Nantucket. In this controversial and upside-down perceived reality, that such movement is still perfectly normal, is equally bizarre!

Much love to all at the Ashram, and of course to you.

Best wishes,
John

14

The Powers That Be

Early on in 2022, there was a clear transition of the world's attention from the Covid-19 and vaccination issues, into the next 'crisis', being the US-UK-EU-NATO proxy war against Russia in Ukraine. It did not take much to connect these events or, for many a contemporary mind, to suddenly but conveniently forget about the fears of the deadly pandemic and being ostracized from their community. This phenomenal effect was not lost on Swami Vidyananda and John, who deliberated the causes, one of which was seen to be a war on the minds of men and women. Swamiji and John discussed the spiritual challenges around the manipulation of the mass-psychosis, especially with an eye on the exponential increase in digital technology.

On Wednesday, August 31st, 2022, Swami Vidyananda wrote:

Dear John,
Hari Om.

Glad to know the boys are well.

Yes, indeed, life carries on. Which makes me wonder whether the powers that be can finally succeed because the human spirit cannot be conquered.

Thank you, and Love to you, Terri and the boys.

Yours in Prem and Om,
Vidyananda

On Saturday, September 3rd, 2022, John wrote:

Dear Vidyananda,
Hari Om.

On the powers that be, perhaps we must begin a new string examining their effects?

To begin: Their 'effects'.

You wrote in your last email: "Which makes me wonder whether the powers that be can finally succeed because the human spirit cannot be conquered."

The changes we see, are changes that in time, we will become accustomed to and we will learn to live with. Like our grandparents and great-grandparents did when, from having been plunged into chaos twice[1], their world emerged in the shadow of the Cold War with a very real threat of total nuclear annihilation. As we know from history, people soon forget the newness of their surroundings - even when it cycles[2] into forms of barbaric authoritarianism. Right or wrong, people prefer to focus on their personal day to day lives. The changes of today however, are irreversible. Even if all stopped what they were doing, shook hands, and went back home, the world of yesterday's choices no longer exists. We will have arrived in the new world of yesterday's consequences.

This is the same with our understanding of humanity - at least, the non-spiritual mechanical part of it.

As for the human spirit being unconquerable: I too, do not doubt this, but neither do I doubt that it will be tried and tested amidst the masses. Besides the physical and psychological suffering that the system's entities impose on society's respective people, we may also see an increasing dilution of psychic awareness due to 5G and vaccine-stimulated behaviour. Added to this is the spread of fear: the number of vaccine-related "unexplainable deaths" is supposedly[3] twelve million and climbing rapidly, and the spike in supposedly unrelated cardiac arrests, (turbo)cancers, and other unexplainable immune disorders, is becoming more noticeable.

This is perhaps a pessimistic outlook - but unless powerful and Divinely Guided 'players' intervene - this is the type of trajectory we may expect over the coming years.

Human civilizations are not only cyclic, but they have previously also been decimated by famine, disease, revolution, and war on a relatively small scale, and by water and fire, cataclysmically[4]. Perhaps the destruction of Sodom and Gomorrah[5] reflects what occurs naturally, when people become too clever for their own good, and put their advanced intellect over Spirit! If one assesses the old myths, it does appear that an increase in intellect-based intelligence can become a double-edged sword. This does not always align with life-oriented intelligence.

Perhaps, all we are witnessing is the beginning of, what one may call, the reverse swing of the Divine Pendulum in the great cycle of what we call 'civilization'. A bit like ploughing the soil in preparation for the new saplings; similarly, for the many dormant seeds of spirituality to be germinated once more. Spirit, expressed in such human or biological form is, in my view, the Creator's very purpose of Life, and perhaps these changes will stimulate such risings.

---

[1] Having experienced World War I and II in Europe.
[2] Referring to anacyclosis: the cyclic rise and fall of civilizations that rise as monarchies to become tyranny, to be ousted by the aristocracy, which becomes the oligarchy that is replaced by the democracy, which (as is evident today) descends into a demagogy, which leads to anarchy, from which arises the next monarchy.
[3] A number based on recorded cases in the West, whereas the true representation of the effects of the untested COVID-19 'vaccinations' will likely never be known.
[4] Referring to the Deluge following the end of the Pleistocene, etc.
[5] In the Abrahamic religions, the two cities of Sodom and Gomorrah were destroyed by God because of their wickedness.

Perhaps you care to share your thoughts on this?

Best wishes,
John

Saturday, September 10th, 2022, Swami Vidyananda wrote:

Dear John,
Hari Om.

Thank you for sharing your insights.

I am now sitting in a cottage within a private nature reserve bordering the southern part of the West Coast Nature Reserve.

I remember our hostess in Calvinia talking about the *Fourth Industrial Revolution*[1] (4IR) as an inevitable change that may appear evil, just as electricity appeared evil to her grandfather. And yes, humanity has adapted to a life of electricity. I wonder though whether 4IR will be so easily integrated seeing that it aims to invade the human body. Will people go along with this? Some certainly will. I have no certainty about it but I do imagine that a great number will not.

I am also not sure whether humanity will rise against this tyranny. I have noticed that more people are becoming aware of the negative effects of the vaccines, and these people are the vaccinated ones, who are starting to talk about their own or their relatives' or friends' adverse events. And these people have spoken to me about this without my asking. The question remains whether they will take better note 'next time'.

Also, I have heard of doctors, who had advised the taking of the vaccine, now realizing the damage. If they speak out, then there may be a game changer, I feel. Since the agendas are being introduced through the medium of health security, doctors and scientists could make a change if more of them (especially those who promoted the vaccines) speak out and challenge.

I also noticed that some movements and organizations have been formed that are fighting the system, at least in the realm of information dissemination.

The two dominant forms of resistance I have noted are legal and creating separate societies.

I also think that these groups will not stop so easily because they understand what is at stake.

On the other hand, I have noticed that many who have been warned and may also see what is going on, are unwilling to investigate further or to do anything at all; it seems they hope that this will all go away, or they are resigning themselves to a new way of life.

---

[1] The 4th Industrial Revolution refers to transformation driven by digital technologies, such as Artificial Intelligence, the Internet of Things, robotics, blockchain, and biotechnology. It blends the physical, digital, and biological worlds, and is characterized by the fusion of technologies that blur the lines between these realms.

So, I have no clue where this all is leading to. Politically I lack any such knowledge.

From a spiritual point of view, I am also unclear whether this will lead to a greater spiritual awakening. Although many people speak about this, I realize that the term 'spiritual awakening' has different meanings to people.

Those who have realized what is going on seem to be a mixed bag of people and those who went along (and still are) are also a mixed bag. By 'mixed bag' I mean worldly and spiritual people.

Whether an awakening to political intrigue and propaganda is a spiritual awakening I am not sure.

Will humanity turn towards spirituality on account of these events? Some certainly are but I doubt whether as a whole. I think it will require more suffering still; and more oppression. The tyranny has to come to a point where a large mass of humanity will pray for Divine Intervention and be prepared to also be part of such intervention.

The key question in all of this however remains with one self. This question is still unanswered by myself: what is the correct response for me to all this?

Yours in Prem and Om,
Vidyananda

On Monday, September 12th, 2022, John wrote:

Dear Vidyananda,
Hari Om.

I am glad to hear that you are in nature, it must indeed be very beautiful there now.

Thank you for your thoughts and observations.

1. My view on your first comment - if people will go with the 4IR idea or not - I differ only in that I believe rather a great number, 90% or more, will go with it. The reason being:

- It will be made popular, like vaccines - but even more so - as 'an easy way to knowledge' and thus being seen as clever. One needs but see how often people use their phones during conversations – they find importance in being able to quote statistics, names, etc, without having to remember them.
- It will be promoted as the way to become a "high-income earner" (as stated by Elon Musk) - imagine, for example, a lawyer who knows every law and every case ever judged accordingly.
- It will be promoted by the corporations, being 10,000% more effective than normal advertising.
- It will be promoted by the state - as they can enforce 'backdoors' through which they can monitor what people think, and as such predict what they will do - and in some cases, control what they will do by manipulating what they know and think.

- The docility of the 95% who just wish to be entertained (as per J Krishnamurti and Swami Venkatesananda[1]) will almost certainly embrace this for reason of popularity, sensuality, profit, greed, or duty.

It is therefore, in my view, not so much *IF* this will occur, but rather *WHEN*, and that also a time may come *WHEN WE ALL WILL,* to some degree or other. On this, therefore, the more relevant question would perhaps be WHERE or rather HOW Spirit will manifest Itself in such beings!

2. My view on your second comment - the rise of humanity against this tyranny – as you may assume from my view above, and as you also infer by questioning the "next time", I do not believe this will occur - for three reasons:

- Like you, I meet people regularly who have - for one reason or another - gone ahead and taken the series of 'jabs and boosters'. I no longer speak out against this as I know that creating fear will only exacerbate any side effects. The increase of adverse reactions and fatalities is already being swept under the rug, just like the logic behind the traditional Flu becoming a deadly Pandemic. Indeed, contracting the flu is, to these people, scarier than Death itself.
- The information war is almost complete. Within a few years, the internet-media will be completely locked in place and only the most persistent hackers will be able to access information that was not censored and pre-processed. If there were parts of the world today where this interference was not occurring to some degree, then I'd say there is a chance - but there are none.
- The 'official narrative', that was bought into and implemented by doctors and officials, will be repeated forever. Like the assassination of the Kennedys, the Gulf of Tonkin, 9.11, and WMDs[2], whereby the externally manipulated and controlled entity ruled over the masses, it, too, will convince the average sincere and good-natured 'mind' that it is probably better for everyone to just go with it. Then, in time, fiction will become factual history.

Although I *appear* pessimistic, I do believe this story has now been written – and it cannot be undone - at least not by the small percentage of open-minded people and organizations within this unprecedented situation. People who are asleep (as in 'without any spiritual awakening'), are in my view automatons – like mechanical entities that follow predictable and controllable patterns. Just consider how, in the last century, tens of millions of people entered military conflicts because of what they were told by their government. The previously stated percentage of 90 - 95% of people, opt to take the easier route, and many of them will thus become irretrievably entrenched within those choices.

However, if one studies the history of the nature of humanity, such tendencies seem natural - as in The Divine's purpose. Perhaps the human being has to endure such conditions for the individual Soul to evolve!

---

[1] During a meeting between Krishnamurti and Swami Venkatesananda, they agreed that between 90 and 95% of people simply want to be entertained!
[2] World-changing motives for war, that have since proven to be false.

Perhaps, therefore - considering that, from our viewpoint, A.I. is here to stay - our discourse should take a slight turn:

- Perhaps we must contemplate the point as mentioned above: '... that a time may come WHEN WE ALL WILL to some degree...' and '...WHERE or rather HOW Spirit will manifest Itself in such beings!'
- Perhaps A.I. will in time, enable us to discover and understand if it is in correspondence or conflict with Divine Consciousness.
- Perhaps there will be a way (or necessity), to carry Divine Spirit, like a Trojan Horse, into the Virtual Reality?[1]

Best wishes,
John

Thursday, September 22nd, 2022, Swami Vidyananda wrote:

Dear John,
Hari OM.

Well, I am back now, have caught up with things and have watched the links you sent.

I see your point that 4IR will be made very attractive and it will be made to be 'indispensable' just like cell phones are today. And looking at the comments below the video clip there does seem to be a lot of enthusiasm.

However, I was surprised that it appears that they are not as far-developed as I thought they were. I say this based on the comments by Elon Musk on some of his concerns regarding the technology itself.

I do wish to make a distinction between political awakening and spiritual awakening. I would call psychological/political awakening an awakening to the fact that we have been brain-polluted as Swami Venkatesananda would say[2], by the education system and propaganda and therefore have

---

[1] As a side note on Artificial Intelligence (AI): When we contemplate our understanding of our Divine Higher Being, we may consider how, through the Divine's Higher Dimensions, we are all connected. As such, we can contemplate if AI - that can also indisputably harm humanity - can create a new pathway for us to interconnect with the Higher Path, one that is without dogma's filtering or twisting of Truth within its emotional translations. It helps to formulate a better understanding by reviewing the views of some of those of very high intellect and knowledge on AI, i.e. those with 'super-brains'. Such review would primarily be to obtain an insight on their views on AI, and how their 'reality' sees humanity's place with AI. FYI: the following link is a 36-minute interview between Lex Fridman and Elon Musk, both well qualified and versed on all aspects of 4IR. They discuss (their view on) the concept of consciousness and whether or not one is able to define the difference between consciousness and AI., if there is one! They also discuss whether interference on a greater scale would be such a harmful thing - considering how, at present, humans are treating each other and their surroundings, without such 'intelligence': (https://www.youtube.com/watch?v=smK9dgdTI40)

[2] Swami Venkatesananda altered the word 'brainwashing' to 'brain-polluting' because 'washing' means making clean, whereas the traditional term 'brainwashing' actually means 'not clean'.

believed lies to be truth and also have been living our lives accordingly. This awakening then leads to a search for 'truth' regarding all the things we have learned etc.

A spiritual awakening I would call the awakening to Spirit. In this awakening there is at least the appreciation that we are not mere mind-body complexes and that we are spiritual beings first and foremost, and there will be an active attempt to discover or attain that spiritual reality.

These two types of awakening are not necessarily mutually exclusive but I believe that a person can have one type of awakening without the other.

My feeling is that Swami Venkatesananda and Krishnamurti may have referred to the spiritual awakening, as I doubt very much that Swami Venkatesananda expected that his fellow disciple brothers should be politically awake when they mention the 95%. Of course, I may be mistaken.

But I would agree that most people are politically unaware, although it appears to me that the numbers may be increasing, especially those who got hurt by the vaccines, and those who witnessed the vaccine deaths. However, whether they make the link to the political agendas (such as 4IR) I would not know. And as I mentioned earlier many organizations are now making a fight, and I wonder whether they will not make an impact. After all, many changes to society were also brought about by freedom fighters.

Now, to the question of whether we can lead spiritual lives whilst being connected to 4IR. Here I am specifically referring to AI being integrated into the body in the forms of technological implants, such as nano chips, etc. These of course would be the instruments of a two-way communication system, which means that the brain will also receive information.

And that is the crux: I don't think it will be possible to live a spiritual life. The reason is that the mind, which is intimately linked to the brain, needs to be still for there to be an experience of Spirit or Consciousness. This will not be possible as long as the brain is being stimulated by technology. Even in our current way of life, it is extremely difficult to enter into Spirit due to the innumerable distracting thoughts that we have. The additional burden of constant stimulation from AI will make it virtually impossible.

In the video they briefly discuss consciousness. But their view of consciousness is incorrect. Consciousness is not a function of thought. Thought covers or hides consciousness. Consciousness is ever-present and is the essence of Being. Consciousness is discovered when thought is absent. Thought cannot create consciousness, and therefore AI cannot do so either. Thought and AI are extremely limited and cannot even understand consciousness. However, they hide it.

Consciousness cannot be measured or objectively studied because it is the Ultimate Subject. It can never be understood by the mind or intellect or AI. Hence pursuit and immersing oneself in that stream is counter-productive to anyone who wants to lead a spiritual life, i.e. a life in Spirit, which is Pure Consciousness or Pure Being.

As we know, Krishnamurti warned about AI and technology and that these will lead to tyranny. And already we have the beginnings of that tyranny.

Can there be any thriving under tyranny? Very unlikely. And my understanding of history shows that usually the spiritual movements either went underground or separated themselves from the tyrannical state so that they could pursue their spiritual goals.

However, I never like to be dogmatic about my views; but if my understanding of spirituality is correct, not so much from a philosophical point of view, but from the practical point of view, then I cannot see a reconciliation of 4IR with true spirituality.

What do you think?

Yours in Prem and Om,
Vidyananda

On Friday, September 30th, 2022, John wrote:

Dear Vidyananda,
Hari Om.

It was enlightening to read your reply; again - thank you for sharing your thoughts and insights.

I agree with your thoughts and views, especially on the consequences of trying to attain (our understanding of) Consciousness through or within the medium of Artificial Reality. Yet still, when one studies the Technocrat or the Academic, one notes that they staunchly believe it to be different. Thus, if one wishes to understand these 'beliefs' better, I feel one has to explore the minds and worlds of such people further.

One could, for example, observe how a large percentage of people **religiously** follow the advances of the 4IR and its Artificially Generated Reality. As such, one can understand how, across millennia, the world's various religions formed and shaped certain parts or peoples of the world; likewise, this 'new idol' has gone global within a few decades. What is of greatest concern is that it has no form, direction, or aim, other than its own enhancement through the seemingly 'irreversible' attention of and thus enslavement of, its subjects. Its end-game is unclear, but it would seem to be the enhancement of something non-biological; a kind of an inconceivable awareness within something that is non-living (inanimate).

It is this rather scary aspect that forces me to consider the following: Would I be passive, and abandon those whose minds have wholly been 'uploaded' into this 'false god', or would I be active? Active being, for example, to somehow insert or 'upload' myself consciously into such a Virtual Reality, whilst remaining in control of the information upload, and from within this invisible mind-prison, attempt to influence or assist people in this 'space' to escape?

This, however, may be like entering a world of potentially irreversible damnation, whilst trying to assist people to switch their talking minds off, and committing what they may perceive as a form of menticide!

Either way, it seems to me that the largest challenge would be addressing the proverbial 800-pound gorilla in the room: How would we define consciousness *within constraints that can be accepted by differing views of what is at stake, and what to look for*? With this I mean that different people have different views of what they believe consciousness is, and if one wanted to assist these potential great many, then some form of commonly accepted definition would need to be considered. To me it seems clear that we (I believe you and I?), consider that consciousness is not a product of mind or thought, but that it is found in the conscious absence of mind or thought. When one wishes to describe this to a room full of people who differ vastly in every way, it would be a bit like defining the idea of Love; everyone has many things they love, each of which has a meaning that differs. One can imagine how each one's 'love' may differ for their God, child, parent, self, country, hobby, dog, or even their football team!

Hence, if one wanted to undertake such a mission, and enter into a 'Neuralink-Metaverse'[1] whereby one would encounter and interact with avatars[2], one would need to be able offer a clear definition of what consciousness is. One commonly-understandable way to do so, would be to define consciousness by what it is not. Another would be to suggest that consciousness is more like a medium.

Based on 'consciousness as a medium', I tried to put together some reasoning on how and why this would be so. The result was that I found the medium of consciousness must differ for different animate species, and among the human species, and it would also differ between different kinds of people according to the nature of their awareness. My notes became rather 'expansive' though and, due to their nearness to the heart, some I felt were perhaps somewhat challenging. Hence, before we entered this 'new and delicate' domain in our discourse, I wanted to ensure you would be open to such a line of thought and discussion.

Let me know your thoughts!

Best wishes,
John

On Wednesday, October 12th, 2022, Swami Vidyananda wrote:

Dear John,
Hari OM.

Certainly, I am always open to discussing any topic, however near it lies to the heart (or in the heart). After all, are these not the very things we should discuss? So, please do share your thoughts on 'consciousness'.

On the question of whether one should dive into this 4IR world, which means being linked through one's brain. I would leave that to an enlightened Master. Since they have attained that level of consciousness that is beyond thought and are therefore not affected by thought, they can handle

---

[1] Neuralink is a company controlled by Elon Musk, that researches brain-computer interfacing using, among others, an implant concept. The metaverse refers to a virtual environment that allows for multiple virtual realities.
[2] The avatar herein, refers to the graphical representation of a user in a digital environment.

the upload.

But as for myself, who has not even mastered my mind, I would not like to take that risk. This is also because I do not regard myself as a saviour nor as an awakener. My role as a teacher is only incidental to my being a seeker, and in that role, I do not see myself as awakening others but rather as one who is sharing whatever I know with those in whom some kind of awakening has occurred, on account of which they come to the ashrama. The rest of humanity is in my prayers and I place them in the hands of God.

My goodness, I feel as if I am talking about the movie 'The Matrix'! Can you believe it!

I pray that both of you are well. Please accept my hugs, not virtual but spiritual!

Yours in Prem and Om,
Vidyananda

15

On Consciousness and the 4th Industrial Revolution

In this part, John expands on his hypothesis by exploring the idea that Consciousness, if perceived as a medium, will differ between beings. This is because beings perceive their realities differently, according to their biological and sentient formation, as well as their dimensional awareness.

On Friday, October 14th, 2022, John wrote:

Dear Vidyananda,
Hari Om.

I trust this finds you, Vani and all at the Ashram, well!

Terri and I are also fine, but naturally keeping a wary eye on the multi-dimensional yet human endeavour, taking place in the various geopolitical arenas. However, as little can physically be done, besides taking care of the basics, I spend much time trying to understand the inner workings of the participants and subjects in our observed reality. This understanding is important to me as I feel that only by doing so - completely and utterly - can I love unconditionally and accept unreservedly!

That said, thank you for your last reply. In my contemplation on these matters, it helps a great deal to be able to share my views. Besides that, your in-depth, wise, and spiritual approach to such things as well as your opinion as my friend, gives me comfort; if, during my journey into some of these deeper, more mysterious, and often darker sides of humanity, I come to a point of compromise, I know that you will 'nod', 'nudge' or 'kick' me back to the Light accordingly!

I admired your description of yourself as one with a role as *'an incidental teacher who has not yet mastered his own mind'*. But is mastering one's mind something that one knows one can do? Or is it rather a process and a way or state of being? This 'mind' being something other than ourselves, often has 'a mind of its own' and as such, even after many years and perhaps even lives, the mind remains vulnerable to *unexpected and unfamiliar external stimuli!*

The analysis of the mind is perhaps a topic for later discussion as I think we have enough to chew on right now. I am however confident, that the review below will not represent an unfamiliar stimulus, as I believe it is a territory you are already well familiar with! That said, it may take a few weeks to digest, but then there is no rush to reply, and if you prefer not to, then that is OK as well!

Best wishes,
John

So then, here goes...

On Consciousness and the 4th Industrial Revolution

If one wondered how one could define the 'contemporary view of consciousness'; one may consider that many New Age[1] participants tend to refer to consciousness as a "Unified Field" and that others refer to consciousness as *something one has or has attained* and call it "my consciousness". Perhaps these are both components or parts of a Whole - so for now, I will refer to this 'Whole' as Universal Consciousness.

During our past discourse, I believe we concluded that the Technocrat defines consciousness as something that the thinking-cognitive-brain-mind evolves into. According to him (or her), it is something that is the product of the 'mind' and as such, if he can create an artificial mind, he should also be able to develop an artificial version of consciousness. However, the result of this will likely be, that their very search, for something which they have already defined, will be so named, no matter what is found. This is – in the material world – a veritable power, as it connects with the Power of Belief, a psychic (and often perceived to be miraculous) phenomenon that manifests, for example, the placebo and nocebo effects.

Whichever way one chooses to look at this, there are a great many who have, in one form or another, surrendered their freedom of choice to this power. Of those who have seen or even experienced its effects, many will be hard-pressed to forgo the perceived comfort and safety of the situation they now find themselves in. It is akin to the misuse of authoritarian power in many countries, whereby the subjects of that country are knowingly manipulated via their suffering and fear but yet, are unable and unwilling to make changes.

The effects of this harnessed energy – whether dark or light – is a metaphysical 'manifestation of the psyche' and it is what many contemporary believers consider as 'spiritual' and the part of them that interacts with it, as their consciousness. As this effect does arise from the mind and thought, it is a feature of the human that the Technocrat will try to replicate in his machine: Behold, the 4th Industrial Revolution transcends into the 5th Industrial Revolution![2]

---

[1] New Age typically relates to a religious movement or community associated with a type of dogmatic spirituality. It involves practices like meditation, energy healing, astrology, and a focus on personal spiritual growth, but is often chastised due to its disassociation with the physical, material and societal world.

[2] Where 4IR refers to the merger of humanity with technology, the 5th Industrial revolution (5IR) largely refers to the battle for the thoughts and opinions of humanity and thus the psyche of humanity.

Some may feel that these views are 'off-track' and even illusory, but only until they see the evidence of 4IR research and its Trillion Dollar budget. The aware and informed observer may also note that often, forms of Satanism and other barbaric rituals and symbolism, as mentioned above, are accepted as normal en-masse. After all, these are not only used in our mind-capturing and idol-cluttered entertainment, but also in the practice of many an authoritarian regime (including certain monarchical systems), the military and certain sectarian religions.

One may, however, also see that these effects are simply the fulfilment a karmic instrument, as you so profoundly wrote in July earlier this year:

"... is it possible that this Plandemic/Genocide is an act of the karmic law, in which depopulation is required? Is it possible that the instruments used are the corrupt elite, who are the 'ideal' instruments, but who due to their weaknesses will still have to pay the karmic debt? And is it possible that all the lambs to the slaughter are unconsciously sacrificing themselves as part of the spiritual evolution?"

In contemplation of these ideas, thoughts and phenomena, I spent some time trying to enter the minds[1] of these 'corrupt ones', to see the purpose of Life and the world of people through their eyes (a practise I do not recommend as it was not always the most comfortable of things to do to my mind!). The result was that I noted how many of them followed a path of fear- or sex-driven greed (but not all). I had to acknowledge that within the higher echelons, some of the elite among these 'corrupt ones', believed in a higher, kind-of dark spiritual purpose (which they of course do not consider as 'dark'). As this is where the real power resides, this was the avenue that I opted to analyse deeply – and I combined my findings with my general understanding of a variety of subjects.

To 'begin', I first observed that different animate beings – including but not limited to the differing degrees of awakened and sentient persons – have different mediums within which they realize consciousness. Second, I noted that these mediums appeared to correspond to the traditional elements of Water, Earth, Air, Fire, and Æther[2], but more on this further down.

From here, I found that many things began to connect. Again, I apologize for the length of this hypothesis but these were complex ideas and the only way to review them, was to do so expansively. This I believe was additionally necessary as the subject matter (that of Artificial Reality, Artificially Generated Reality and the 4th Industrial Revolution), is by far the most dangerous threat humanity has ever faced. Its singular nature is just so far beyond our understanding of reason, logic, *and what we consider as necessary*, that to attempt to 'visualize' this, I feel, can only be done by placing it within the greater 'dimensional' perspective, as follows:

---

[1] This was naturally not a physical process, but a purely mental or imaginary one.
[2] Also called "the five elements", they originate from ancient Greek philosophy, as well as other early belief systems, where they were used to describe the fundamental building blocks of the universe and the natural world. Each element was thought to embody specific qualities and forces in the world around us, and together they were believed to account for all physical matter and phenomena.

The Reality of Dimensions

In the inability to logically describe *what something is, separate of other things and on its own*, our Creator's Duality always provides an alternative, which is describing *what it is not*. Of these two options, 'what it is' and 'what it is not', the identification of anything begins with what is real and what is illusory, or what is true and what is false, and what – in the three-dimensional reality of Space-Time – we observe is physical and what is metaphysical or even conceptual.

Just as a one-dimensional line is a mathematical concept, the perceived reality of the one-dimensional man[1] is one whereby he sees all things surrounding himself and his world as either being one or the other, and thus equally conceptual. This does not mean his reality does not exist, it simply implies that *without the greater entity that it forms a part* of - it has no substance; the nature of such 'substance' in other words, is defined by the 'greater entity'. (One can see this, for example, in a person who identifies himself as a member of a collective or organization, be it military, academic, social or other, and who, when outside of such surrounds, no longer values himself).

The same can be said of the two-dimensional plane or surface which, due to its absence of depth, has no form; as substance, in other words, it does not exist. In the same way, the reality of a two-dimensional person, whose picture-like perception has no depth, is also equally conceptual. This person's state of mind is consequently in perpetual flux: infinite in its possibility, unable to have a defined opinion for very long, and supporting a reality that is absent of anything substantial. This too, does not mean his reality does not exist; it simply implies that, like the one-dimensional person, it is a reality that, *without the greater entity that it forms a part of*, is absent of substance, and thus conceptual and even illusory.

If we next observe the three-dimensional reality that man perceives, including its feature of 'Time', we again encounter something that is paradoxical to his reality. This is the inability of his three-dimensionally conditioned mind to comprehend a thing that exists outside of it; in other words, he is unable to acknowledge that something exists outside of his space-time reality. Consequently, when something has no actual boundaries defined by space or time, in other words, it is 'spaceless' or 'omnipresent' and 'eternal', then his mind will automatically attempt to fabricate boundaries[2] to define it.

To attempt to explain this in physically descriptive terms, we could try to define the dimensions by attempting to describe the beginning of a mountain, or a wave, or a single thought. As none of these are of their own origin but the effect of a multitude of causes, we would have to go back to the

---

[1] The terms 'man', 'him', 'he' or 'his' do not refer to gender, but to the general human being or humanity.
[2] One could consider the Big Bang theory as a created example of an artificial boundary – a theory proven to be unsubstantiated (especially since the recent discoveries from the NASA launched James Webb Space Telescope, amongst which galaxies that are older than that the Big Bang was 'calculated' as).

beginning of all things – if there ever was such a thing! As such, limited by his three-dimensional reality, it is beyond his ability to realize that his own reality is equally undefinable and thus illusory[1]. In the case of the mountain, for example, the earth below is an integral part of it, as are the climatic elements that shape it, and which in turn affect and are affected by the sun and moon. The same occurs with the three-dimensional observation of a thought, that has causal relations which are even more immeasurable – in both its time and space.

It should therefore be considered that, in the three-dimensionally perceived reality, every aspect of man, including that upon which his history, knowledge and the very concept of Space-time itself are based, is non-fundamental.

This kind of thinking is naturally not very popular, but I must persist! If for example, we maintain an open and unbiased mind in our wish to understand the Higher Dimensions, because we know they exist, we may see that the perceived reality of the three-dimensional space-time world is as conceptual to a Higher Dimension, as are the one- and two-dimensional ones to the three-dimensional. Hence, if we follow this line of thought, and see how a collection of intersecting one-dimensional lines create a two-dimensional plane, and how adjoining two-dimensional planes can create the three-dimensional solid, we may consider that there is indeed something separate of space and time that gives origin to the time-based three-dimensional world.

If we were able to continue this flow of reason, we would arrive at the veritable presence of the omnipresent, omniscient, and omnipotent Consciousness!

In our previous writings, we discussed the mind-capturing 'entity' or 'possession' phenomena. Seeing the trends of ill behaviour by both the individual and his collectives, as conscious and intelligent phenomena - with an identity and life of its own – is not popular among academia, science, psychology, or contemporary thought. To these, these phenomena are described as the effects of fractured or disturbed minds. However, as we have noted, most of the observed 'bad behaviours' are fear or greed-based, and are often defined by an absence of conscience, combined with narcissistic, apathetic, and even violent behaviour. Of note as well is that these tendencies are, when observed across a wider spectrum, destructive and 'unnatural', seeing that they run counter to what is naturally good and enables a harmonious existence for the individual and collectives of men and women.

Still; it is preferred by modern psychology to classify the causes of such destructive behaviour as genetic, or due to an abusive childhood, or because of external and environmental elements such as excess, violence, perverted sex, drugs, and also cult-like practises.

---

[1] Except perhaps when he applies philosophical or mathematical logic and reason, but since these can be seen as portals to higher dimensions, their realization still requires a higher dimensional influence!

Whereas these are all veritable factors, they are seldom considered as the effects of an underlying metaphysical phenomenon.

In the same way, we can see how the influences that cause a disturbed and fractured social or familial environment are seldom seen as isolated. As a result, these influences and environments are often academically categorized under acts of social desperation related to the bad influence of a sociopathic and absent-minded herd. *The presence in these, of a metaphysical 'vibe' or entity that is repetitive, alive, intelligent and identity or shape-shifting, is also seldom considered.*

All this aside, and regardless of whether we refer to these phenomena as causes or as effects, as possessions or entities, or merely as the results of disturbed processes of thought and ego; the relevant point of this narrative is that they are typically one- or two-dimensional in their nature and they can be identified by their *effects*, which change constantly, as the need arises, and can be seen in the actions of those who are subjected to them.

I believe this differs from Divine Consciousness, as Divine Consciousness does not manifest Itself in the actions or thoughts of the individual, but rather by his *inner state of being*. The description of the "inner state of being" however, is to the one- and two-dimensional observer equally confusing, as he is more likely to consider the "inner-state of being" as the state of his thoughts, moods, forms of belief, or other sentiment. Therefore, depending on the varying background of the respective one- and two-dimensional person's views, one may attempt to describe to them what Consciousness is, by describing what it is not. To do this, in turn, we must become aware of such observable inner and outer effects. To clarify my view on these 'effects', I have broken them down along their respective categories:

The Contemporary[1] Definition of Consciousness

To the one-dimensional being everything is either this or that, with me or against me, have or have not, good or bad, and so forth. For these beings, nothing is ever neutral, as even when it appears to be, it will be considered liked or disliked, with an approved or disapproved 'opinion'. *For the two-dimensional being*, the primary focus is on appearances, and anything that may reside underneath such an appearance is, to them, a non-issue and virtually non-existent.

For these persons, their emotions or feelings are what dominate their physical and thinking centers, and even their sentient centers. If such ones are doing physical labour or sport, for example, their focus of mind will be on how they feel about their performance. The same will apply when they work with their minds; thinking, studying, analysing or other, they have 'feelings' about the outcome of such, as well. We can even say that everything they

---

[1] The term 'contemporary' here, is not used to define people by their education, occupation, or affluence, but rather by their perspective on reality; persons who are closely associated with the attributes and norms of their current space and time, which in John's interpretation applies to existing in dominantly one- and two-dimensional realities.

see, do, think, say, or have, will have a 'feeling' of sorts, dominating it. This 'feeling' will then form its own opinion, and consequently, affect how they think and act. Regardless, therefore, whether such a person is a manual labourer or a politician, a soldier or a doctor, a wealthy businessman or an academic, in the contemporary (or one- and two-dimensionally oriented) ones, their emotions and feelings will dominate them and their mechanism.

Thus, the contemporary one whose focus of mind is oriented around their emotions or feelings, will consider Consciousness with an emotion-based feeling attached to it. Instinctive and intuitive impulses will be regarded as 'signals from their Consciousness', as will their acts of being compassionate or empathetic.

The contemporary ones whose focus of mind is oriented on their thoughts, will likely consider their cognitive consciousness as related to Consciousness. Often such intellectuals – as found in academia – will offer deductive reasoning, that may include religious and spiritual considerations, on *how the mind of the intelligent cognitive man evolves to attain Consciousness*. Thus, they see Consciousness as the result of an 'effect' that the psyche of their intelligent mind manifests, which they then 'have' and which then somehow connects into a collective of others who are similar. Consequently, they exist in considerable confusion when that which they manifested in their state of 'being Conscious' abandons them, and with the passage of Time, they begin to observe the now inevitable death of their personal identity or ego.

Science and Technology's Definition of Consciousness

The Technocrat's aim is to replace the biological man, which is perceived as 'limited and imperfect', with something that does not require high levels of sustenance, and which is not subject to humanity's inherent weaknesses, such as an undefined lifespan. Subsequently, the Technocrat searches to re-create man along certain inanimate designs and criteria, ones that science can understand, control, and continue to improve.

The Technocrat formulates a belief that this is feasible and achievable by Technology, and if not now, then at some point in the future. This is partly due to a related belief that, what he perceives as '*his* Consciousness', resides in man, and is processed from and within his formatted, uploaded, and conditioned intellect. He thus sees Consciousness as something that evolves from the thinking and contemplative mind, following a process of learning, especially from subjects such as mathematics, psychology, sociology and philosophy, theology, etc, combined with a collection of memories or memorized details. Consequently, within this limitation, the Technocrat cannot envision the ancient knowledge and tradition that *the truly conscious man, is the one who enters Consciousness, within which he follows an opposing path, one that is thoughtless*.

As a result, the Technocrat, like the Academic, considers Consciousness as a conceptual 'process of Emergence' and one that is not too different from Artificial Intelligence, whereby the machine begins to think and reason by itself. He consequently convinces himself that his ability to manifest combinations of new programs within his physical self, will not be too unlike a spiritual revelation. This is substantiated when he is enhanced by access to instant knowledge, processed through Artificial Intelligence, and such that he can create distant horizons with new views and realizations. These will include designs and formulas of such grandiosity and with ever increasing levels of technological breakthrough, that their origin will be beyond comprehension, at least along the lines of human reason and logic.

The Technocrat, however, will not see nor acknowledge the irreversible danger of 'Hell on Earth' that he may be creating for himself; one in which the control of his mechanical and cognitive abilities are external to himself, and which may also include the control of his sentient ego. Once he has crossed such a technological threshold, the android[1] he has become will be unchallenged by things that previously made him stronger, and he will struggle through what little remains of 'his conscious life'. He has become a mere component of a form of intelligence that is an independent, artificial, and external program; one that may have little consideration for his deeper human feelings and needs. In addition, his now artificially enhanced mind is capable of resolving long-reviewed and complex questions, such that he finds there is no longer a reward in seeking the answers for himself. Further, in this state, all he discovers are questions that even 'it' cannot answer.

Religion & Spirituality's Definition of Consciousness

(As a side note; I apologize if this part appears disrespectful, lecturing, challenging or as a criticism of religion and spirituality – this is not intended in any way. To enhance my analysis, with its aim to understand, I felt that this angle needed to be included; that is if I wished to attain a full scope of understanding. I also felt that it was important to review this angle, as so much harm is committed in the name of the Divine. However, please feel free to correct or re-align my thoughts and views as you wish).

Many of the followers of the world's 'contemporary' forms of religion generally seek – or believe they seek – to save their 'soul' by appealing to one form or another of the Holy or Divine Spirit. This they regard as the Spiritual Essence of God, and one which they can merge with, as long as they are without sin or karma. The spiritualist does not differ much from this, as he, too, generally seeks to merge with a form of the Divine Spirit, or that which he sees as a Spiritual Essence, and a path to a form of salvation or a state of Unified Eternity.

Both religion and spirituality are generally based on compassion, forgiveness, and truth, but where they tend to differ, is that the former follows mostly sets of doctrine recorded in scripture or expressed by its prophets, and the latter primarily follows a way of living. To the unobservant eye, these may appear similar, but they do differ, as most religions typically aim to serve the collective and the individual through the collective, whereas spirituality seeks to enhance the essence of the individual, and its collective via the individual.

---

[1] A robot or synthetic being designed to closely resemble a human in appearance and behaviour.

What many cannot or will not accept is that the 'ego-entity', that has possessed the psyche of the normal thinking mind, is neither the essential self nor that which is regarded by him as Consciousness. The ego-entity, however, 'knows this' and being cunning, also knows how to convince the unaware and perhaps biased 'id-entity' of the host, that it *is* the essential self or consciousness. The ego-entity does this with visual deception, that can even appear to the host as miraculous.

Another of the ego-entity's means of deception is to 'grow itself' using the invisible and undetectable web of psychic connections that exist between beings of a similar species. This is a natural phenomenon and is known as 'morphic resonance' (a term coined by Rupert Sheldrake[1]). It is this very feature in man that enables individuals, unrelated to each other, and in different parts of the world, to inexplicably and almost simultaneously, attain similar skills and knowledge. This feature occurs subconsciously among most animate species, but in the unaware man, it becomes relevant when this ego-entity, subconscious to his awareness, psychically links into its collective network. It is often the element of morphic resonance that the ego-entity in man uses to empower himself and to make himself feel that he is on top of the world; invincible and untouchable.

Believing in his own prowess, or even that he is being 'guided' by the Divine through *his* Consciousness, he proceeds through life, doing as he pleases. If he is clever and oratory, he may draw many others into his 'congregated wake'. In the belief that he acts in the name of god, he goes from strength to strength and often realizes only too late if and when he has gone too far.

The Trance- and Psychedelic Definition of Consciousness

Inducing trance states, using sound, exercise, and forms of yoga are well known. These methods are old and are perfected by the practitioner over many years of received teachings and devoted practice. The use of plant, succulent, and fungi-based psychedelic substances to attain the trance state are illegal in many places and are considered by many as unorthodox or as 'short-cuts'. They are, however, very powerful, and in addition, Great Nature has provided thousands of variations, many of which have been used amongst animist traditions all over the world, and for thousands of years[2]. The complex process of plant combinations and brewing methods, amplified through very specific ceremonial practices under the watchful eyes of a trained and initiated shaman or curandero, is equally ancient. Its origins can only be guessed at, and moreover, the incorrect plant, plant-combination, or system of brewing can lead to the brew being deadly toxic, and when used within the incorrect ceremonial practice, can have the worst of outcomes. These were by no means discovered by accident or on a test-trial basis. It is my view that these discoveries were attained through the

---

[1] Sheldrake describes morphic resonance as a process whereby self-organising but disconnected systems inherit a memory from previous similar systems. See https://www.sheldrake.org/research/morphic-resonance

[2] There are Neolithic petroglyphs and cave paintings discovered in Algeria, which contain features of psychedelic mushrooms, dating back to 7000-5000 BC.

teachings and guidance of higher dimensional beings; beings that are closer to that realm or space of Universal Consciousness, than man himself.

If I compare this phenomenon with man-made enhancement using Information Technology, or man-coercion through dogmatic guidance, there is a vast difference. It seems to me that the use of psychedelics enables *a sincere and willing* Seeker to be reformatted and illuminated, and to become more conscious by actual spiritual entities. This process can be considered akin to raising the veil that obscures the 'afterlife', and from where great teachings, healings, and realizations are said to be attained.

As a point of interest; the use of psychedelics, both chemical as well as plant-based, was popularized in the 1960s and applied creatively or experimentally – but often with disastrous consequences. As with all things to do with attaining Consciousness, it is not something that is attained by 'throwing a switch', drinking a pill, or which occurs automatically or accidentally. One cannot expect to simply 'evolve' into being conscious, without having done the work. Ultimately the process of psychedelics requires that the participant already be conscious to some extent; meaning self-observant, absolutely sincere, and with a good as well as a strong intention. Any mental or emotional imbalance in a participant may become highlighted in him or her, and not be rebalanced unless the participant is willing to do what it takes. A participant using psychedelics who is, for example, emotionally unstable, may come out of such a journey absent of any enhanced changes and perhaps even more confused. A participant who thinks too much may try to analyse visions or teachings that are immeasurable, and a person who is too physical may attempt to undertake even more extreme physical challenges. However, a person who is balanced across his or her centers may, after only a single such ceremony, return spiritually fulfilled, with a great inner understanding of Universal Consciousness.

The Realistic Definition of Consciousness as 'a Medium'

A clearer understanding of our merging with 'ego-less' essence, whereby neither the 'I' nor the 'I AM' features, is by its very nature, relentlessly resisted by the ego. Many follow a belief that it is their name-ego they say 'I' to, that will be 'saved' and welcomed in Heaven, or Paradise, or that will gather with ancestors or clan members. There are probably elements of truth in all of these beliefs, but there is often also a personal bias. Seldom do these believers contemplate much on these matters or the fate of others who are not like them (or *with* them). They also do not wonder what will happen *after* they eventually get 'there' and the absence of such contemplation is often simply because the ego does not really want to know the answers to such questions, as the answers will not support its unique existence.

Perhaps, if we tried to follow a certain kind of deductible and comprehensible logic, such as that of hierarchy and correspondence, then a clearer understanding may be established. This logic would have to be one that can be justified to every person ever born, regardless of their religion, form of belief, class, manner, or ethnicity.

I have approached such a perspective, and for this, returned to some of the old known traditions found worldwide, ones that survived across the millennia. I found that there are among these, very specific, primary, alchemical, or traditional elements. These seem outdated to modern or contemporary science, which claims the periodic table[1] to indicate otherwise, but to me this seems to be due to their inability to see beyond their limited dimensional views. Of the predominantly five traditional elements, some vary to a minor extent, but in general principle, these are summarized as:

Water, Earth, Air, Fire, and Æther[2]

I do not see Fire as an element, but rather a destructive or cleansing process or force, such as a tornado or tsunami for the determination of Consciousness. This may make more sense if we can consider how each of the four remaining elements represents a medium for animate beings of a different type, nature, or complexity. Fire, however, does play a pivotal role in the other four; as with the presence of a medium that accommodates the manifestation of things, there must also be one that accommodates their dissolution.

Water as a Medium of Consciousness

By taking the presence of humanity out of the cycles of Great Nature, it is easier to recognize and understand the principles of the natural food chain, whereby the little fish consumes the shrimp, which lives off the microbe or flea, and the big fish then eats the little fish. At the top of this food chain resides the shark or whale; large, ancient, and indomitable, it has (besides man) no predators. Seeing this integral chain, we can envision how the life force of each microbe and fish consumed is absorbed 'as a whole' by its predator, and how the consumed life-force then becomes a part of it, too. The sardine thus becomes 'at one' with the shark, and the quantity of its absorbed life force determines the impact or component part of 'the whole' that it becomes 'at one' with.

At the end of this cycle, the shark or whale used in this analogy, naturally also dies. It then decays and disintegrates into millions of small parts, some of which may remain dormant in a nutrient or mineral form for extended periods, or even eons. The nutrient-based life force is then, in time, absorbed by plant life, microbes, shrimp, and small fish. As such, the life-force of the shark or whale used in this analogy, is re-distributed among millions of organisms, and the next cycle is seen to continue – beautifully and unendingly.

As we are unable to communicate intelligently with these aquatic creatures, we do not know for certain if there is a single form of awareness

---

[1] The periodic table is a tabular display of the chemical elements, which are arranged by atomic number, electron configuration, and recurring chemical properties.
[2] Classical elements typically refer to earth, water, air, fire, and aether, which were proposed to explain the nature and complexity of all matter in terms of simpler substances. Ancient cultures in Greece, Tibet, India, and Mali had similar lists which sometimes referred, in local languages, to "air" as "wind", and to "aether" as "space".

within them, whether individually or when they exist within schools and pods, or colonies of countless organisms such as those that form a coral reef. When, however, we observe the interactions in schools, pods or colonies, it seems evident that something does indeed 'morphically' connect the respective creatures, into a larger organism or greater being. It is along this form of logic that we may consider the medium of water as the blood of such a larger being, as the absence or quality of water directly affects the presence, strength, and quality of each of these creatures and therefore, indirectly, the greater aquatic being.

It could therefore be deduced that, to an aquatic organism's 'awareness', the water that makes up the bulk of its physicality and surrounds it, is its medium of consciousness.

Earth as a Medium of Consciousness

For land-based life, the life-cycles of organisms will differ somewhat from the aquatic ones. This is because, beyond the level of insects and small crawly things, animals are seldom consumed 'as a whole' by another single organism. This means that the life-force of a single animal that has fallen prey does not merge in its entirety with that which consumes it, and consequently, its life-force is distributed among many other organisms, including those that are plant-based.

This wondrous design still corresponds with the aquatic one though; the grazer consumes plant-based material which has grown out of the minerals and nutrients that were deposited there through different processes of various creatures, such as excretion of waste, decomposition of bodily remains, and decay of material remains of small insects and lower forms of life. As with the aquatic analogy, the large predators at the top of the food chain that do not fall prey to other creatures at their death, are still consumed by countless smaller organisms and the cycle continues in perpetuity. We may therefore deduce that, to a land-based organism, its medium of consciousness is Earth.

Air as a Medium of Consciousness

Following the preceding analysis of aquatic and land-based organisms, we now transcend to the next level of complexity, and observe the cognitive, sentient, and thinking man. Since he exists in artificial surrounds, outside of his natural ones, his physical remains are not generally consumed as such, but upon death, are either turned to ashes or left to decompose within the constraints of a cemetery. As such, a different type of transition of life-force occurs, that is not transferred through Water or Earth, but Air.

The human being differs further from the aquatic and land-based creatures, in that he has a psyche. As described earlier, this is an identifiable entity, and regardless of what some choose to believe, it remains a force or a form of energy, that grows in substance, complexity, and strength with time, and unnoticed by the unaware man. If one can see this for what it is, one may then also note, that not all identified psyches function along the same principles; human beings differ along very particular centers of attraction based upon where their 'focus-of-mind' is dominant. Following the traditions of Gurdjieff and Ouspensky[1], I would like to divide humanity into Man # 1, Man # 2, Man # 3, and the Spiritual Man, and describe them as follow:

In Man #1 – the Physical Man – the psychic forces are absorbed at death by those who follow his ways and adopt his perceptions of reality. These are typically his followers, subordinates, and in part, spouse and children.

In Man # 2 – the Emotional Man - the transition of psychic forces at death are similar to *Man # 1*, except that much of the psychic force is 'radiated-out' or surrendered to others through forms of psychological intimidation and its consequent trauma during life.

In Man # 3 – the Thinking Man - his psychic forces are preserved at death in writings, recordings, and other created forms. These are then absorbed or consumed, physically, emotionally, or intellectually, by others – across extended periods of time.

The psychic forces of Man # 1, Man # 2, and Man # 3 described herein, differ by *how* they are transferred from one being to another. Although these forces are of a non-biological composition, the entities they are transferred to, are still physical in nature, and as such, they remain part of the earth's biosphere. It is due to this that one may reason that, to the psychic elements of an aware ego, the medium of consciousness is metaphysical and thus considered as Air.

The Æther as a Medium of Consciousness

The next levels of being are also divided along certain criteria, and categorized herein as Man # 4, Man # 5, Man # 6, and Man # 7. As the purpose of this essay is to define the medium wherein each one realizes consciousness, they are herein simply described as one form, the Spiritual Man.

The Spiritual Man is the one who, through his or her work of self-observation and focused awareness, exists in an environment that is instinctively balanced across the three base centers described above. He may be ordained or live a normal life, he may get married and have children, run a household, a business, or even have a position in public office of some sort. Exposed to the attraction and repulsion, the challenges, distractions, and duress of a normal life, he must, within this experience of love and loss of Life, maintain the balance if he is to attain, what some refer to as, enlightenment.

(As a side note – if I may – I would suggest that the good monk, priest, yogi, or ascetic will fall herein, as they are the ones who, in service, unconditionally surrender 'normal life'. Acting as teachers, mentors, and guides, one could say they provide the counter-balance - one that preserves the access to mediums of consciousness against evil and the Darkness-of-man. Without their work and sacrifice, the attainment of balance amongst the centers for Man # 1, Man # 2, and Man # 3, would likely become problematic, and the freedom or possibility of attaining consciousness, in the

---

[1] GI Gurdjieff (1866–1949) was an influential mystic, philosopher, and spiritual teacher, known for his development of a system of personal and spiritual development referred to as "The Fourth Way." Ouspensky worked with Gurdjieff.

medium of Æther, from the perspective of a contemporary man, would likely remain absent).

The Spiritual Man is therefore one whose medium of consciousness is Æther. As such he finds himself liberated from the draws of the 'contemporary life'; he maintains his psyche with awareness and simply serves his day-to-day necessities but enhanced by the Instinctive Center. Although his psychic elements at death would be absorbed similarly as to those described above, every part would be evenly balanced across the three - physical, feeling and thinking - centers. In other words, the Physical Man or Man # 1 who is exposed to the Spiritual man, will attain a balanced amount of Physical, Emotional, and Thinking based psychic energy, and the same for Man # 2 and Man # 3.

The Spiritual Man, such as described herein, is therefore one who has applied his focus-of-mind, sentience, and physical life, in consciously observed, sincere, and truthful ways. At death, all that is pure and real, being that which is True and Good, can then merge with others who walked, are walking and will walk as such in his path, and to later emerge as one into a Higher Dimension. All that is false and untrue, in other words, is washed off or shed and 'left behind' as, from a Higher Dimensional perspective, such things do not and cannot exist in that which is real, pure, and eternal.

That consciousness that is realized by the Spiritual Man, would therefore be in the medium of Æther itself.

To Conclude: The Purpose of Fire

It can now be concluded that the purpose of Fire, mentioned as one of the five traditional elements, does have its place. It is to eventually and ultimately, consume the falseness of the psyche that was purged and shed.

One could say that the term 'Fire' is therefore not necessarily a literal translation, but rather a descriptive one. Ultimately, something that is false is not real, and as such it carries no substance; hence it is not something that can 'burn' either. Like the shadow before the Light, it simply ceases to exist, not only in essence but even in human memory. Perhaps, therefore, when all is said and done, and the illuminating Fire of Chaos has swept across the plains of falsehood, then contemporary life will re-emerge as it was before. All that has passed will no longer reside in fact or memory; except for those who attained their Consciousness in the medium of the Æther, where all that is and always was, forever will be.

Best wishes,
John

On Tuesday, November 15th, 2022, Swami Vidyananda wrote:

Dear John,
Hari OM.

Thank you for your loving wishes; and yes, we are all well. And we pray that you and Terri and the boys are also well.

We are also keeping an eye on developments, more so to get an idea of what is going on and what may happen; but also with the view to understand the other, which of course is also important. However, I venture to say that compassion need not arise only from getting a thorough understanding of the other, but if we gain a thorough understanding of our mind, we may be able to appreciate the workings of other minds in general, which is sufficient to have compassion. Compassion also is the natural characteristic of one who has realized his/her oneness with all creation. Realized, not in terms of thought, but actual direct experience.

It has taken me some time to read through your essay, especially since I wanted to understand it as best as possible. So, here are some of my thoughts.

So, to be clear on consciousness. Consciousness is not in the objective realm. It is purely subjective, it is the stuff we are made of, i.e. we do not have consciousness, we are consciousness. Consciousness however is masked by thought etc, and since we have identified with thought, etc, we believe consciousness to be something we possess or can acquire.

So AI is based on this fundamental error, as we both agree, and therefore it cannot replicate anything at all, because consciousness (being the substratum) cannot be replicated. A so-called replicate is artificial, and that which is artificial is artificial and not real. So AI can never be real, as its name indicates. Anyone who enters into this world is entering into great illusion and delusion.

And the thing about being deluded is that one thinks that one is not deluded, and not only not deluded but very intelligent. This is a great recipe for disaster.

Anyhow, I am merely repeating what we have already discussed.

You mention satanism briefly in your essay. I am interested to understand what you mean by the term and how it is being played out in the '1st world civilization' and also how it is built into 4IR.

You describe what may be called the 'self-fulfilling prophecy': we determine what consciousness is, and then when we find that which resembles our definition, we believe we have it. And in this manner, the various groups that you have described (including the technocrats), may feel that they have been successful in discovering consciousness. That is their own trap that they fall into, and the trap that those who follow will also fall into. To reiterate the point: consciousness cannot be described, not discovered as an object of perception, hence all the views that believe consciousness to be some-thing are false.

To make sure I understand you correctly, the lower dimensions exist due to the presence of an immediate higher dimension. And the existence of the higher dimension is the very substance of the lower dimension. Therefore, to understand any dimension, one needs to understand the higher dimension. Furthermore, the question arises whether the higher dimensions continue ad infinitum in their 'highness' or whether there is an ultimate dimension which is the ultimate dimension of all dimensions. The first option is an impossibility. Hence this leaves us with the ultimate dimension, which is not a dimension but is pure (or cosmic) consciousness. This means that all dimensions (and therefore all things) exist because of consciousness and that consciousness is the Ultimate Substance of all things and dimensions. This means also that this cosmic consciousness cannot be observed as an object because the observer is also that consciousness. Hence consciousness can only be known by being consciousness.

Now, the phenomenon of possession I understand is a view or belief regarding reality based on any of the lower dimensions being regarded as ultimate reality. And because these beliefs are regarded as reality and shared by everybody, they have real effects such as all the disturbed thinking and actions etc that we observe. Our individual problems are not in reality confined to the individual, they are collective in their nature, however expressed and experienced through the individual as an individual. This is the illusion.

Your analysis of consciousness in terms of the elements is interesting and very different from the understanding that Vedanta has of the elements. However, I do not regard these as contradictory, since both systems are ways of understanding. They may use the same words for different 'things'. Hence these views are complimentary.

In the Vedanta system, the elements are regarded as the different dimensions that creation is made of. Ether/Space is the 'container'. Not in a limited sense though as space is infinite, but in the sense that all creation is contained within it. All created objects also contain Space as a thing cannot exist without Space.

Space gives rise to Air, which is movement. All things move or vibrate.

Air gives rise to Fire. Fire relates to heat. All things have heat, even if we call them cold.

The first three elements are not visible but we can infer their presence.

Fire is what gives rise to Water. Water is liquidity, which again all things contain, at least to some degree.

And finally, Water gives rise to Earth, which is solidity. All things have some form of solidity, even if it is very subtle.

If we look at the human body, then we can understand the presence of these five elements. The body occupies space and is made up of space, the various cavities. There is movement within the body, such as blood, lymph, and nerve impulses, as well as the locomotion of the body's limbs. There is fire in the form of temperature and digestion, for example. Water is the fluids. And Earth is the solidity of the body.

Now these five elements relate to the chakras. The lowest is at the perineum and the highest chakra is the throat. Depending on which chakra an individual is identified with, so will be their state of consciousness. The lower chakras deal mainly with survival and desire (and therefore fear and hate). The higher chakras deal with spirituality. The fire element is the will and that is either directed toward the lower Cakras or the higher cakras.

However, even these chakras and therefore the elements, are transcended through the third-eye chakra and the head chakra. The third eye is a symbolic term for clear vision. Here the individual has a clear vision of what is and all efforts are directed toward enlightenment, which is the seventh or head chakra.

So, there is an ascent of consciousness taking place within the seeker.

However, having said all this, the Vedanta will still say, that regardless of the level of consciousness, there is still only consciousness, whether we call it un-consciousness, sub-consciousness, lower consciousness or higher consciousness, cosmic consciousness, etc. All these can only exist due to consciousness and all of these have consciousness in common. That consciousness (as mentioned above) can only be discovered through being that consciousness.

Consciousness is therefore independent of thought or any thought processes. It simply IS.

And the Upanishad so beautifully put it: That Thou Art.

I'm not sure whether my response makes much sense or is very coherent. Please forgive me if it is not.

Love and Blessings to you and Terri.

Yours in Prem and Om,
Vidyananda

16

Delusions of Reality

On Sunday 20 November 2022, John wrote:

Dear Vidyananda,
Hari OM.

I trust this finds you and all well, and that life at the ashram continues without too much interference. Terri and I are well, and I was very appreciative of receiving your response on AI and consciousness!

Our last exchange I believe was well concluded, and although these are not necessarily definite-outcomes, I am taking the liberty of starting a new string...

Firstly, thank you for taking the time to provide a very detailed and explanatory response to my essay. The essay was long - but it is complex to address a substantial subject such as consciousness, and to do so effectively, one has to level the ground so to speak, so that the correspondents can clearly see where one is standing and then understand one's point of view.

One thing this exercise has given me is a clearer picture of the following: Although as human beings we share the same three-dimensional space-time, and observe the same things and events, the *reality experienced* between different groups of people, differs vastly. Whereas this – from a social cognitive point of view - is considered a typical psychological feature, to me it seems as if the reality of different groups of people, differs so much, that they may as well be from or on different planets.

For example: Consider the recent midterm elections in the USA[1]. In these midterms, the incumbent party lost a few votes in "the House", but they won an additional seat in the Senate. This is all quite boring but what I found fascinating was that the majority of Democrats still voted for the Democratic party[2]. I mention this because the leaders of this party (especially the president) appear more as 'misleaders'; seeing that they do not represent the will of their constituents at all, but rather that of external entities. From that point of view, they are like marionettes whose strings are controlled by people who are unaccountable, being that the laws they write for their citizenry, do not apply to them. Consequently, they often do incalculable harm to the lives and economies of billions of people, including the

---

[1] The U.S. midterm elections are held halfway through a president's four-year term and determine the composition of House of Representatives and the Senate.
[2] John's view had nothing to do with party politics, but the fact that the ruling Democratic party had a President affected by dementia, and whose actions were the leading cause of pointless wars, internal conflict, and corruption at the highest levels.

very American citizens who vote for them – and yet, all seem to be at peace with that. It is a strange trend; most of the many Americans I know are, across-the-board, good, hospitable, kind, intelligent, and God-fearing people, yet still, they continue to fanatically support this obviously one-sided system. [Note that I care little for politics or any system of democracy that promotes a centralized form of rule that is authoritarian and which, due to the simple nature of contemporary human beings, gives too much power to too few and thus leads to corruption and perversion. (Power corrupts, Absolute power corrupts absolutely![1])]

This, however, is not just an American phenomenon, we see it in pretty much every country and among all races, religions, and ethnicities.

The *Power of Belief*[2], as documented by Dr Bruce Lipton and as observed in the placebo and nocebo effects[3], indicates that contemporary belief has *both psychological and physical* effects on the individual and his or her life. Human beings are therefore able to manifest their actual - not just perceived – reality, through their belief (which beliefs in turn affect the perceived and therewith experienced reality). This indicates that beliefs can run so deep that inherently good people, who are made to believe that others in their neighbourhood (who they do not even know) are evil, will eradicate these people, their families, homes and even entire towns. Beyond seeing that belief can heal you or make you physically ill, it also influences the outcome of events, and one could even say that it affects Great Nature. (This is evident in the power that prayer veritably has, *when it is focused, sincere, and supported by an unwavering Belief*).

In your last email, you wrote consciousness is the "stuff we are made of"[4], a view that I wholeheartedly share. I would add that human beings, due to their complex nature within consciousness, can become conscious of this.

This then leads me to ask:

1. Is Belief a 'Supranatural Force' (for lack of a better word)?
2. Would this 'Force' - in our observed reality - be psychic? Or does it originate from a higher dimension?
3. Is it possible for the psychic power of human beings to affect the reality of those who are unaware of it?
4. What are your thoughts on Belief as a higher dimensional 'Force' that can be harnessed for both good and evil?

My reason for posing these questions is because you asked me about my views on Satanism - and it is my view that this is connected. The practice

---

[1] Originally stated by Lord Acton, a 19th-century British historian and politician, who wrote: "Power tends to corrupt, and absolute power corrupts absolutely. Great men are almost always bad men."
[2] This view, based on Dr Lipton's book by the same, describes powerful forces that shape who we are and what we can achieve. By consciously cultivating empowering beliefs and letting go of limiting ones, individuals and societies can harness this power to manifest changes in thought patterns, emotional feelings and physical aspects.
[3] Based on these beliefs, the placebo is a positive or healing effect and the nocebo is what leads to negative outcomes.
[4] See: Tuesday, November 15th, 2022.

or 'craft' - real or believed – of Satanism is rooted in the ancient occult sorcery, which includes necromancy, and is believed to gain its power by accessing the psychic (fear and desire based) power of contemporary people, *by altering their beliefs.*

Those who use these practises believe they can capture and harness the psychic powers of the deceased - which is why the use of elaborate and ceremonial practices like entombment, embalmment, and mummification were (and still are) practiced.

Best wishes to you, Vani, and all at the Ashram,
John

On Monday 21 November 2022, Swami Vidyananda wrote:

Dear John,
Hari OM.

Indeed we are all well. And I pray that you and Terri are also well. Please convey our heartiest love to her.

Lord Krishna in the Bhagavad Gita states, "As is a man's faith, so is he." We are our faith. Faith is not merely that which we believe in but that which we have identified with. That is what gives it its power of reality. Whatever we identify with appears as real. And therefore there will be physical and psychological outcomes; and I guess at times social ones too, if enough people share the same belief or faith.

Faith as a force (or movement of energy) has its roots in the Divine: it is a matter of what form it takes and on what it is focused, that will lead either to evil or good outcomes, or preferably to enlightenment. The form it takes is based on our thought structure, which is the belief or faith.

I would also agree that some people may have learned the ability to tap into sources of energy outside themselves to add to their energy to bring about certain effects. Even acts such as prayer draw on an external source, where we draw on God's Power for some purpose.

Recently I have come across a few references and documentaries in which the so-called Elite is accused of being satanic. If we view satanism as the misuse of energies to harm others, then to me, that seems the appropriate description.

And all that needs to be done is channel the same energy that is used for evil toward good actions and spiritual uplift!

There was a great Tibetan Buddhist Yogi called Milarepa. There are wonderful biographies on his life which are worth reading. He is a great example of turning away from a life of Black Magic to Enlightenment.

Hence my regular prayer is that these people may realise what they are doing and change course.

Are you still in Croatia? Any new developments?

Yours in Prem and Om,
Vidyananda

On Friday 25 November 2022, John wrote:

Dear Vidyananda,
Hari OM.

Thank you for your reply.

We are well and yes, we are still in Croatia. We have moved from the city of Dubrovnik to the island of Korčula. It is peaceful here, and life here is very much rooted in the old traditions, family values and mostly an ordered system of decency. There is the creeping-in of western influences, but this is gradual, and I believe the statists, who are still foolhardily pushing their NWO[1] style reform, are being met with more and more public resistance.
There are some rumblings of Serbian resistance against Bosnian rule in areas that are ethnically Serb, but these are largely political and geopolitical. It is more so a 'handy-dandy' 'ready-to-use' potential flashpoint since Serbia is landlocked and surrounded by EU / NATO countries, and allied with Russia. There are about a dozen of these flashpoints in the world that 'they' have and like to 'keep warm', in case they need to start a war.[2]

It is unlikely that another Serbian rising will flare-up and either way, unless the Croats are attacked, they are unlikely to get directly involved. In addition, our far-off island of Korčula is a good place to be, as even at the height of the very intense Balkan war, the effects here, were only economic. Korčula sustains itself quite well, and people here still prefer to trade with cash!

As to our life here: I am in the process of buying a small house, and I may rent this out as a small investment, or we may live there. We have not yet decided. Whilst I must wait for a few business-related developments that are in the hands of outside parties, we remain patient and spend time on our studies and writing – and as the house needs some work, this will also keep my hands from getting idle!

Then: Matt flew into Amsterdam from the US this week and is spending a few days with Nick before coming here. Nick has a few exams left and will then join us as well. We are very much looking forward to spending almost a month with them!

As to the subject of our correspondence - thank you for your response and thank you for your continued willingness to entertain my philosophical deliberations!

The Teachings on Faith by Lord Krishna - as you explained - are the purest Truth; they are, as per our preceding conversation on consciousness, *all-encompassing*.

---

[1] The New World Order, following ideals such as those of the World Economic Forum (WEF) and UN Agenda 20 and 30, as discussed earlier.
[2] These comments largely refer to the bloody Balkan War of the 1990's when, following the breakup of Yugoslavia, its various territories ceded from the central government, which was located in Belgrade, Serbia.

I do not question this, but when one looks at the contemporary[1] masses, it does seem that 'faith' to some, is more like 'hope' for others. It is difficult to believe that so many let themselves be injected due to their 'faith' in the authorities behind the pandemic and others acted on fear-based 'hope' that the outcome would be OK. The same can be said for many actions in the past, too, including crimes against humanity. These range from the crusades and inquisitions, to the war on Islam (and vice versa), as well as numerous religion-based brutalities against civilians and the genocides of past and present!

It is this state of mind that puzzles me, as it is so contrary to common logic and the teachings of enlightenment across millennia. I wonder what it was and still is, that drives so many to such extreme, bizarre, and opposing ends; it is as unnatural as water flowing uphill! Perhaps there is a purpose in it? After all, the arduous journey of the Tibetan Yogi Milarepa, required him to awaken from a place of dark magic and evil, to attain one of the highest forms of enlightenment. Perhaps is it essential that humanity also take such a journey, and as a global-whole!

When I take *a very broad perspective*, that includes the wider spiritual, physical, psychic, and metaphysical realms, as well as the sciences of psychology, sociology, biology, geopolitics, economics, history and a few others, I see that, if one wishes to, one can begin to understand what this purpose is. This perspective has led me down the slippery slope of analysis of the differences between 'faith' and 'hope' and I find that this is determined by the reality that is perceived - *or that which I am made to perceive*.

While 'faith' and 'hope' have the appearance of same-ness, it seems they are opposites; when outcomes are not favorable or as expected, they diverge.

'Faith' is that which is sincere and characterized by a certain level of acceptance - but for this a higher form of awareness is necessary.
'Hope' is that which carries bias and is characterized by disappointment, disillusionment, fear, or anger - such as one may find in a contemporary one or two-dimensional environment.

Still, it is strange that not every man and woman follows guidance naturally and logically, to forms of acceptance. This is especially relevant, as it could make life simpler and more harmonious. Instead, people consciously or subconsciously prefer to identify with an outcome that is not yet known. Perhaps therefore, all that *is* 'was written' and what 'was written' were the Divine Laws by which the Kosmos and the illusory three-dimensional reality of man was made manifest. This observation can be substantiated when one observes how the effects of these laws are miraculously influenced more so by *why* and *how* one chooses, rather than by *what* one chooses.

Still, what we 'see' is that so very many are choosing on the behest of a relative few whose purpose is dark and quite evil. What we also 'see' is

---

[1] Referring to the larger percentage of humans, who perceived reality through one and two-dimensionally-oriented perspectives.

that this is causing the demise and suffering for so very many, and even for Great Nature herself.

If we again consider the arduous journey of the Tibetan Yogi Milarepa and that of humanity, which must now take a similar journey as a global-whole; besides meditation and prayer, what else can one do? Are we to remain passive whilst we observe what occurs? Must we merely persevere to remain neutral, whilst simultaneously remaining vigilant to ensure we do not become infected by the mass psychosis that surrounds us? How can we do this and not become separated from the whole, and blind to the world? Perhaps all we can do is focus on preserving the teachings for future generations, and for when the tide turns...

... I will end this review here, on this uncertain note - but please do let me know your thoughts and observations, if you have!

More importantly, though, we send you and Vani lots of love; we think of you and all at the Ashram and are most grateful for the seat in our hearts, that you have taken.

John

On Monday 28 November 2022, Swami Vidyananda wrote:

Dear John,
Hari OM.

Love to you and Terri and the Boys! As you know you are all in our hearts.

Thank you for keeping me in the loop of your developments. I am always keen to know what is happening with you.

Please keep our friends U. and her husband G. in your prayers. He is undergoing cancer treatment and is very weak.

On the subject of faith: As you conclude, people have different interpretations and usages of the word faith. And you correctly make the distinction between faith and hope. In this context, I would say that faith is to be steadfast in Consciousness or steadfast in the pursuit of Consciousness. In this, there is no seeking of any specific outcome other than to be established in It.

So, hope is based on desired outcomes and/or delusion. This is what we see in the world. And since most people are not seekers or established in Consciousness, they naturally live in hope. And since hope is based on desire and/or delusion, how can one see clearly? It will not be possible, since desire and delusion will cloud the mind. So, even a seeker, if they come under the influence of these (which of course happens frequently unless there is constant vigilance), can slip from faith into hope. It is then that people will act contrary to logic, reason, etc.

In fact, the Bhagavad Gita makes these distinctions as well. You may wish to read Chapter 17, which is the chapter dealing with the threefold distinction of faith.

As to what can we do for others? You have told me many times that it is not possible to help those who remain unawakened. And it has been proven to me over and over again during these last three years. No matter what we say, it seems to make no difference. But maybe seeds are planted, and with God's Grace, these seeds may sprout at some time. And sprouting cannot be forced, we can only keep watering. So, I am learning to await appropriate moments to say something without the desire that I should see fruition. This applies to all teaching. Maybe we should share what we know at the appropriate time in the appropriate manner and leave the rest to God.

Thank God for having friends like you and Terri.

Yours in Prem and Om,
Vidyananda

17

Comments on
The Schiller Institute's
Ten Fundamental Principles
for
Establishing a New Paradigm

In a review of the structure of civilizations, and their inevitable decline, alternative systems came under review. While some systems clearly had physical growth in mind, whether by militancy or capital support, others had more ideological or spiritual designs in mind. Regardless of the angle though, all systems, without the presence of consciousness, ultimately carried within their design, the seeds of corruption. Whether this corruption was fuelled by financial, authoritarian, ideological or religious principles, it none-the-less enabled the growth and stability of a selected few, maybe 20%, against the hardship or even suffering of the rest, maybe 80%.[1] The purpose of this deliberation was to determine which systems produce the more tolerable degree of hardship and suffering.

On Sunday 11 December 2022, John wrote:

Dear Vidyananda,
Hari OM.

I trust this finds you and Vani well, and that the year-end celebrations at the Ashram are progressing harmoniously. Terri and I are well and are currently in Austria where we are experiencing a beautiful rendezvous with both Matt and Nick. We will spend a few weeks here before separating to go our various ways; some of which are known, some are aspired to and guessed at, and others are, as yet, unknown. In Croatia, we completed the purchase of that house, but since it was built 65 years ago, and inhabited by the same gentleman (who is now 87), it, as you may imagine, needs some work and upgrading. It will be an interesting project though, and in addition, I also believe it will tick many 'constructive-purpose-boxes'.

---

[1] This follows the idea of the Pareto Principle, also known as the 80/20 rule, which states that roughly 80% of outcomes result from 20% of causes.

Thank you for the depth and wisdom of your last reply to my writings on the Delusion of Reality - it closed off this topic beautifully!

The email below is for your interest (and comment if you wish). It is of a geopolitical and geo-economics nature and one where I address an organization that offers an alternate form of world government.

Some time ago, I was introduced to the Schiller Institute and the LaRouche Organization[1], and asked what I thought of them and their approach. As a result I followed their work for a while. Although I believe they see things for what they are, and although I believe their intentions are noble and correct, I also believe their proposed solution will not last and will potentially end poorly. The reason for this is that their methodology is a repetition of what enabled and led to the current catastrophic situation, and their suggestions contain elements that lead me to be very sceptical, indeed, to the point of being suspicious. Similar to Elon Musk, whose release of revealing Twitter Files made him the hero of many, but who really is a front man for very large entities with other agendas; there seems to also be one made up of a belief mechanism in the LaRouche background that enables the organisation to exist and which actually controls it, too. You see, it is this controlling entity that is contained in the seeds of such organisations, and that seeks to germinate an agenda that is in-line with agendas such as those of the WEF[2]. These are agendas of a social order through corporate control that require the controllers to manage the collective, rather than to allow for the liberation of the individual.

Following some thought and contemplation on recent publications and announcements by their commentator Harley Schlanger, I offered Harley some thoughts on their "Fundamental Principles".

The reason for my sharing these comments with you is that I think it may be interesting for you. The reason for my thinking so, is that it lays bare the first layers of the root of the problem of the human dilemma of today. It highlights the absence or biased distortion of the Divine purpose of humanity. I doubt that I will hear back from them on this, and if I do, they will likely not be in support either. I chose to write these nevertheless, as I felt guided to do so. I am keen to hear your comments and observations on the spiritual angle of my comments, even if yours are critical of mine.

As it is a longish read, my request for your thoughts is *only if this is of interest and you have the time to ponder on these comments*. If not, or not soon, then naturally, this is not a problem at all. Then let us simply consider the purpose of this message as being to wish you and Vani blessed holidays and all that is good and beautiful for 2023!

With much love and best wishes,
John

---

[1] The Schiller Institute is an offshoot of the LaRouche Organization, a political and ideological movement founded by American political activist and economist Lyndon LaRouche (1922–2019).
[2] World Economic Forum

From:	*John*
Date:	*On Sunday, December 11th, 2022*
Subject:	*Comments on the Ten Fundamental Principles for Establishing a New Paradigm*
To:	*Harley Schlanger*

Dear Harley (if I may),

Thank you very much for your informative daily updates.

As you have asked the audience on a few occasions, to offer views on Mrs Helga Zepp LaRouche's "10 Fundamental Principles", I have chosen to share mine as I noted certain fundamental problem areas at the core of each of them. Even though I have persevered to be as brief as I can, I apologize for the length of it.

One could say that this commentary addresses the idea of a centralized authority that the principles (largely) promote and which is largely technocratic. As we know, such power will in time corrupt absolutely – and when it is in the hands of a mere few who control 'the levers' of this technocracy, this will greatly exacerbate the risk. The largest cause is usually the lack of accountability that occurs at a certain point, and which has to do with the mechanical and thus predictable nature of the one- and two-dimensionally orientated man*, who covets and attains such power. (*Please note that I use the term 'man' to refer to the human being, or humanity).

To begin, the "10 Fundamental Principles" are mostly based on the reason and logic of comparative and historical observation. This, however, excludes the undeniable metaphysical and spiritual context of man.

These 'metaphysical' aspects for example, are not merely philosophical; they factually represent the greater part of that which we simply call 'man' as, due to their higher dimensional (or vibratory) nature, they dominate the physical realm (the 'physical realm' being that which is detected by the 5 physical senses). By ignoring the metaphysical realm - especially man's 'spiritual context' - one takes away the largest contributory part of that which is considered as 'man'. In your presentations, you make regular reference to the dark satanic practice of many of the current authorities – and one sees that these in turn are very much active in the dark side of the metaphysical realm. By distorting the psyche of the contemporary man, they alter his systems of belief, which in occult circles, is considered as none other than black magic.

Then, when observing these "Ten Fundamental Principles" through the lens of these realities, I would comment as follows:

1. **On Sovereignty:** *As Einstein's saying goes, one cannot solve problems using the same ingredients that created them; one simply needs to see how, after Westphalia[1], history continued its repetitive or cyclic patterns. The repetition is the use of force or vote or forms of hypnosis such that one*

---

[1] The Peace of Westphalia refers to two treaties signed in 1648 that ended the Thirty Years' War in Europe and the Eighty Years' War between Spain and the Dutch Republic. These treaties established principles of state sovereignty and religious tolerance, significantly shaping modern international relations.

central authority generally ousts another to show all 'how government was meant to be' and then takes measures to ensure it stays that way. Regardless of the noble intentions behind and within these movements, 'measures' or principles; one sees the continuation of centralized forms of sovereign power, that are always corrupted in time.

The <u>primary</u> problem with every such design, is and has been, that their structures and ideas are ultimately 'top-down' in their arrangement of control. Even though many of these are painted as democratic or as some form of nationalist, communist, or other 'ist', they are not 'bottom-up'. They are only so in appearance as, in reality, these 'top-down' systems cannot function with bottom-up influence for very long; this is because people simply differ too vastly across all plains. For any centralized system to function, it must always control how its people in different regions think, speak, learn, specialize, eat, love, and live, and it cannot have differing moral codes. The paradox occurs as it is not possible to forcibly or artificially 'make' people be that which they are not – the human (metaphysical) spirit will simply not allow this. Perhaps such rule-based implementation can be done temporarily – such as was done with Covid – but not permanently; at least not without simultaneously creating unintended and disastrous consequences for future generations.

Thus we see how after a sequence of empires and other forms of 'central authority', across millennia and in recent centuries, the political, corporate, financial, military and even religious institutions continue to remain 'top-down' governed – with the same types who are clever (only to become cunning) and influential (only to become powerful), reigning at the top.

Therefore, to blame the state of the world on a handful of super-wealthy or psychopathic individuals, does not consider all the factors. Without condoning anything, it is clear to me that these unfortunate powerful ones are ultimately just side-effects and victims of these same 'top-down' systems as well. It would therefore be better if one were to begin by observing and acknowledging that the term "sovereign" in the first of these "Ten Fundamental Principles", still implies the same problematic top-down execution of "sovereignty".

2. The artificial or external interference on any naturally occurring order of things, will always have a downside. Looking at the "Second Principle", being that of **'Eradicating Poverty'**, one may observe that the existence of 'Poverty' is regrettable but, in any civilization, it will always remain a natural occurrence. If one believes one can eradicate poverty through affluence, then one disregards the consequent complacency that will create sterile minds, and one has not considered the 'metaphysical' meaning – that perhaps its existence has a purpose. It must not be forgotten, for example, that the healthy mind stimulates creativity and ingenuity, just as the absence of such, stimulates the kind of laziness that causes certain people to refer to these as "useless people." Sometimes being poor but honest is considered better than being complacent and ignorant – and where the former can be realized by the individual, the latter is not. Perhaps the problem of poverty is one that must reside among the morals and priorities of an affected community, and not any central authority.

3. **The extending of Life Expectancy**: 'Life Expectancy' is not realistically definable by the number of physical years lived, and in addition, it is simply not the same everywhere. Such an approach must therefore begin by taking into account the fullness of life, as well as the natural average of a particular way of life and lifestyle, in a particular region.

   In addition, the 'Health Systems' referred to are no longer what they imply. These systems are, due to similar centralized controls, now more focused on the profitable enablement of abusive lifestyles, rather than repairing and healing. Where care may never be denied, a form of accountability must still be determined, but again, this accountability must be at a local or regional level – where it is managed with consideration and with locally based intelligence. In an intelligent and understanding environment, the balance between 'live and let live' and 'compassion and consideration' will be more inclined to evolve naturally.

4. The wording in Principle #4, is selected to make the contemporary man 'feel motivated' about an **advanced technocracy**, but this circumvents the factual and fundamental issues it creates. It again - indirectly - suggests the need for a centralized authority:

   - First, it bases its view on the observation that human beings are the only 'creative beings known in the Universe'. This would be better worded as 'the only beings creative for the benefit of the self, within a single lifespan'. Must one not also consider that there are other ecosystems with creative forces, ones that co-exist – even in a hop-scotch way - as if they were a single organism over many centuries, such as certain co-existing types of animate and plant species, or over millennia such as certain types of fungi?
   - Next it refers to the concept of 'education'. This is one area wherein much of the present problematic system's root causes lie, but I do not want to expand too much on this. One must however consider that compulsory and centrally managed 'education' is very controversial, as today 'education' is designed around certain needs, needs that are determined by this 'authority', and not the community. Today, for example, we see how practical skills are no longer valued because one can get technology to do the needed tasks, cheaper and quicker. The proponents of this, forget or ignore, that mankind needs to develop some of these skills for the various facets to do with their personal development, as well as their ability to adapt, live and survive (and sport does not replace practical skills).

5. I shall not elaborate much on the complex **system of Finance**, but 'Credit' is, evidently, not something that may ever be determined or controlled by a non-participating central authority. Money must always be supported by a tangible asset, and any credit must remain physically accounted for at the local or regional level at least. This way, if a nation or body corporate wishes to grow beyond practical considerations, and defaults, then the accountability (such as employment or supply lines by third parties) that affects those who are local or regional, remains and is managed locally or regionally. If one region is then to assist another, then that must be decided by such regions separately.

6. **The idea of infrastructural tunnels and bridges** is noble but absent of what happens thereafter, in the decades and centuries that follow. How will such an already perfected infrastructure doom the creative thought by individuals in our future generations? (that most divine of elements as claimed in the Fourth Fundamental Principle). Sometimes the perfection of something must be seen or acknowledged in its relative imperfection.

7. The concept of **global security** that firmly divides 'the world' into blocks. This too refers to a need for a central authority, and who determines and manages these blocks? It again seems to refer to the illusion that 'the world' consists of people who are all the same in their physical, ethnic, and metaphysical make-up. It suggests that a central authority will consider the need of an individual or an ethnic group over that of 'the world' or a 'a block' in it, but only up to a certain point. This 'point' will then be determined by how many people are affected, and this again, would be decided along certain authoritarian agendas. I may refer here to Brzezinski's[1] grotesque view on the statistical difference between 'killing and controlling millions of people'.

8. Many of the views expressed above will be reflected in the 8th Principle. **The concept of God** being seen as something that serves the many, however, is extremely dangerous. As God, in whatever form or name, can only be found in the heart of the individual man and woman, and can only be germinated and discovered by his or her aware and thoughtful being and actions. As such, the idea of an authority 'managing' this process, will likely continue to lead to more friction and division instead of unity.

9. The 9th Principle about **the settlement of "quarrelling opinions"** appears feasible and noble when considering Eastern and Western philosophies. In the scope of the nature of man, as has been historically proven however, this is unlikely to be practical without an authoritarian backing which – in the light of the many concerns to do with a centralized authority – is unlikely to be long-lived, and most likely to end chaotically. As it is, conflict arises out of unresolved quarrels, or issues where a minority do not agree with a majority perspective. To prevent these from spiralling out of control, these are best managed on a local or regional level, overseen by resident elders who are familiar with the ways and perspectives in such territories, and who were appointed by the resident citizens for such tasks. Even if minor conflicts arise as a result of such quarrels, the chances of an amicable arrangement between regions would still be more harmonious between such elders. This is even more so than, for example, politically appointed judges who must consider the ludicrous opinion of so-called politically correct non-participating and without-ability parties.

10. The 10th Principle begins correctly but then deviates with the view that **evil lies in the lack of development**, rather than an excess of development,

---

[1] Zbigniew Brzezinski was an advisor to several US Presidents and a key figure in shaping U.S. foreign policy. His intellectual contributions and strategic insights have had a lasting influence on American foreign policy. He infamously said: "In earlier times, it was easier to control one million people than to physically kill one million people; today, it is infinitely easier to kill one million people than to control one million people".

as is apparent in the world at present. This principle further and regrettably also promotes the technocratic state over the sovereign individual man.

I can expand much on each of these observations and can also offer certain 'bottom-up' alternatives, but I have found that very few are interested in any suggested changes whereby central control is waived. Fewer even will acknowledge their effectiveness. The reason is <u>not</u> - as you mentioned - that "man is inherently evil", as in fact, man <u>is</u> inherently good but that man is, however, inherently lazy. Consequently, it is when man mechanically surrenders to this laziness, that he becomes subjected to and easily coerced by false promises or he becomes reconditioned by becoming identified with more powerful others and things. It is this that leads man to 'evil'.

The topsy-turvy or backwards perception of this phenomenon is the cause of the now absurdly altered reality which the bulk of humanity perceives as 'the world'. Subsequently, if man does not find a way to re-establish his civilization with forms of individual sovereignty, that make every human being absolutely accountable for himself, his kin, and his clan - mankind as an intelligent and advanced civilization will undoubtedly falter and die out. This is only a matter of time.

Individual Sovereignty can perhaps be categorized by principles such as habeas corpus and natural law, but in the application of these, there must also be absolute accountability by those with authority. Any form of immunity for one's actions is absurd in principle – but the corrective actions must be determined by those afflicted and affected, and not by a supposedly unaffected few who judge and rule from thousands of miles distant.

In conclusion, and in the event that you have managed to read this letter thus far and:

- that I have not bored you too much with these views, and
- that you are able to follow this higher logic, and
- that you feel there is a seed of merit in it,

I have inserted below, for your interest, a philosophical elucidation of the greater physical, metaphysical, and spiritual context of Man. Frankly speaking - the understanding of each of these beings represented in man is vital if there is to be hope for the continuation of humanity as a happy, stable, and prosperous whole; the misunderstanding or ignorance of these can be considered a travesty to the preservation of the individual human soul.

Best wishes,
John

An Ode to the Sage (and His Purpose)

The sage was asked by his devotees about his life,
other than that which his listeners saw him as:
did he enjoy it, did he feel fulfilled,
and what will become of him at its end?

He took a deep breath and said:

*I am only the Speaker through which the message reached ears,
that were not distracted by being entertained and opinionated,
but who listened, carefully.
As such this Speaker also listens and observes,
and perseveres to become That.
For one to seek something other than That,
is for one to seek to be only an idea,
a fleeting moment in time,
like a thought that arises and passes soon forgotten.*

*When one desires to know the 'I', who it is, or who it serves,
one can only do so, by seeing it as something separate,
and other than all that one is, which then adds division,
and as this is not possible, one may see 'I' as this:*

*I am the link between my father and his fathers,
and my sons and their sons,
I am the daughter of mothers,
whose mothers know my daughters' daughters.*

*I am the gender half of an existent and complex whole,
the harmonious merger, in existence with the opposite half,
creates emergence as Creation intended.*

*I am the body and the mind
that forms the temple and vessel for the formless spirit,
I am the formless spirit that,
by residing in this temple and vessel, embodies it.*

*I am the merged body-mind-spirit in one,
who mutates into Higher Being,
of both form and formless, temporal and eternal,
and enlightened as such,
can become one with the All and Everything.*

He then continued and said:

*I am a cell amongst trillions of others in an organism,
where my temporal but harmonious existence as such,
in service to the whole,
leads to the whole's acceptance of me as a part of the whole.*

*I am therefore the whole whose trillions of beings,
be they cells or stars,
serve me out of selfless love and wish,
and as such I am at-one with each and all.*

*Oh ignorant man, you with such profound and diverse imagination,
of riches, fame, and technology aimed at star-travel and immortality,
in your blindness, you remain food for a cell among trillions,
the wavering leaf on a tree among others in countless forests,
a seasonal blade of grass on endless everchanging plains,
a grain of sand that was once a recurring mountain.*

*Only when you do and can truly see,
will you not desire the stars and count your days as a mortal being;
you will find that you are the stars eternal,
and all that is manifest among them.*

On Monday 12 December 2022, Vidyananda wrote:

Dear John,
Hari OM.

Thank you, we are well, and I pray that you and Terri are also well.

How wonderful to receive this email from you, as I had just logged on to briefly write to you!

Thank you for sharing the links and your comments with me.

I think that it is good that you wrote to them. Sometimes we need to act for the sake of the action, even if there seems to be no tangible outcome.

When I read their principles, it immediately reminded me of WEF[1]. I even tried to find out whether Helga Zepp-LaRouche was a member of the WEF. I could not find any info though.

I agree with your comments re centralised power, which seems to be the inevitable outcome of any system. If we have an invested belief in a system, we are bound to become dogmatic and authoritarian.

I also fail to see how technology can be the answer to any social problem.

For that matter is there any system that can solve the basic human problems? Are not all systems destined to become the problem itself, the very problem it is intended to solve?

Alas, we do not wish to look within, to look into the maker of our problems, the solver of our problems, the implementer of the solution, or the administrator of the solutions. As long as a mind full of inner problems is any of the above, naturally, there will be outer problems.

The problem is that the 'saviors' of mankind do not see that they are full of problems. They always regard themselves as righteous and truthful. So, from the outset, they are doomed to make the same mistakes they accuse the 'unrighteous' of.

I further agree that to leave out the spiritual element of man (which is the essence of man) is a mistake. Now, it is interesting that although these institutes refer to the soul and Schiller's 'teachings', they don't seem to include these in their applications in any tangible way. So, I would be interested what their reply to you is, especially regarding this point.

Wonderful that you wrote to them. The thoughts are in the ether.

---

[1] The World Economic Forum is a private international organization that brings together business, political, academic, and civil society leaders to discuss and address or align global issues.

I came across two interviews that may also be of interest to you: one is Schwab's involvement with the SA Apartheid Government[1]. The second is an article that comments on the future of Smart Cities, or Zero Carbon Cities, of which Cape Town is destined to be one, especially since our mayor, actually serves on the WEF committee for Zero Carbon Cities.[2]

Love and Blessings,
Vidyananda

On Friday 16 December 2022, John wrote:

Dear Vidyananda,
Hari OM.

I trust you are well and enjoying your Riversdale Retreat,

Thank you for the clips on the history of collaboration between Schwab and the old SA regime, and the aspect of Smart-Cities; they were interesting and very informative and thank you for your thoughtful and sobering views.

Some perspectives arose when I observed these developments, but what is most astounding is the fact that the exposure of evidence of *'wrongdoing with ill-intent'* is ever-increasing on many platforms, yet the 'globalists' (for lack of a better expression) continue their bizarre and destructive paths unabated. One may even say it is with exponentially increasing intensity, which to me means that:

- either their 'operation' has already reached its 'tilting effect', having attained sufficient critical mass for it to now run its course and unstoppable; or
- it means that they are desperate and that their increased madness is akin to an all-or-nothing death struggle.

It is my view that it is, or will be, a combination of these. Many of the changes that were implemented and caused are quite clearly irreversible:

- the world of pre-lockdowns no longer exists, for example, and what they claim they have in mind - as per my email to Harley - cannot ever work, at least not for very long.

Consider the effects of vaccines as just one example: in our tiny little Croatian village a 36-year-old mother of 3 recently died of an unexplainable 'heart attack'. Further, I am in a village in Tirol, where last night we had dinner with some locals who are childhood friends of mine, and they were talking about spates of 'unexplained deaths' as well as suicides, which they generally agreed among each other, to be occurring at an average of 2 per week.

Thus, it seems to me that the 'reality bubble' for many contemporary people

---

[1] Klaus Schwab is the founder of the World Economic Forum.
[2] Cape Town's mayor at that time was listed as a member of the World Economic Forum Net Zero Carbon Cities:
https://web.achive.org/web/20220208203516/https://www.weforum.org/nzcc/leadership/

has been popped, but due to their identified attachment to these now dissolved or evaporated realities, and the alternative one of madness and absurdity that is being spoon-fed to them, they have become subject to what was referred to in one of those clips as "the beast" or "the beast system". Perhaps along with what we previously discussed; for one reason or another, people's fragmented beliefs cause them to fall deadly ill, to simply choose not to live, or, as we saw with the rapidly growing rate of assisted suicide concepts, to suffer a combination of these two.

As sad as this tragedy already is, the effect of this mass-psychosis is likely made worse by numerous 'vaccinations', especially the ones that caused blood clotting and compromised immunity, and also most likely due to a shortfall of spiritual realization of the self... This thought then brings me to a few observations regarding this 'Smart City' project:

These are *the inevitable* consequences:

- There will be a separation of those who will be 'in' the grid and those who remain outside of it.
- At the time of its implementation, one's geographical location will determine if one is in it or off it - no choice.
- If, by the time the separation is implemented, one has not left but stayed behind, then the one's choices will further decline along lines such as:
    - Psychological dependency (information control)
    - Chemical dependency (vaccines)
    - Mechanical dependency (movement control)
    - Economical dependency (all transactions via monitored cryptosystems)
    - Biological dependency (the necessity of implants, drugs, etc).
- This may not mean one has to comply with all of these requirements, but when one is within such a Smart City, life will become exponentially complex as without the central authority's approval, one will have difficulty moving around, obtaining essential services and goods, or doing business.
- This will not mean that those outside these zones will live much more comfortably - I have a feeling that access to many services, including medical ones will be limited, as will certain transportation facilities. Life outside will likely become more agrarian.

And then there are the *unintended consequences*:

- I do not believe humans can exist as civilized beings, without the presence of spiritual realization among a certain percentage of the people. Further, the number of unconscious or unawakened people, 'zombified' or in various states of hypnosis from hypnotized states through chasing dollar- and sex-driven power, or from being distracted by entertainment, was, in my view, prior to Covid, increasing to dangerous levels.
- While Covid caused many to descend into enhanced states of distraction and entertainment-seeking, now in the aftermath, many people

are waking up, particularly those who would otherwise have remained in their pre-Covid 'zombie' states.
- Many of the people outside the Smart City will be more inclined to rebel violently against the city; this will place both them and the city in physically *and* spiritually precarious positions.
- Many of the people who find themselves irretrievably trapped inside the Smart City system, may now actively revert to the only place or space of liberation: that of a correct path of meditation, prayer, and a conscientious lifestyle.

Then,
- A Smart City's system is dependent on electrical, electronic, and electromagnetic circuitry – all of which are highly sensitive to CMEs (from the sun) and EMPs (from man-made devices).
- A Smart City will require a rule-based order to function, that must be strictly and harshly enforced 24/7/365. This will be complex to maintain and have various side effects, ranging from a lack of creativity to a lack of compassion - both of which are equally essential for basic human existence.

Thus, when things go wrong people will get hungry, and as the famous Bob Marley foresaw and sang, "a hungry man is an angry man!" If one considers how the average city has only 3- or 4- days' worth of supplies at any given time, one can imagine that this program would already be destined to implode, even before it is implemented.

I do not believe this whole cycle will take very long - and I do believe that we may still see its turn within our current life cycle. Hence, perhaps one must simply let these not-so Smart City systems just proceed along the path of their doom - and simply plan and prepare to be able to look after our people in the interim and to remain strong so that we can help those who will seek help in the aftermath.

I believe it is the quality of this ability, that will determine the quality of the next cycle of civilization, and the ability for those in it, to find divine liberation.

With high regards and best wishes,
John

On Thursday 22 December 2022, Swami Vidyananda wrote:

Dear John,
Hari OM.

I meant to tell you that I started reading your trilogy. In fact, I am now on book three. You certainly have done a tremendous job of bringing in so many angles and aspects and tying them together. Well done! Lots to contemplate for the inner challenge.

In regards to the continued agenda regardless of the increasing publicity of their wrongdoing: In addition to your two observations, could it also be the deluded belief of the elites in being untouchable, as well as the ruling class believing they are protected by the higher authorities/elites?

I noticed that many people are waking up to the adverse effects of the vaccines (although many are still in denial even though they had adverse effects). But whether they make a connection to what is really going on, I wonder. Generally, there is very little receptivity when I talk about these things, even amongst some of the 'un-injected'. It seems that people in general do not want to hear about these diabolical agendas, hoping that everything will be alright.

Re Smart Cities: I agree with your view on the division that will be created and that life outside the Smart Cities will be agrarian. In fact, the WEF talks about it in a visionary article, that those who opt out of Smart Cities will live in 19th Century towns. Well, I might prefer that! This is I think where the so-called energy crisis and load-shedding agendas will lead to: they are preparing to create 'green energy' exclusively for smart cities, whilst the rest have to do without.

I pray that you are right about the self-created doom and failure of these Smart City projects, and I too have a feeling that it cannot actually be done. I feel that there will be a point where people will not wish to go further with enslavement and artificial living because these cannot satisfy the heart, and hence these will be either abandoned or rebelled against. It seems to me that the oppression of people can always only go up to a certain level before the bubble bursts. As Swami Venkatesananda said: "Oppression leads to compression leads to explosion". Unfortunately, the rebellion for freedom will itself lead to oppression again and another cycle is started. And technology is only as imperfect as the human mind, so one can imagine the endless technological problems in such a city.

Your point that people will revert to a spiritual life as the only option within an oppressed environment, such as a Smart City, holds true also for those who opted out. Because regardless of what system of living we choose, the spiritual path alone is the road to freedom, etc.

Two of our friends have properties in Barrydale. One has lost her husband recently and the other is about to (or so it seems). I am encouraging them to keep their properties, as these may be of value if the Smart City Project in reality gets cracking.

Yes, you may have guessed from my last sentence that our friend's husband may pass away soon: he is seriously ill with cancer and from what we are witnessing, I don't think he has long to live, especially since he too sadly took the injection.

I agree that we cannot live without spirituality as a society, otherwise that would be like the oceans existing without H^2O. Hence that is what I finally turn to again and again, meditation and prayer.

I hope your time in Tirol (which I believe is very beautiful) is rewarding.

Love to you all.

Yours in Prem and Om,
Vidyananda

On Saturday 24 December 2022, John wrote:

Dear Vidyananda,
Hari OM.

We are well. Tirol is indeed very beautiful and I loved coming to its mountains and people as a child. It has also been nice doing long walks in the snow, even having to dodge and return the occasional stray snowball, and our time with the boys is very special. Next week we all head back to Croatia and soon thereafter they will go on their respective ways and lives and face their respective endeavours and challenges.

I am impressed and elated that you undertook to read the Pilgrim trilogy![1] Indeed, there is so much to contemplate and yet, to have even a glimpse of understanding our Creator, and the absolute perfection and beauty of His Creation, one must opt to observe all things and from all angles! The beauty to me, is when I see that there are paths to the Light from every angle, albeit they differ, but in this difference lie whole galaxies of depth...

We trust this finds you and Vani and the Ashram well, particularly within these complex times and with the various developments. I can imagine the neutral acceptance you maintain is not always seen as such by those who believe that surely all must have a judgemental opinion. You mentioned Barrydale: it is indeed an interesting place, and as you know, I have some interests in the Pagoda there[2], which is something that may still turn into a wholesale project! Do keep me informed on the developments surrounding those two houses - perhaps some guidance will come from this.

Also, thank you for letting us know about our friends U. and G. Yes, I was in contact with her a few weeks ago, and our daily prayers and thoughts are with them.

As for our conversation, I would like to comment on your statement: "Could it also be the deluded belief of the elites in being untouchable, as well as the ruling class, believing they are protected by the higher authorities/elites?"

I believe that yes, the elites are deluded, but they are as unaware of the depth of their delusion as the multitudes to whom they subject their false reality, are. Within their one- and two-dimensional perspectives, they have created an illusory 'higher' dimension, and its deceptive ways feed the desirous and desperate. It is, however, a psychic illusion within a sensory illusion, and from within this, they cannot possibly see or even envision the higher, truly spiritual dimensions - nor that their 'illusions' exist by feeding off them.

Thus, I see these deluded ones opting for the path of sensory stimulation

---

[1] John's books, a trilogy titled The way of the Pilgrim
[2] The Barrydale Kaba-Aye Peace Pagoda in South Africa is a Buddhist structure inspired by the original Kaba-Aye Peace Pagoda in Myanmar. It serves as a symbol of peace, promoting the teachings of Buddhism and fostering intercultural and interfaith understanding in the local community and beyond. John was its custodian during the process by which it was officially protected as a Heritage Monument.

and submitting themselves to the dark deceptive *entities* that their collective psyche feeds. (Although I previously described these 'entities' as demonic, they are of course still naturally occurring phenomena, designed by Great Nature to feed or protect the earth's biosphere). These deluded ones are usually oblivious of this process though, and will live perfectly normal lives, until they are put in a uniform or costume of sorts, or if they are cornered. Then, they will deny or defend such influence - calling it normal and necessary, or a duty and calling. I have even observed this phenomenon in myself in the past, when at times I ventured 'out' quite far.[1] I believe though that I was guided to pass through such life phases without compromising myself *irreversibly*. Today, living a normal life and not dependent on a physically 'protected' space, I can still sense these challenges almost every day (like when driving in traffic!). Consequently, I occasionally find I have 'fallen asleep' and am then responding to something the ego 'I' in me sees as 'stupid' or 'undeserved' with irritation or anger and by which I feel the old angry wolf pulling at its leash! Further, occasionally I find I am being unnecessarily stubborn!

Either way, as long as I catch these reactions in time, these spells are not necessarily bad. I find that 'waking up' from the distracted or hypnotic sleep reminds me of that blessed Light we experience every day, which is otherwise perceived as normal! The process of re-discovery or re-awakening is always spectacular, but risky as it does require one to fall asleep first... And yet, even this I believe is natural as at times, I sense the phenomenon of our cyclic or pendulum-like existence within my psyche, and it effects my mood from elated to being periodically sombre, and then back to elated - independent of external conditions or my actual physical status quo!

Returning then to the expanded delusion of the 'Ruling Class'; they seem to me, to descend dimensionally, beginning in three-dimensional awareness, and then gradually following their elites like two-dimensional idols and then further, down to a one-dimensional 'with or against' environment.

Yet still the existence of all this, I find, is perfectly normal and natural in the mechanical duality of our conceptual reality. The awakening process must be opposite to that of falling asleep, as must be the results of such paths - and for one to be, so must be the other!

Thus I leave you to enter 2023, with some more thoughts for contemplation...

Wishing you well, and with much love as always,
John

On Monday 26 December 2022, Swami Vidyananda wrote:

Dear John,
Hari OM.

I can just imagine the 'stray' snowball! Love to the boys and Terri.

---

[1] John refers to his time in military uniform, within an active war.

Delusion is such that the deluded does not know that he is deluded. In fact, the deluded believe that he is very wise. The wise have stepped out of delusion, and the seeker is becoming aware that he has been deluded and is vigilantly observing himself regarding any further delusion. One cannot for a moment believe that one is out of the woods of delusion. As you point out with your personal examples (which we of course all undergo) the potential for the activities of delusion to arise is there all the time. Swami Venkatesananda and Krishnamurti both emphasize the need for constant self-observation.

And as you rightly point out this is also part of the world. And according to Vedanta delusion is sometimes in the ascendancy, individually or collectively. And these are the times when this seems to be especially so. But it seems to be also possible, that the delusion can come to a point where it itself becomes an awakener. For example, whilst dreaming a scary moment in a dream itself wakes one up, and with that, the dream disappears. This is because the Ultimate Reality is omnipresent, and hence also present even in delusion, albeit It is hidden: just as a fire can be hidden by the smoke.

My prayer is that more people wake up. The suffering of many is intense. Yet again, this suffering may be the awakener.

I pray that you had a good Christmas. We had a wonderful Christmas Eve Satsang with a nice group of friends.

Thursday we are celebrating the Birth Anniversary of Swami Venkatesananda.

God bless you.

Yours in Prem and Om,
Vidyananda

18

Fate and the Depopulation Agenda

On Friday 13 January 2023, John wrote:

Dear Vidyananda,
Hari OM.

I trust this finds you and Vani and everyone well!

We are well, and after a blessed 7 weeks of having our sons with us, Nick has returned to university in the Netherlands and Matt - who was asked to resign due to his unwillingness to 'take the jab' on his last position - has obtained a new position on another yacht in the Caribbean and is leaving tomorrow (14th). As the timing of all things is always interestingly guided, I have since yesterday been crutch bound with a torn Achilles, which tore for no particular activity-related reason. I am elated to say though, that it chose to do so at the very end of the 7-week bliss! Interestingly enough, when I look back, I notice that such injuries have played very distinct and directing roles across the journey of my life thus far. It is on this topic that I wish to share and hopefully exchange a few new lines of thought with you; especially when reviewing one of your last comments surrounding 'delusions', where you wrote:

"...according to Vedanta delusion is sometimes in the ascendancy, individually or collectively. And these are times when this seems to be especially so. But it seems to be also, that the delusion can come to a point where it in itself becomes an awakener. For example, in a dream, a scary moment in the dream wakes one up, and with that, the dream disappears. This is because the Ultimate Reality is omnipresent, and hence also present even in delusion, albeit it is hidden: just as a fire can be hidden by the smoke"

It is interesting to observe a perpetual and cyclical nature present in all things to do with Time and Space (or Matter). Following some recent contemplations, I reviewed the lives of my parents and in particular, the times and circumstances of their and their parents' formation. I observed how the course of their various lives flowed like a river, along a 'cause-and-effect' route that was determined and defined by these turbulent times and circumstances. Now, it must here be said, with utmost love and respect to my forebears, as they were mostly very good and considerate people, that I do not believe any of them practiced a particularly spiritual life. There was the occasional one who was religious in the traditional church-going way, but this would follow the kind of practice that did not entertain concepts of deep meditation and observation of the inner-self; let alone the awakening of a non-attached higher and unified Being.

That said, when observing my parents' 'ups and downs' across the years, as well as the various life-changing events of their eras, or decisions that were made as a result of these events, it became clear that there is in life the presence of inevitable cycles that are unavoidable. In addition, I noted that there is a rhythm present in these cycles that determines 'how' one lives through them. Whereas the cycles are seemingly Cosmic in design, and can therefore not be affected by us, by becoming aware of them we can affect 'how' they are perceived. As such, an 'up-hill' can then be seen as a creative force, rather than a punishing one! Consequent to such awareness, the rhythms present in our formation and conditioning that make us repeat similar mistakes or routines or perspectives throughout, without ever realizing it, can also be observed and therefore affected by us.

I noticed, for example, how my parents' lives went through very distinct cycles *roughly* every 7 years where, as such, one way of life ended, and another began. What was particularly interesting is that I discovered this *after* having noted (some time ago) how my own life was following such 7-year cycles. [One can call it confirmation-bias but in mine, I saw 7 years from the planning of my conception to young childhood, 7 years school in NL, 7 years school in SA, 7 years military to specialist, 7 years single to entrepreneur, 7 years married in Sint Maarten, to family with young children, 7 years SA focused on building Welbedacht and the physical foundation, 7 years Welbedacht focused on the inward journey, and the next 7 year cycle started early 2022 with our leaving SA!] The separation between these cycles is defined by not more than 6 - 9 months perhaps; they were not planned as such, and just fell into place. Looking from the present into the past, as a whole, I can clearly see that 'how' each cycle was lived, determined 'how' the next one was presented.

Consequent to this, I noted certain rhythms to do with 'how' life was experienced and lived by both my parents, and these trends continued in my own life. I noted how their inability to see these rhythms caused their lives to be physically challenging and complex, and at a time when they should have been able to focus on the intuitive-spiritual (golden-age) phase, they still struggled with the physical. Their 'way of life' however, did guide the formation of my own, and it was this supporting element that largely enabled me to live my early years in relative comfort, to adjust along the way, and consequently to discover what I did. As such, therefore, it seems that my life is a continuation and perhaps even a culmination of their lives, and even the lives of their parents.

Personally, I am not too keen on contemplating the Law of Karma as I find it gives too many who do an excuse for being this way or that way, and thereby avoiding the present Now. It does however appear as if the above observations indicate the presence of a Great Wheel that turns across consecutive and perhaps even parallel generations, and which our lives form mere spokes of. That said though, I would be very interested to know what light your teachings reflect on the existence of such cycles and rhythms across a single life, or that of consecutive lives.

Setting the above aside, I wish to comment on a phenomenon that appears to be related; that of the seemingly imminent population decline.

Whether one observes this from the geopolitical perspective, such as those to do with the effects of vaccines[1] that you and I have reviewed to some extent, or whether one looks at this from a perspective of chemical-and-pesticide-and-radiation effects causing reduced sperm counts among men and reduced fertility among women[2], or whether one looks at the establishment of fewer families due to gender (mis)identification, economic reasoning, or later childbearing, there is none-the-less quite a lot of concerned chatter on this particular issue.

There are of course certain population control agendas, also known as eugenics, behind many of these factors, but there is seemingly also a 'natural' angle present. This view is based on realizing the perfection of the Divine Creation in every way, and which would therefore include accommodating the formulation of such eugenic agendas! One need but look at the greater Design of Things to note how there are numerous such cycles in the physical reality we refer to as Space-Time, that are supposedly Cosmic in their design[3]. Further, there are other, much larger cycles that occur across eons, and which we cannot observe over a single life, or even across a series of generations. One of those great cycles I am referring here to is that of the Great Year, the 25,920-year Precessional Cycle, which has component parts that are also found in canonical numbers such as 72, 81, and 108. (I believe we already exchanged some notes on this a few years ago).

As you know, there are definite correlations between these great Cosmic cycles and those that are found in mathematics, harmonics, and even our directly observable Solar System, such as the dimensions and positions of the Sun, Earth, and Moon, which I recall we also discussed previously[4].

These lines of thought then bring certain questions to the fore, and where some of these may appear somewhat profane, ultimately, when considering the bizarre reality that we see erupting everywhere, I would like to raise them nevertheless:

Perhaps the fate of humanity, the influence of certain agendas, and the fear of a 'depopulation phenomenon' are cyclic features we can become aware of, and perhaps by being aware of them, we can reform or transform our perceived reality.

Perhaps the aware but unbiased / impartial observer can consider it plausible that such thinking is present among those who are manipulating the levers of geopolitics. Perhaps such thinking among these manipulators

---

[1] Bill Gates said in a 2010 TED Talk: "The world today has 6.8 billion people. That's headed up to about 9 billion. Now, if we do a really great job on new vaccines, healthcare, reproductive health services, we could lower that by perhaps 10 or 15 percent."
[2] There is sufficient scientific evidence to suggest that certain chemicals, pesticides, and radiation contribute to reduced sperm counts in men and fertility problems in women.
[3] Under Cosmic origins, would fall CME's (massive solar flares), and meteor strikes, and scientists have even found a correlation between earthquakes and volcanos and the sun's activities.
[4] See correspondence dd Saturday, April 5th, 2014.

considers that the high and unprecedented population of the present has led to a reduction-by-dilution of life-force among the average contemporary person? Perhaps such thought considers that people who have a reduced life-force, will sooner move away from a natural spiritual realization, and be more inclined to go toward the physical and tangible, as represented in the artificial. Perhaps, if there was even a grain of truth in such views, then this kind of thinking could convince the proponents of such schemes that in time, their agenda would lead to a renewed Golden Age?[1]

I have contemplated these thoughts for some time. It seems this is the direction the current agenda aims at. When one listens to the words spoken on this by some such as Sadhguru, who also speaks for the WEF on the depopulation agenda, one notes that there is much of this kind of thinking. What would be your or your teachings' message on such?

With best wishes,
John

On Tuesday 16 January 2023, Swami Vidyananda wrote:

Dear John,
Hari OM.

I am happy to receive your email, as I have been thinking of you. We are all well and I pray that you and Terri are still well since your email.

Good on Matthew. I wonder whether it is not possible for all those who actually would not take the jab to also have such courage and to have faith that some other job can be found. I am sorry that you are on crutches. How strange that you should get a tear without any accident! I pray for your complete recovery.

Regarding cycles and depopulation:

The scriptures such as the Bhagavad Gita and Bhagavatam speak of Cosmic Cycles. The largest cycles are those of creation and dissolution: the universe(s) come into being for a period of time (billions of years) and then they dissolve back into the source for an equal length of time. All enlightened beings merge with the Source and the unenlightened enter into the new cycle of creation, continuing their journey.

Within these cycles are ages, which in Sanskrit are called Maha Yugas. These cycles are of a length of 4,320,000 years and repeat a thousand times within one cycle of creation. There are four yugas in one Maha Yuga: Satya Yuga, Treta Yuga, Dvapara Yuga, and Kali Yuga. Satya Yuga is equivalent to the Golden Age. With each yuga righteousness as a whole declines by a quarter. We are now in the Kali Yuga, which began with the parting of Krishna.

The Bhagavatam gives an interesting description of the Kali Yuga:
"In this yuga, day after day, righteousness will decline, along with the

---

[1] The Golden Age is a term used to describe a period of great prosperity, cultural achievement, or excellence in a particular area, often in the context of history, civilization, or art.

health, strength, and longevity of the people. Wealth alone will be the criterion for the worth of one's birth, conduct, and character. Strength alone will determine who is righteous and just in his dealings. The relationship between husband and wife will depend on mutual liking. Cheating will be a common business practice.

"Masculinity and femininity will be judged by sexual efficiency. Brahmanas will be distinguished only by a thread they may wear. Even the administration of justice will be perverted by bribery and corruption. Hairstyles will determine beauty. The vehemence of speech will determine truth! People will do good to society only to gain fame. The four stages of life (celibate-student, etc.), will all become one household life!

"During this period the good people will flee the corrupt cities and isolate themselves in mountains and forests, being content to live on roots, fruits, and honey. Elsewhere, people will be overtaken by famine, pestilence, drought, and storms. Their wealth is drained by taxation and robbery and their energy is depleted by their own unrighteous living, they will die young. Even trees will become stunted on account of their ruthless exploitation by unrighteous men. Cows will become emaciated and will yield little milk.

"In kali yuga, tamas (darkness) predominates. Hence, women become unchaste. Even men of religion are after pleasure and wealth. Women become unsexed and harsh in their behavior. Servants are disloyal to their masters who, in their turn, mercilessly dismiss incapacitated servants. Even so, barren cows are starved. Unqualified people masquerade as hermits, to earn their livelihood. People who are ignorant of religion preach it. People kill one another for a petty sum of money. Greedy fathers disown their sons, and ungrateful sons fail to maintain their aged parents. And, worst of all, people do not worship lord Visnu, the highest object of adoration in the universe. Only when the Lord is enthroned in people's hearts will the evils of kali yuga disappear from there."

Then there is the belief that there will be a Divine Incarnation to restore justice and spirituality. But I think that if this were to happen, it would be in the far future when things are really unbearable.

Here is a quotation from the Yoga Vasishta re depopulation:

"However, when the people become predominantly sinful, Yama the god of death sometimes engages himself in meditation for some years during which the population increases and explodes.

The gods, frightened by this population explosion, resort to various devices to reduce it. All this has happened again and again countless times."

So, it appears that this is a natural cycle and we may be witness to this.

Then the question arises: If depopulation is the workings of the Divine, why does it involve what we consider evil actions and agendas? Paramahamsa Yogananda writes about this, either in his writings in the Gospels or the Bhagavad Gita. He says that when the Divine initiates destructive action it uses appropriate instruments, and these are those people with evil propensities, or those in whom evil is dominant. However, these people still have to face their karma due to their attachment to their actions. An example is Judas. His betrayal was necessary for the crucifixion of Christ and his greed and misunderstanding were the means for the betrayal. So, although it was part of the Divine Plan, he still had to endure his karma, which ended up in his suicide.

Then there is also the concept of mass karma. It is possible that a large group of people have performed the same karmas and therefore they are subject to a single event that affects them on-mass?

A note on using karma as an excuse. This is a misuse of the concept. A true understanding of the law of karma would actually bring one's attention to the now because one would realize that the action performed now is vital to the future. Also, Swami Venkatesananda emphasized that although we may recognize that someone else is suffering on account of their karma, the question arises as to what our karma now is in response to being witness to that suffering. Karma essentially means action: thought, word, and deed.

In response to your thoughts at the end which you have phrased as questions, hence I presume they are open-ended contemplations:

I am not quite sure what the first question means, but if I understand correctly, are you suggesting that people are waking up to the depopulation agenda and therefore questioning the truth regarding COVID, etc?

It is interesting that I suddenly find people I would not expect to, talk about depopulation. I think more people are starting to realise that there are nefarious activities taking place; and it may also be that they start connecting the dots between the various agendas. However, it is difficult for many to envision that there are people who would initiate a depopulation agenda on such a scale.

The reduced energy in people may be due to their limited thinking. The Yoga Philosophy teaches that energy is limitless and that a person can have unlimited energy if they are one with Consciousness. When we are limited to the body's consciousness, we experience limited energy; and if we abuse that energy through wrong living, then we are depleted even more. And so I would agree with you that the loss of energy can easily lead one to the vegetative artificial digital world. It's like surfing the channels of the TV, which is much easier than the self-effort of spirituality.

I was a little surprised to see that Sadhguru is involved in the WEF. I only saw a short clip about a comment regarding the population. Other than that he thinks that there are too many people, I don't know what his views are on how it should be reduced.

Anyhow, I think that if a person believes that the population should be reduced, they should be the first in the row to submit themselves to the depopulation program. Only then are they genuine. Not too sure how many volunteers there are. We always think that the 'too many' are other people; we don't realize that we too contribute to that number. And anyhow, why must we do anything? Let Nature take care.

Wishing you and Terri well. Sending much Love.

Yours in Prem and Om,
Vidyananda

On Thursday 19 January 2023, John wrote:

Dear Vidyananda,
Hari OM.

I trust this finds you and Vani well!

We are well, the boys seemed to have settled into their routines for 2023 and my leg seems to be healing - albeit too slowly in my ego's opinion. I was reminded of my unshakable fate on this damp winter morning, when I, on my crutches, speedily hopped up some steps, tripped, and bounced my way back down into a nice little puddle after having sprained the ankle on my good foot. I calculated that by the end of this current recovery period, I would have spent around 6 months of my life walking on crutches, and probably twice that hobbling around whilst my injuries healed! Hence I meant what I said when I previously wrote "...such injuries have played very distinct and directing roles across the journey of my life thus far", and that I must still learn to be a patient patient!

Thank you for the very detailed reply.

On your response on cycles:

I previously read some of the quoted texts, but your provision of them in the context of this discussion made them even more profound. What is interesting is how applicable they are to what we are witnessing today, and it is clear they were written by one who had knowledge of this occurrence before - and/or who keenly understood the mechanical nature of an unawakened human society. Indeed, such corrupt conditions were typical at the end of many empires, including the Persian, Greek and Roman ones, and these endings often coincided with the climatic cycles that lead to famine, disease, and revolt. Still, we know the Bhagavatam texts predate all of these though, which makes them additionally interesting! This is because their details confluence with not only very advanced mathematical and in particular, geometric features, but also climatic (solar) cycles and other aspects that correlate with knowledge only obtained since the start of the space-age, about 60 years ago. One notes, for example, how the Yuga cycle is very similar to the contemporary estimate of the age of the earth, being 4.5 Billion years, and that the 432,000 Kali Yuga number matches the radius of the sun in miles [...and it is also the address of a little house I bought here last month, which is on Ulica 43 2...].

As for Sadguru:

I am entirely in agreement with your views here. I have listened to many of his talks, and when I watch him speak and listen to the content, I do believe him to be wise and genuine. Perhaps his view was just misrepresented by the media, or perhaps he does believe that the maladies of civilization do have to do with the number of people. Perhaps he knows something we do not! Either way, I personally believe, with a high degree of certainty, that there is more than sufficient food, energy, and goodwill on planet Earth to sustain this many people, and probably more. It is merely the workings of those who are corrupted and who have lost their knowing of the difference between governing and controlling, and who then fear numbers that they believe they cannot control. As a result, the balance of delicate ecosystems are intentionally tipped, causing misery, artificial crisis, and war that was avoidable. I do therefore hope he knows who or what he is being associated with, as the transhumanist ones do not seem to care much for the human soul (or at least, the spiritual version!).

As for depopulation itself:

It is evident that human nature has not changed, especially when one considers the devastation it continues to enable. Just consider the many millennia of perpetual and cyclic rhythms of conflict; these have led to war and misery and were ultimately caused by the desire to control by those without the actual ability to do so. The recorded events of the past centuries show that the causes then, were not different than those of today; and why would they be? The only difference that is clear to me, is that the 'numbers' are higher, but this too is relative. If we consider that humanity consists of around 8 billion people, we see that it is only extraordinary when we consider that the total amount of people that have ever existed, is *'supposedly'* 108 billion[1] (a powerful canonical number that also has many occult purposes). Either way, if one applies the logic of infinite possibility to the stimulation of an environment by the improvement of its conditions, one sees how the current population growth has been stimulated by stable climatic conditions, combined with an Industrial Revolution (which was also enabled by a stable climate).

Hence, the currently changing climate (*which is largely sun-related, NOT man-caused*), will see population adjustment coming gradually and naturally and this is in fact, already happening. The projected problem with the present and imminent decline in numbers in the 1st world is what is stimulating the need for robotics and AI - a development that can therefore be seen as a natural process as well, and with a positive element!

Summarizing these topics:

I believe that Robotics and AI will therefore have a positive purpose as well, but that the meddling of globalists using the WEF, WHO, UN, and other politicised entities, may cause these to become destructive, and beyond comparison. It does therefore seem that humanity's rise and fall is inevitably cyclic and that these cycles are integrally connected to climate cycles, which are of course cosmic and solar in design, and which one could then say are, in reality, the breath and word of God. Either way, whether one finds oneself at the rise or fall of such periods, it is ultimately what one does individually with one's time that matters. Although I worry about our children and their, as yet, unborn children, witnessing the coming storm is likely to be harder on us, as we have witnessed the changes over the past half-century, and not just the changes themselves, but the accelerated change of changes!

On a positive note, therefore: Ultimately, we (humans) mostly live well and live longer, and experience fewer wars and less famine and poverty than a century ago. This, even with the massively increased population. And, certainly, a higher percentage of people have more choices now than ever

---

[1] According to the Population Reference Bureau.

before. We may lament that so many are still drawn into the dark side of corruption because they are complacent, or lazy, or distracted, and this is of course regrettable, but it is also the law of cause and effect. As per our previous discourse on a hypothetical "morality pill"; such a thing would take away that one gift we have that is most Divine, and which is one step short of Life itself: and that is Choice. Ultimately, some will work and sacrifice to enhance their bouquet of choices, and some may freely give theirs up in exchange for entertainment. Then, when some will awaken and become conscious, perhaps it is only possible to do so because the opposite also exists.

On a somewhat 'bleaker' note, perhaps we must contemplate a more complex question: If these *non-violent so-called vaccines, which were ignorantly but mostly innocently accepted do then destroy* the lives of tens of millions, would this be a worse calamity than having tens of millions *violently and intentionally* kill tens of millions?

With much love and best wishes,
John

On Saturday 21 January 2023, Swami Vidyananda wrote:

Dear John,
Hari OM.

We had a peep on a website where we think you are staying. It looks very beautiful!

Oh my, I am sorry that you had a second accident. Yes, they do teach us!

Re Scriptural Predictions: Paramahamsa Yogananda explains that the sages have the ability to see how the collective karma will unfold. They may not know the details but can see the general trends. Even we can do so, I guess, to some degree if we understand the workings of the mind and the trends of thought current in society.

This does not preclude the possibility of the course of collective karma changing if humanity makes efforts towards a spiritual awakening as a whole. And it seems to me that the great spiritual Masters have some 'hope' in this, on account of which they offer warnings and alternative ways of being. Alas, they are not heard; and if, only by a few. Even if there is a large following, it is usually mechanical and not spiritual. Not surprising, as we realize how difficult it is to be truly spiritual.

What has always amazed me since I first read the description of the kali yuga (which is traditionally believed to have started app. 5,000 years ago) is the detailed description of the mindset of people. This impresses me more than the predictions of events. The mindset after all is what really matters. And how accurate the description of our current mindset is! And I say 'our' because I can see that my mind also is tainted with these mindsets. It is only due to the Grace of the spiritual life that a more wholesome mindset arises, hopefully fulfilling itself in enlightenment.

Of course, we should also remember that the mindset described is the dominant mindset and not that of all people. The yuga is characterized by the dominant mindset, although all other forms of thinking also exist at the same time. Hence the declaration that the 'good people will flee to the countryside'. How ironic that one of the WEF's concepts is that outside of Smart Cities there will be the 'unfortunates' who will live in 19th century villages! I think I prefer that!

It is also on account of this statement re 'good people fleeing' that I keep that option open. Not that I believe that I am good but the advice of the scripture seems to be that at some stage one needs to get out of the corrupt cities when it becomes unbearable to live there.

As for Sadhguru, I am surprised that he associates with the WEF. But as you may be implying, he might not be aware of their agendas. I wonder whether many of the people who become members of WEF actually are aware of these agendas. For the WEF it is a plus to have someone like Sadhguru because he has a large following and influence: just the man you want to influence the spiritual crowd!

I also agree with you that the Earth provides enough. And if She cannot, then she will take care of the problem. We don't need to do anything! This is the problem: the saviors of humanity, as Swami Venkatesananda called them. The philosophers, scientists, politicians, and priests believe that they know the solutions to the problems of the world. And in that, they create only more problems and suffering!

On a by-note: I noticed in the last few years that Swami Venkatesananda and Swami Krishnananda[1] and Krishnamurti (and probably others) here and there have made remarks re socio-political trends. Most of us (including myself) never really took notice of these remarks, mainly because these remarks were made on the side, and were not the main features of a talk. However, these comments were made.

Interesting that by now there have been 108 billion people on the planet. However, from the Yoga Vedanta point of view, these are all replicas. How many of these people are actually rebirths?

And yes, one is concerned regarding the future of the world if the globalists get their way. Not only for our children and grandchildren etc, but for ourselves because we may be reborn into this whole mess! A good motivation to rise above the cycle of birth and death!

You pose an interesting question regarding the vaccine deaths vs violent killings. I wonder whether the manner by which one dies is really that important when it comes to the question of death itself. It is of course the suffering that is always of concern. And there may be as much suffering (or maybe more?) from dying from a vaccine-induced aggressive cancer as from a bullet.

Swami Venkatesananda had an interesting thought on this: The problem may not be that someone was killed because death is inevitable. What is

---

[1] Swami Krishnananda was the General Secretary of Sivananda ashram, Divine Life Society, Rishikesh, India form 1958-2001. He was a profound philosopher sage. https://en.wikipedia.org/wiki/Krishnananda_Saraswati

objectionable is the violence involved. So, I wonder: it may not be important what the method was but the fact that one killed. As an example: were the gas chambers less violent than the machine gun? Somehow the systematic cold-blooded administration of these methods seems to me as violent as any physical method. And I feel that the psychological suffering that is caused is the real violence.

Although there is all this darkness, there seems to be also a lot of Light. From what I have read and listened to of late, there is more and more resistance, more and more law cases, etc, and I have a feeling that there may be a relentless backlash against these agendas. So, I wonder whether there will not eventually be a curbing of all of this. Anyhow, I am grateful to these heroes who fight on our behalf. May God bless them!

Please send our love to Terri, and we pray for your recovery. Please look after yourself.

Yours in Prem and Om,
Vidyananda

19

The Turkey Earthquakes

On February 6, 2023, Turkey[1] suffered a series of devastating earthquakes that struck southeastern Turkey and northern Syria. The primary quake had a magnitude of 7.8, followed by a powerful aftershock of 7.5 later the same day. It was one of the strongest earthquakes in the region's history, causing widespread destruction, loss of an estimated 50,000 lives, and the displacement of many more.

On Thursday, February 9, 2023, Swami Vidyananda wrote:

Dear John,
Hari OM.

I pray that you are healing well and that you will be completely mobile again.

Just a quick sharing of this interesting article about the recent earthquakes in Turkey earthquakes:

https://truthcomestolight.com/turkey-withstanding-a-modern-day-5th-generation-and-silent-war-natural-catastrophes-may-not-be-so-natural/

I'm interested in your perspective.

Yours in Prem and Om,
Vidyananda

On Friday, February 10th, 2023, John wrote:

Dear Vidyananda,
Hari OM.

Thank you for your email and for sharing this article.

I am well, and just past the halfway mark through the projected healing period - at least according to the course of nature and the opinion of the specialist. This is fine as I feel the injuries of the two ankles are connected as a single event, which in turn is connected with other events and 'work'. Already it has caused me to take a different view on letting go of physical control over certain projects, and also of the course of our movements within this new region and community (which includes the pros and cons of living on an island for example).

As to your article on the catastrophic earthquake in Turkey, and the

---

[1] Recognition is given to the change in the country's name, from Turkey to Türkiye

possible link to human activity or technology. My first thought would be that the perspective is conditional on the form of 'belief' one was exposed to - and I have divided my views according to a few of these versions:

Technocracy:

There could well be truth in the views of human-caused earthquakes. The HAARP system[1] is well written about and publicly known, as is its ability to even influence the natural vibrational frequency of the earth. These could be seen as acts of sheer stupidity, and whereby the 'Law of Unintended Consequences' becomes buried under a range of hyped-up and self-imposed necessities. These and many other geoengineering techniques, such as sky-spraying, otherwise known as chem-trails, are weaponized programs that have been active for 60-odd years and are even officially patented[2]. Yet they seldom get attention in the mainstream media and even when they do, the contemporary mind is unable to absorb the reality of what this even means.

I experienced a 'similar' anomalous event when I got stuck in a category 5 hurricane in 2017.[3] There were, at that time, no such hurricanes on record, yet the summer of that year saw three category 5's in the Atlantic and 4 in the Pacific, almost simultaneously! These storms grew from normal category 1 or 2 systems and, within 24 hours, powered up to become category 5's. It is my view that the ocean water in front of these traversing systems was artificially heated, which would then cause such hurricanes, and which is possible to do with satellite-based laser technology.

Cosmology:

It is common knowledge that the sun's activity plays a dominant role for life on earth. What is not commonly understood is that it has acted up a lot over recent years. Besides the number and intensity of solar flares (also known as CME's), the variation in solar wind affects the earth's magnetic field, and subsequently this field's capacity to protect life from the sun's harmful effects. Further, the sun's influences also affect the earth's tectonic plates, and this can lead to volcanic eruptions and earthquakes.

Spiritual Interconnectedness:

One may discover comparable and corresponding phenomena when combining deductive reason and historical, but supposedly co-incidental, occurrences. Through these, one may observe an evident link between the purpose and function of the higher or awakened consciousness of man and the Sun. Following the view that nothing is Random, and everything has Reason, it is my view that, from the Sun, our Creator emits varying dimensional and vibrational forms of Life throughout our Solar System, and

---

[1] HAARP is the High-Frequency Active Auroral Research Program, which is a research program primarily focused on studying the ionosphere and its potential uses for communication and surveillance technologies. Part of this research investigates influencing weather patterns and the Earth's vibrational pulse.

[2] See https://patents.google.com/patent/US20120117003A1/en.

[3] A Category 5 hurricane is the highest classification on the Saffir-Simpson Hurricane Wind Scale, with sustained wind speeds of 252 km/h.

for that matter, every other solar system in the Cosmos. I strongly believe that the very purpose of Creation, and all its components, is to enable 're-alization' or 'enlightenment' by forms of 'life'. I also hypothesize that this is symbolized by the 'missing' or invisible capstone of an unfinished pyramid. As Nothing is random, and Everything exists in support of such Awareness, without a sufficient amount of such Awareness, Reason becomes 'diluted'. This would then have a direct effect on how the Sun's solar winds strike the Earth.

Evidence of Historical Cycles:

Man, as is evident, messes with the weather and all things. But as real as this is, it is obviously not comparable with the Divine's influence. Consider the end of the Pleistocene[1] about 12,000 years ago for example - I have written quite a bit about that. The energy release that caused the ending of this 240,000-year era is supposedly comparable to every nuclear bomb going off simultaneously, and many times over. This was a time of mass extinction but supposedly, many new species evolved out of that! Then I have reason to believe that there was another major cataclysmic incident that occurred about 6,000 years ago. This one was as violent, but its effects are intermingled by historians and geologists alike with the previous event, which's occurrence dominates much of the evidence, and thus it was not as well recorded[2]. By then the massive Pleistocene icecaps on the northern hemisphere were already gone, and the expected floods and effects and adjustment to the Earth's crust had occurred. Then one notes how the era in between these two cataclysmic events was filled with smaller cycles, and while Great Nature simply and rapidly recovers in one way or another, each cycle has a shock effect on the collective psyche, and therewith, the fall and recurring rise of human civilization.

Basic Geology & "Letting no crisis go to waste":

The region in Turkey that was struck is particularly geopolitically sensitive; as you can see, it is close to the Turkey - Syria border area. Although the earthquake's artificial nature, as described above, is possible, such incidents, when their causes are natural, are easily weaponized through propaganda. Blaming the US for the regional problems is not unfounded, but either way, people can be made to believe almost anything these days! Through the media it is, for example, very easy to start an ethnic war, even among the so-called intellectuals in 1st world economies; one glance at the nonsensical causes and purposes of the current Ukraine conflict should answer that.

This Observer's Reality in Relativity:

When this earthquake's destruction is compared by some to that of war-torn Damascus, Yemen, and much of eastern Ukraine, one will see that it is relatively insignificant. Yet this is largely overruled by panicky contemporary sentiment. Consequently, I must regrettably turn my back on such

---

[1] The last Ice Age
[2] An event explained by Emanuel Velakovsky, in his book *Worlds in Collision*, and Graham Talbot's *Saturn Myth*, and researched by a large field of scientists as part of the Electric Universe or Thunderbolts organization.

reporting, as I do not know how much is true, and how relative it is to the greater human dilemma (as a whole). In addition, as tragic as such disasters are; where war and man-made destruction brings out anger and hate, the desperation from natural disasters can bring out beautiful qualities in people. Having experienced cases of both war and disaster, I know this to be true, where I experienced how, in the latter, it was visible in both those affected and those in a physical position to assist (i.e. not just financially).

All that said, your shared link led to a string of views for further thought and contemplation, and I would naturally be very keen to hear your views!

Best wishes,
John

On Tuesday, February 14th, 2023, Swami Vidyananda wrote:

Dear John,
Hari OM.

I am glad to note that your ankles are healing and also that you have a positive attitude towards these, in that you take these incidents as a learning curve. May we all be able to do this.

We are well here. Not much to report on a personal basis.

Re the Turkey Earthquakes

Thank you for your detailed replies. I also felt that the article I sent you was rather emotional, yet I did not want to ignore the possibility, especially since this was the time I heard about HAARP and its capacities.

I am also aware that there is the tendency now to immediately believe that there is some conspiracy, whereas of course not all events are of that nature. I have noticed that every time I hear someone is sick, I think it must be the injection! So, one does get biased and we have to be careful.

I read the article below as well. I am not good at reviewing articles but they do at least acknowledge that they don't have proof and that they are only suspecting foul play.

I agree with you that architecture certainly plays a role, especially considering that Turkey is an ancient country with very old buildings, which would (I would think) get damaged easily.

However, whether the events in Turkey were natural or man-made, it is important to know that man-made events are possible.

Generally, the population (including myself) is unaware of what advanced technologies already exist, and what kind of technologies are being worked on. We are generally not aware of what insane ideologies are involved in shaping technology and to what degree technologies are used for destructive purposes. Who would think that using weather and earthquakes would be considered a technology of warfare? And yet, this is precisely what they are working on. And this is not new. The ancient Hindu scriptures described the use of weapons that could precisely do these things: cause severe weather, fire, immobilize people, create illusions, etc.

Thank you for pointing out the Sun's activities. I was not aware of this. And your view on the Sun being a transmitter of the Divine Will (if I understood you correctly) is also interesting in that the Sun has been worshiped by many ancient cultures, as you know. In the Ishavasya Upanishad, the Sun is described not only as the life-giver but as a disc that covers the Ultimate Reality[1]. That means that the Divine is the real life-giver.

Thank you for the link to the Interactive Earthquake Browser. Although Turkey is prone to earthquakes, it is interesting that the amount of earthquakes that were recorded in the last week is almost equal to the amount of earthquakes from 1900-2016. See these two websites:

https://www.statista.com/statistics/269648/number-of-earthquakes-by country/ and https://earthquaketrack.com/p/turkey/recent.

Also, if you adjust the dates on the Interactive Earthquake Browser, it is surprising that so many dots remain. Of course, there are the aftershocks, but I would think that they would make that distinction between aftershocks and epicentres. So, I think it either is a very unusual natural event or it is man-made. So, I am keeping both options open.

Yes, you are quite right that the other atrocities are worse, however, what strikes me is the possibilities of warfare technologies and how mean the whole thing is.

On a slightly different note: I was listening to a talk by the late Swami Ranganathananda[2] who was the President of the Ramakrishna Mission and close associate of Swami Venkatesananda. He made an interesting point, and that was that that person who knows the Self (or the Divine) has no fear and does not cringe in front of anyone. He cannot be made a slave. And we come back to the same thing again: Enlightenment is the key to the whole thing. Whatever we learn about the world and its dynamics, let that lead us closer to the Divine.

Blessings to you, my friend.

Also, regarding the law case: Yes, I have been following the WHO Pandemic Treaty saga. I agree that all these lawsuits are lagging. As you are aware, there is a court case against Dlamini-Zuma, and she is supposed to be held in contempt of court. And yet, South Africa again is in a State of Disaster and she is 'leading' it! The saying that the wheels of Justice move slowly is true. Sometimes they don't seem to move at all! Except the Divine Justice, which we cannot witness unless we have raised our consciousness to that level.

My Love to you and Terri,

Yours in Prem and Om,
Vidyananda

---

[1] The Ishavasya Upanishad is a classic text dealing with the relationship of the world and God.
[2] Swami Ranganathananda (1908-2005), born Shankaran Kutty, was a Hindu monk of the Ramakrishna Math order.

On Saturday, February 18th, 2023, John wrote:

Dear Vidyananda,
Hari OM.

I trust all is well and trust that the festivities around your and Vani's birthdays were enjoyable. All is well with us, I still have my cast but with my other sprained ankle now sufficiently healed, we are somewhat mobile again.

Thank you for your very interesting response, I enjoyed seeing your perspective.

I also appreciated your expression of the late Swami Ranganathananda's view, which I translated as one who knows him or herself, does not fear or cringe *and* that such an ability cannot be attained by wearing blinkers[1]. To truly know the world of our experience requires us to remove such blinkers, as only in doing so are we able to find an understanding of what would otherwise be considered incomprehensible. It is my impression that without such basic understanding, one cannot actually accept another unreservedly. I personally very much enjoy our correspondence, and this exploration, too, has considerable learning value in this regard.

Thus, on the topic of knowing the functioning of the material world:

When I consider the passage of the first 40 years of our (your and my) lives, I see, more so now than ever, how strange and inexplicable the nature of our *physical and material* world seems to be. And this, even if I review the distant past! This is perhaps not so noticeable if one lives within an established and sectarian community that perhaps spans across generations and has a specific way of life. In such contexts, a degree of naiveté (for lack of a better word) makes it easy to miss the greater reality 'game' taking place. These types of biased communities, which of course represent the larger percentage of people, will likely not choose to look for agendas that are buried within layers of carefully narrated propaganda, and are subsequently more easily swayed by the 'information' that tells them how they should perceive their immediate 'reality'.

On the analysis of Information:

When referring to an 'information' based 'reality', we may consider both that which comprises our immediate surroundings and which is subject to all five senses, as well as that of our perceived worlds which is subject to the stimulus of just one or two of our senses. For the latter, artificial forms of information are often provided to replace the missing senses; such as a smell, taste, or feeling that is then expressed by an actor's visual and verbal expressions. In this way, reality becomes artificially adapted through the application of artificial sensory stimuli. This in turn becomes a grotesque version of what is 'real' in the Divine's Great Nature.

The one thing that these real and adapted or artificial 'realities' have in common, is that they are comprised of 'Information'. Whether this

---

[1] Blinkers refer to blinders used for horses that prevent them from seeing objects on the side. It also refers to limitations of discernment.

information comes to us in the form of light, smell, sound, taste or feeling, or selected combinations of these, ultimately it is all reformatted in our thinking brains as 'Information'.

I recently read an article written in 2016, where it stated that:

"The International Data Corporation (IDC) estimates that there were at least 4.4 zettabytes (4.4 trillion gigabytes) of digital data in 2013 and that the total will rise to an astounding 44 zettabytes by 2020."[1]

This means that the 'Information' that surrounds, permeates, and defines our reality, increased 10-fold over 7 years! This includes everything we can 'know', true and 'otherwise'. Further, this total is supposedly increasing exponentially. The article then goes on to say that:

"The explosion in the amount of information circulating in the world, and the increase in the ease with which that information can be obtained or altered, will change every aspect of our lives, from education and governance to friendship and kinship, to the very nature of human experience."

The rest of the article goes on in great detail about how the author believes a form of 'non-authoritarian truth-measure must be established'. This is naturally a pipe dream as the statement in itself is contradictory. The point however is that the density of our information-based reality is increasing, and not just in randomness, but often in carefully crafted layers.

As an analogy, information today is comparable to an ever-expanding ocean, with currents, tides, and waves, and with beautiful states of calm that are contrasted by catastrophically destructive storms. To those who have not yet become aware of their spiritual essence, this ocean is their world and sole reality. Consequently, it is upon the design and nature of this so-called ocean, that many today make their living. This is especially true of those who practice law and marketing, and have become very skilled navigators on this ocean! Others have learned to combine their talents and have built data-collecting fleets of magnificent vessels that are capable of great but also terrible feats. The existence of 'terrible feats' is of course nothing 'unfortunate' because, in the Divine construct of our perceived reality, these simply obey the mechanical law of polarity that follows the dual nature of the cognitive man.

Thus, we see how so much of our 'information' is designed by those who know well how the contemporary mind perceives reality so that they can channel the information through a strategically controlled media who timely release it to obtain the maximum and desired effect.

When taking this reality formation into account we can, for example, observe the 'information' surrounding a reported train derailment that caused a massive chemical spill in Ohio a few weeks ago[2]. CCTV information showed flames before the train derailed, and the reports that followed said that after the derailment, the chemical spill was set on fire by the

---

[1] The International Data Corporation is a global market intelligence and data provider for the information technology, telecoms, and consumer technology markets.

[2] A freight train derailed in East Palestine, Ohio, United States on February 3, 2023. The freight train was carrying hazardous materials.

authorities, which caused an even worse disaster in the form of a deadly toxic cloud looming over a small town called East Palestine. There were many details that seem to steer this incident away from being an accident or act-of-God, and towards being 'intentional'. What makes the reported event more bizarre is that last year, Netflix released a movie of just such an event, also in Ohio, featuring a derailment, a chemical spill, a fire, and a toxic cloud[1]. Supposedly, even some of the extras in the movie were from East Palestine!

Anyway; whatever this event or story represents, and whatever levels of truth or deception are present in the information transmitted, we are unlikely to ever really know. What is certain though is that fiction and reality become blurred – and such concurrences are, I believe, important point to note.

If we now return to the earthquake in Turkey and Syria and take into account what we know from the hyped-up Covid and vaccine publicity, as well as, for example, the 9.11 event which is now known and proven to have been engineered to implement the Patriot Act[2] and to facilitate the US and UK invasion of Iraq[3], we see that statistics are often tampered with to initiate the required narrative. If, for example, one removed the 'information' of the actual earthquake, one would see that the same political rhetoric is at play and the same propaganda tools are being used, as have been used for at least 20 years. The only difference, of course, is that today the desired effects of the selected propagandised versions are more easily obtained with the rise of technology. The more likely and dominant influence on the applied geo-strategies is the fact that Turkey favours Russia, China, and Iran for reasons to do with economics, geography, and ethnic stability over the West. They all serve each other's needs and do not, actually, pose any existential threat to each other. The Turkish relationship with the US, however, has been unstable for decades, largely because of this relationship with these three, and also because Turkey does not, in reality, need the US but fears their military, financial-economic, and therewith geopolitical power. Hence one may see how the news reports, modified by Turkey and suggesting the US is responsible for the earthquake, can fan the already hot tempers of the public in Turkey.

My somewhat sceptical mind then considers the Dlamini-Zuma case[4]. It sees how the media, and consequently so many of South Africa's intelligent minds are stuck two years in the past, seeking justice for what no

---

[1] A movie named "White Noise"

[2] The Patriot Act is a U.S. law enacted in 2001 (written in 1996) to enhance law enforcement and intelligence agencies' powers to "prevent and combat terrorism", however, it has been widely criticized for its broad and vague provisions that infringe on civil liberties and privacy rights.

[3] US, UK and Israeli intelligence knew before the invasion that Iraq had no weapons of mass destruction, and that it played no part in the events surrounding 9.11. Yet their governments still used this narrative as the pretext to do so.

[4] Dr Nkosazana Dlamini-Zuma, Minister of Cooperative Governance and Traditional Affairs, was in contempt of court for failing to submit records concerning her decisions during the 2020 COVID-19 national state of disaster, such as the rationale and processes behind her decisions, including the ban of alcohol and tobacco sales.

longer has any strategic purpose, except perhaps further destabilization. Putting another Zuma in jail will only destabilize the country then and this brings little healing. This is whilst the energy, corruption, and economic turmoil are overheating, *all of which are substantially very strategic*, but the consequences of which are not given the same priority by the contemporary mind. To many artificially stimulated minds, the now considerable media-hype around the shooting of an unfortunate rapper-celebrity[1] regrettably carries more weight, even though around 60 persons die violently in SA, *every day*.[2]

Therefore, although the process of 'Enlightenment' that was described as "the key to the whole thing" becomes very complex within this ocean of information, perhaps *understanding* the process is actually simplified. If one has given control of one's mind to others, then naturally such a one simply does not have a mind anymore!

All that is seemingly then left is the physical self; but for many, this too has been surrendered. Then perhaps one who has drifted this far from the 'self' may say that they can still 'feel', apply sentiment; but this kind of feeling, without a mind and body to sustain or stimulate it, cannot be much more than a dream state. Consequently, I doubt that enlightenment along this path is possible, as it seems to me there is nothing to enlighten.

This is a tragic state, but it is one that creeps in whilst the host is asleep (or being entertained) and as such, has gotten lost in a plethora of artificially stimulated 'Information'. Hence we may guard against such states by learning "about the world and its dynamics". Indeed, this may then lead us closer to the Divine, or it may also distract us *from* the Divine! I'd compare this process to taking the small 'boat' that is our mind and using it to enter that unpredictable ocean-world that is encoded in 'information'. Alone, and with only our very small boat, we would surely be lost and become food for the fishes; this, were it not for a little Divine Intervention which, I believe, we may experience, when we seek it.

Food for thought for the idle mind!

Best wishes,
John

On Tuesday, February 21st, 2023, Swami Vidyananda wrote:

Dear John,
Hari OM.

I am glad that your ankle has healed quite a bit for you to be more mobile again. I pray for further healing and full recovery.

Thank you, Vani and I enjoyed our respective and shared birthday celebrations. We also observed an all-night vigil this last Saturday night, called

---

[1] Kiernan Forbes, known as AKA, a celebrated rapper, was shot and killed in February 2023 in Durban.
[2] In 2024, based on recent crime statistics in South Africa, approx. 70 to 84 people are murdered daily.

Maha Shivaratri. It consisted of 12 hours of devotional singing and four pujas (as we did to the 'lingam' at Blue Butterfly), one every three hours[1]. It was quite wonderful! The great challenge is the day after to remain awake after the function is completed. Not always possible!

Swami Ranganathananda[2] seemed to have been one swami who was quite aware of the many problems of society. In his talks, there is often a call to righteous governance. Fearlessness certainly does not come from 'blinkers': are these not worn due to fear? True fearlessness comes from not identifying with the body-mind complex but rather with the soul (or consciousness) which transcends the body-mind complex and which is eternal. When we identify with the Eternal, then there cannot be fear.

I agree that 'information' is a key problem. The way we generally experience life and ourselves is via information, be it sensory, mental, emotional or intellectual. The realm of information is always dualistic and finite. Even concepts of infinity are finite as long as they are concepts. Finally, we have to negate **all** information, to have clear apprehension. I am using the word apprehension in the sense of non-dualistic perception. (Sorry about the contradictory language but this is unavoidable due to the observation that verbal (or written) communication is by nature dualistic). Whether the information is artificial or natural, it is still limited and dualistic. But when there is apprehension, then there is Truth. That Truth will guide our thoughts and actions. That Truth also includes natural perception but at the same time transcends it. It is then that we are beyond the illusion.

On the other hand, it is possible to use information to dislodge information based on propaganda (like using a thorn to dislodge another thorn), but I can also see the danger in that: because one can also get conditioned by the counter-information (what we usually may call correct or true information). That information is also incomplete and can lead to a conditioned response as well, which is of course then incorrect information. For example, I noticed that whenever I hear of someone getting ill or dying, I immediately attribute it to the injections. And although it is correct that many people are suffering or dying of these, it is not true that every death and illness is due to these. So, there is the danger that in our attempt to counter propaganda (which is conditioning) with information, we create another form of conditioning. This will also keep us in ignorance. So, it appears to me that to really be established in Truth, one needs to go beyond all information, all sense of duality and limitation.

Not easy! But what else to do? Except have a cup of tea and coffee with my friend John!

Love and Blessings to you.

Yours in Prem and Om,
Vidyananda

---

[1] Puja is a form of worship. Traditionally the lingam is a symbolic representation of God in Hinduism. At The Blue Butterfly Retreat Centre is a labyrinth whose centre stone looks somewhat like a lingam.
[2] Swami Ranganathananda was a prominent monk of the Ramakrishna Mission

On Monday, February 27th, 2023, John wrote:

Dear Vidyananda,
Hari Om.

The all-night vigil sounds like an event to behold. I am not sure how I (or any of the other unfortunate participants witnessing my singing performance) would fare over 12 plus hours, or of how much use I (or they as a result of this) would be the next day; I believe my singing talents to be comparable with your cooking ones![1]

Thank you for your deep thoughts and reflections within this multi-dimensional field of contemplations that we have entered! Your view on "apprehension" and "when there is apprehension, then there is Truth" was therefore very interesting, and one I intend to borrow from time to time!

I agree that the 'blinkers' could indeed be worn out of fear, but this could also be done consciously, for the sake of improving focus, and preventing distraction from one's intention. I find for example, that by not following daily 'bad-news' updates, I am in a better mood and more able to focus on my daily tasks. Also, when I was actively corresponding on business matters across time zones, I would avoid checking my email in the evenings, before sleep, because if a problem came up, I knew it would affect my sleep. For the same reason I avoid wasting my time and attention following political debates: such acts could therefore be considered as putting on 'blinkers'!

To wear or not wear the blinkers, is indeed the question because there is, of course, the law of consequence. If one lives in a hurricane or tornado-prone area, not following the weather forecast can prove to be fatal!

Like you, I must focus on not getting carried away, such as seeing an unexpected illness or death and automatically relating it to an injection, or such as relating any economic downturn as part of a conspiracy. This kind of thinking can lead to levels of paranoia. Likely or not as these things may be, we must still apply unbiased intelligence to our learning so as to understand the feasibility and relativity of the information that comes to our senses. This is because, as illusionists have shown, even the eyes are easily deceived.

To define Truth using the senses and the conditioned (programmed) thinking brain can therefore be very complex. This becomes especially so when there is the addition of a constantly changing physical world of things and people, and a metaphysical world in-between these things and people through which the exchange of all of this information is taking place. Where in the physical world the perspective of Truth can be defined through a basic understanding of the facts through measure and comparison, in the metaphysical world, Truth in the exchange of information is more complex to define as it lies not in 'what' is being exchanged, but in 'why' and 'how' it is being exchanged.

---

[1] Swami Vidyananda is well known for his shortcomings in the culinary arts.

And it can be made even more complex than that. Consider when people say things like, "It is not what you said, but how you said it", or "It is not what it looks like", or "Believe what you want, to me it is what it is". It is here that a *'Believed Truth'* (being one that is based on an opinion on something), in either of the physical and metaphysical worlds, may be compromised in favour of a *'Higher Truth'* (being one that has a higher meaning, such when one wants to avoid a confrontation, especially one that may turn to metaphysical trauma or physical violence).

I believe that the problem of not knowing something, simply because one has not yet learnt, is an irreconcilable one, unless one practices meditation and obtains a form of inner or intuitive guidance. This is because an absence of awareness of the existence of both of these worlds will lead to each of these two worlds to consider the other as illusory, imaginary, or even irrelevant. Depending on which world one then sees as dominant, will be the one that one will support and to which, for such duration, one will belong. Thus, when looking at it from this perspective, we may see why and how so many are stuck in repetitive cycles.

As my beloved and good friend Swami Vidyananda wrote: Not easy!

Thus, wearing blinkers in the paradoxical affairs of Life does little more than assist in the conditioning of an unguarded mind. Hence, I will leave my blinkers off to see and hear you, when we have our imminent tea or coffee!

With high regards and best wishes,
John

On Saturday, March 11th, 2023, Swami Vidyananda wrote:

Dear John,
Hari OM.

I pray that you and Terri are well.

The weather in Cape Town makes one wonder about climate change and/or geoengineering, or simply if it is as it is! ;-)

Indeed the day after the vigil is always challenging, and usually, we succumb to a nap in the afternoon.

You are quite right regarding the 'blinkers'. The whole situation does influence one's thought processes and it is a challenge to remain focused on the spiritual path, which, as we understand it, ultimately requires a whole-souled attention to the Divine within. And I think that is a reason why many people, although they have some idea of what is going on, choose not to look at it because they simply want to get on with their lives. But I also find that after reading certain articles or watching a video, I can feel fear creeping up, and I have to make efforts to remain calm. All-in-all a delicate affair because the blinkers can also obstruct useful information, which is helpful, not only in gaining an understanding of what is going on but also in becoming aware of our conditioning, part of which is a result of decades of propaganda. So many things that we took for granted as truths are turning out to be false! This recognition, as you know so well, is very helpful in our spiritual awakening.

It is interesting to me, that when I currently listen to talks by the Swamis or other spiritual teachers of a few decades ago, I am aware that they were alluding to many things that we are witnessing now. Although their focus is not on these things, they are often mentioned on the side and probably went unnoticed. For example, Swami Venkatesananda once mentioned that vaccines are poisons and that the so-called immunity that is supposedly derived from vaccines is actually the effect of the injected poisons assimilating the viruses (which are also poisons). Hence, when the bodily system is polluted, it no longer reacts to new pollutants, and then we believe we are immune. Whereas if the body was pure, it would reject any foreign poisons (such as viruses, etc). This rejection we call disease. This reminds me that Mother Yogeshwari always called her flu and colds detoxing.

Re Truth: Vedanta speaks of two types of truth: Absolute Truth and relative truth. Absolute Truth is what the religionists would call God. This Truth cannot be known through the senses, mind, or intellect, only through that in us which is of God, which is Pure Consciousness.

Relative truth is based on the intellect, mind, and senses and therefore variable. There will never be consensus on this, due to variations in perception and the instruments of knowledge (intellect, mind, and senses) being limited and conditioned. So, I am not sure whether we can ever know the TRUTH regarding any of the events that take place. However, we can become aware of the falsehood as well as our conditioning (most importantly) so that we can hopefully get established in the Absolute Truth.

I pray that you and Terri are well. I hope that your ankles are recovering well. Any plans for a visit to Cape Town?

Love and Blessings to you and Terri.

Yours in Prem and Om,
Vidyananda

20

A Brief Update

On Wednesday, May 10th, 2023, John wrote:

My dear Vidyananda,
Hari Om.

I trust that this finds you, Vani, and all at the Ashram well. We naturally think of you and talk about you often, and I am also comfortable envisioning you in co-meditation, during my own morning routine!

Terri and I have been very well, even though our new life has changed many things. In particular, our perspective on the material world and its various dimensionally-orientated, cycle-subjected, and rhythm-prone peoples is much clearer. At times it is complex to find one's footing and to maintain a calm physical presence (i.e. ego). Although this is and was anticipated, and although one knows it is 'ok' whilst doubt clouds the mind, it still requires considerable work. I'm sure you have experienced such on your own path. Fortunately for Terri and I, and even though we are in the midst of strange people, countries, and cultures, we are very much in sync with each other; when one feels it, the other does too, and this helps to keep the anxious moments brief!

It does remain interesting to observe, even after years of practice and study, how much we still see our 'beingness' and 'purpose' in God's Great Universe, placed within an identification and attachment of sort, to things like social place, house, country, career, thoughts and other!

We just returned from a road trip where we drove about 4000 km from Croatia to the Netherlands and back. The yacht that Matt works on had just arrived from St Maarten in Vlissingen, which happens to be a few kilometers from where Nick goes to University (clearly, the 'coincidental' miraculous crossing of paths and destinations continues, unabated!).

Either way, the timing of the trip worked well for us, as we are still in the midst of renovating that house we bought, and the very slow progress required me to remove myself from the situation for a bit. It was also necessary for me to see my sister and my brother, and it fitted in nicely before our upcoming trip to SA in June (more on this below).

We took three days to traverse Europe, crossing the length of Croatia, Slovenia, Austria, and Germany before arriving in the Netherlands. Traveling from the more classical Balkans to the technocratically perfected Netherlands, was fascinating to say the least. On the way up we drove mainly on fast highways, but on our return south, we drove through most of Germany and across Austria through the Alps on small by-roads, and through the small villages where the old and balanced ways are still well engraved.

What made this fascinating was that, besides traversing the differing European tribes and their cultures, there was also such a stark contrast between the small traditional towns and the cities that are noticeably dominated by immigrants. The resultant culture clash seems to erase the traditional ways of both the European cultures and those of the respective immigrants' origin. This loss, I find regrettable, as the traditional cultures in all places are so rich in creativity, and this is often integrated with a kind of productivity that, in turn, I believe, creates innovation and a natural harmony. While most would consider this 'non-pro-multicultural-view' of mine as not very "Politically Correct", one would only need to see the deplorable state of so many of these European inner cities, and the lack of vibrancy of many of the people and their youths in them, to reconsider. (For this to reverse would probably take many generations and even centuries, and although they kind of succeeded in doing so in geographically ideally-placed cities like Istanbul, it was largely due to the presence of a very dominant authority.)

Within all this, both of our sons are doing well. They are healthy and strong, physically and emotionally; and intellectually they are already well versed in the workings of the world. Their minds are free from the random oppression that has become a pandemic of its own. We are very blessed to have these two treasures as our sons!

Getting wind of the rendezvous, my sister flew in from Portugal, and my brother arrived from the Eastern Netherlands with his wife, daughter, and aspiring-son-in-law in tow. For this gathering of 3 nights, we rented a 4-bedroom farmhouse just outside Vlissingen (which is in Zeeland, the south-eastern Dutch province). As I'm sure you know, there is in every family a little 'history'; however, we none-the-less experienced beautiful magic in the numerous and various exchanges between us. (Among family, this is not always appreciated.) Hence, our goodbyes were warm and sincere, and I believe a lot of 'stuff' was 'offloaded' and much personal healing could begin.

As mentioned above, we have scheduled our trip to SA and arrive on the 17th of June and stay until the 11th of July. I realize you have a retreat early in July, and I know you must do much preparation before, and likely have much Ashram work at the end of it, but if we were to be able to schedule a cup of tea and perhaps a biscuit or two before or after your retreat, that would be great. Let me know if you can.

I look forward to hearing from you.

With the highest regards and best wishes,
John

On Thursday, May 11th, 2023, Vidyananda wrote:

Dear John,
Hari OM.

How wonderful to receive an email from you. You both have been on my mind and I have been intending to write to you.

We are well here at the ashrama, thank you. By the sounds of it, you and Terri are also well, and I presume that you are off your crutches now.

I am glad to note that you had a pleasant trip with positive exchanges with your family. Yes, indeed, most of our difficulties are experienced with family. And when the biological family is replaced by a spiritual family, then the same dynamics seem to arise again!! A wonderful lesson that we need to resolve all the issues within ourselves.

Thank you for sharing your observations re the cultural landscape of Europe. I am reminded of the teachings in the Srimad Bhagavatam. According to that scripture, we are now in the cycle called Kali Yoga, which is the age marked by destruction, which would also include the destruction of culture. It seems to me that two things could emerge from this destruction: 1) a deeper search within to find the Good within ourselves, which is what culture is meant to give us, or 2) deprivation and the rise of unrighteousness. I think we are witnessing both: more people are turning toward the spiritual life, but there appears to be an increase in unrighteousness at the same time, as we have been discussing at length.

I was most surprised and amused to learn that there was an oath of allegiance to King Charlie in which the entire world was invited to participate, and some (or maybe many) did. What a strange 'democratic' world we are living in.

There is not too much to report from our side, other than that we continue with our 'quiet' ashram existence and life. I did go on retreat in April, this time spreading my visit over three 'establishments'. The main stay was at Bhaktipriya's home in Barrydale. She has a separate cottage on the property and has made it freely available for us residents to use when we wish. So, I stayed there for a week's retreat. Vani had also booked me in for two nights at the Bontebok National Park for two nights as a birthday gift. Wonderful! So, this I did before going to Barrydale. And then there was an additional night at a friend's place in Suurbrak, where our friend Nikelwa had established a get-away with also separate huts, in one of which I stayed for the night.

I am delighted to know that you and Terri are coming to Cape Town and I hope to see you every day!!! (Of course except when I am away.) Except for 29 June and 3-11 July, we are available on any of the days that you can make it. We look forward to seeing you. Vani just walked in as I am writing this to you and she was all smiles to learn that you are coming.

Yes, we'll have lots to share.

With Love to both of you,
Vidyananda

On Monday, May 15th, 2023, John wrote:

Dear Vidyananda,
Hari OM.

My apologies, I received your earlier reply and had the good intention to reply today - but then I had the same intention yesterday and the day before... so I must now thank you a second time for giving me a well-deserved wake-up reminder!

As my first line of defence (this is my ego making an excuse): I was a little under the weather or 'out of sorts' the past few days. Perhaps something to do with an energy shift or perhaps just the effects of a variety of smaller factors that influenced my mind to become unmotivated. But since both Terri and I felt it, it could be something other - *perhaps it was to do with the weather!!* (which currently is cold and wet and well below the annual spring normal, and which harmonizes with my 'global cooling' instead of 'global warming' hypothesis!).

As a second line of my defence (also ego): responding to my good friend Vidyananda takes some contemplation and is not something I do 'off the cuff' as you may have noted over the years!

Thank you for your insight on the Srimad Bhagavatam, and your observation that more people are using the remains of culture and technology to assist their turning to *or from* the spiritual life (if I understood you correctly). I have not studied the Srimad Bhagavatam but have, over the years, done a little correlative research on the yugas. It is my view that there is a sequence encoded in these prophesized periods, which is, like in other cycles, numerically aligned with the sacred numerology represented in the physical, measurable, and observable Creation. The keys to this code are the numbers 3, 9, and 81, and anything with a number that adds up to one of these (such as 72, 108, 144, 432, 864, 1080, etc), and they offer an insight into the Divine Mechanism. This view is also mirrored in Gurdjieff's analysis of the enneagram and Nikolai Tesla's "key to knowing the universe" with the numbers 3, 6 & 9. The Kali Yuga seems to correlate to the Sun as well, which has a radius of 432,000 miles (exactly half the Kali Yuga), and a day (or night) which similarly has 43,200 seconds!

My point with this is that it seems to me that the Seeker does not necessarily need to wait for 864,000 solar years for the Kali Yuga to end. To me it feels that this code also points to both the life-creating Sun as well as the 'ruling' level or degree of conscious awareness, with which the Seeker passes through the dimensional or spiritual boundaries. This is perhaps a somewhat simplified 'nuts and bolts' perspective, but it is closer to (my understanding of) our perceived reality. The events that unfold among the collective humanity within these cycles of 'Time' are simply causal. There are, of course, dark, sinister, conscious, and intelligent forces at work within this, but *the depth of this 'darkness' is directly related to the 'absent-of-light' choices made by its mesmerized followers*. Whereby one empowers the other, the other puts the one to sleep. They seem to be - energetically speaking - linked and subject to mechanical and vibratory influences that are very similar to those that one observes in chemistry. Consider when heat is added to a mixture of things, or when a mixture of things is force-compacted to create heat, and the internal vibrational process is exacerbated, which then creates more heat!! This process - if continued - leads to Chaos, which is not unlike a wildfire and therefore also a part of Great Nature! Hence, if these processes were left alone, civilization and humanity would inevitably self-destruct, and enable all life to restart from scratch again. This is, of course, unless a timeous 'cooling force' is brought into play that mechanically reduces the vibration (or states of sleep). This 'cooling force' could also be considered a form of Divine Intervention (Light) or the cyclic nature of the Divine Cosmic Mechanism - and perhaps, all these are the same.

As we concluded in our past correspondences; besides waiting patiently and lovingly, there is seemingly little one can do when the eyes and ears of those one wishes to help are firmly closed. Whether such 'Divine Intervention' would be good or bad, I suppose would depend on the observer, but until then, it seems (to me) that the path and destiny of the Seeker does not depend much on such cycles.

That leads me to your mention of the oath of allegiance to King Chuck[1]. I had not followed this occult circus, but upon receiving your note, looked it up. Wow, what a charade and what a sight to see so many people bowing and parroting such profound words and swearing "so help me God" thereafter. Seeing so many desperately clinging to these occult processes was puzzling; who or what did they think this blinker-wearing god was! My only remaining logical guess, was that they were not actually thinking. If their minds were conditioned to function along lower dimensional and mechanical perspectives, then one can see how their subsequent processes of 'thought' - without the harmony of sentient feeling, doing, and living – would be a veritable prison, which is locked from the inside!

Anyway: It was nice to read of your "three establishment stay". It is really great to have such care from loving friends, and knowing you a little, it sounds like it was also a bit of an adventure, too! From our side, we have of course lived in and out of suitcases on several occasions, and all that seems to be missing is the wagon and a pair of oxen! Not needing to exercise this talent for our upcoming 3 ½-week SA stay, we opted to pick one relatively central place and stay put. For this, we made a very fair arrangement with a former colleague who has an apartment in Sea Point - just around the corner from you!

This then leads me back to a more important part of our exchange - our next meeting, as Yes, we do have lots to share! Perhaps we can begin by passing by for tea on Monday afternoon the 19th?

With love and best wishes,
John

---

[1] Since 8 September 2022, Charles III is King of the United Kingdom and the sovereign over 14 other Commonwealth realms.

21

On reports of Child Abuse and Sacrifice

On Sunday, August 6th, 2023, John wrote:

Dear Vidyananda,
Hari OM.

I trust this finds you well!

Following an intense and busy trip in SA, followed by a turbulent few weeks since our return to Croatia, we have settled into our new house and all is well.

There are still many tasks and chores, but we will now gradually be returning to our original schedules. Both our boys are still here, and although our sojourn between temporary homes has been hectic, it has been a time of great bliss with them as well.

FYI, I saw an interesting excerpt from an RFK Jr[1] interview and his views on 'God'. Not sure if he will get far in politics, as he doesn't have Big Money's interest in mind and therefore not their support, but perhaps that is just as well. I fear that if he were to become popular, he'd not be left alive for very long. However, the Divine works in mysterious ways, and perhaps people like RFK Jr will stimulate a larger awakening and awareness. I'd like to know what your thoughts on this 'lesser-dimensional reality' would be!

With much love and fond regards.
John

On Friday, August 11th, 2023, Vidyananda wrote:

Dear John,
Hari OM.

We have been thinking of you and Terri a lot, although it may not show through communication.

Thank you for sharing the YouTube link, which in itself was an interesting and useful teaching, which I shared with my Meditation Group. Constant God-remembrance does help us to do what is appropriate and of course, also raises our consciousness.

I was a bit disappointed when I learned that RFK Jr was running for

---

[1] Robert F. Kennedy Jr is an American politician, environmental lawyer, and anti-vaccine activist, who was running for President at the time of this writing.

president, as that can be a trap and could detract from his current good work. However, if he can keep to the practice of God-remembrance, then he may not succumb to any of the traps of politics; which must be a very difficult thing to do!

From various articles and clips I saw he mentioned that he feels that his running for president gives him a better opportunity to address the issues he is tackling, especially the health sector. He also mentioned that it will spread awareness of these issues.

It is amazing to see how much he is censored. And it is astounding that this is happening to a potential president. It just goes to show that democracy is out of the window, and those who are in power are holding on and fighting to remain in power tooth and nail. Who knows what's in store for humanity?

I have also been watching a few interviews that Reiner Fuellmich has been conducting on his website https://icic.law/. You may wish to have a peep.

I am glad that you have finally settled into your new home. It sounds like a lovely place! May it bring you much Peace.

Vani is currently visiting Uma in Barrydale, which has come a little into the limelight, as it seems to be on the radar for the "One Small Town" movement[1]. Are you aware of this movement?

Please convey my LOVE to Terri, the Boys, and Yourself :-)

Yours in Prem and Om,
Vidyananda

On Sunday, August 20th, 2023, Vidyananda wrote:

Dear John,
Hari OM.

As ever you are in my thoughts and heart. And so too, is Terri. I pray that both of you are well.

I watched this interview between Reiner Fuellmich and a scientist/spiritualist called Harald Kautz-Vella, which I thought was very interesting. The first time I came across an interview that looked at the spiritual dimension along with science as well. The interview is quite long, so if you are not up to watching, I understand.

I am very interested to know your thoughts on the content of the interview, should you watch it.

Also, I have recently come across the disturbing topic of child sexual abuse and ritual sacrifice of children. This topic is also discussed in the German interview. Have you come across this in your studies? If so, can you share some thoughts with me?

---

[1] This is an initiative to create independent towns:
https://www.onesmalltown.org/landing_page.php

Be well.

Yours in Prem and Om,
Vidyananda

On Tuesday, August 22nd, 2023, John wrote:

My dearest friend Vidyananda,
Hari OM.

It is always so good to hear from you. But even without these emails and even though we are on different continents, you and Vani (and Uma of course) are in my daily prayers and meditations, and it always brings me much gratitude and warmth to see your beautiful Beings there.

I am sorry for only responding now; I began my reply to your RFK Jr response last week, but some chores around the house stopped me from completing it. However, those done, now we must and will address these profound phenomena that are attracting our mutual attention.

The subject of child abuse and sacrifice is naturally one which, of all things in life, weighs heaviest on our hearts. It is however, a smoking gun[1] that proves the presence of darkness and evil in our midst. Yet, it is a subject that is very complex to discuss or address openly and objectively. This is because it tends to draw an emotional response (a mix of fear, sadness, anger, etc) that distorts the ability to see and think about it objectively. In addition, this phenomenon also crosses many different dimensions that we (you, I, and a very few others) are beginning to undoubtedly observe simultaneously. The problem here is that the ignorance and denial of what is evident and verified, is what perpetuates the cycle of abuse. It is happening everywhere, often in plain sight, and yet it is ignored and denied by many.

What makes this subject even more complex to discuss is that, I fear, it is a force that is unstoppable (at least by any one man or woman). To halt it, would require a 'scale-tipping' awakening of people. Since 80 – 95% of people merely seek to be entertained (as confirmed by S.V. and J.K.[2]), and the development of gadgetry to provide this ever-enhanced and freely available entertainment is accelerating exponentially, I believe this force is both unstoppable and inevitable. Some of the ancient writings recorded it as such, but a little more on this a bit later.

As always, I apologize if I appear to lecture, condone, condemn, or offend, but to address my views even in 'brief', I have to elaborate on some seemingly unrelated facets.

The dark force that has taken control over many an individual ego, does so with immense material / financial power. This dark force will often use 'entertainment' to distract and corrupt these egos. As an example, think of

---

[1] Something that serves as strong evidence or irrefutable proof, especially of legal liability or criminal guilt.
[2] During a talk between Swami Venkatesananda and J. Krishnamurti in 1969, they agreed that 90 – 95% of people are not interested in the teachings and prefer to be entertained.

Jeffrey Epstein, his private island, his Lolita Express, and his long and considerable list of recorded patrons that included celebrities, tycoons, royals, and politicians[1]. Here, 'entertainment' took the form of sex-orientated activities with minors, even the very young, and boosted the psyche of this dark force and thus, its psychic power. Further, the accumulated wealth and ordained power of the participants, enabled them to obtain pretty much anything they wanted; their increasing and highly addictive demands continued to seek ever expanding extremes and to go entirely 'off the reservation'. As such, the participants of these orgies, entered a lower dimensional realm where their addictive search for ecstasy crossed the threshold and became an addiction to forms of agony – in both masochistic and sadistic ways.

This type of sociopathic and psychopathic trend is usually beyond the perceived logic and comprehension of the everyday contemporary person, who continues to believe that all people are essentially the same and live by the same moral principles. This, in my view, is erroneous as people differ as much from each other as that various species of animals differ – especially if species are to be defined by their psychic state or *dimension of awareness*.

To find oneself in the 'dimension of awareness' requires an at least in-part knowledge of how the world functions within the differing dimensions. I would say that those who have not made an unopinionated study of humanity, or who have not been exposed to the contradictory nature of these dimensions, or who do not meditate contemplatively and deeply on such matters, simply do not know how the world works. And what makes this problem worse and disastrously so, is that they often think that they do know! Consequently, they may witness the obvious, but cannot make head or tail of the contradictory and paradoxical realities they observe on pretty much all societal spectrums.

The question then returns to "Who then, is running the show?"

As per our previous discourses, I now reiterate my view that this dark force is not just an effect of psychosis, but it is an independent, non-human, ancient, and conscious entity. It is one that is aware of being separate from the human host it possesses. Although it is not a spiritual force, such as that of Divine Light, it looks like it is because it is both formless and timeless. It can take form (according to some of the ancient writings, such as the Emerald Tablets[2]) through the practice of dark magical rites and blood. Once embodied, it supposedly continues to exist by transcending from life to life, consecutively and in parallel.

Although it does not actually live, as in any biological way, the only way it can 'die' (as symbolized in the Bram Stoker Dracula-vampire story), is through the Power of the Light of the Sun – which can of course be translated in various ways. But then, for this demonic entity, this is not a

---

[1] Jeffrey Epstein (1953-2019) was an American serial sex trafficker, paedophile, and financier, with deep ties in Washington DC and Hollywood.

[2] The Emerald Tablet is a cryptic text attributed to Hermes Trismegistus, a syncretic figure of Greek and Egyptian gods. It was a foundational text for Islamic and European alchemists, and it contains the famous phrase "as above, so below".

permanent death anyway, as the dark force will continue to dwell in the unguarded shadowy corners of society. From here, it will await, or seek to occupy, the emotional hearts of unaware people; and when their complacency causes them to surrender their freedom of choice to others, it rises and possesses again, as it has done before.

Where the Divine Light or Spirit and this demonic or psychic force differ from each other, is that Spirit manifests directly from infinite Divine Light but the dark demonic force functions off the psyches of people. It is the people's unawareness of the effects of their fear-based greed and desire, that enables 'entities' to manipulate (and hi-jack) their psychic energy. As a result, they individually and collectively become hosts to this dark psychic entity. This same entity (like the parasite) then begins to shape the affected host-psyches to favour its bidding[1]. The excessive and unusual psychic energy that is resultantly drawn off the host(s) by the entity will now become a drain on their Life-force[2], which is a higher-dimensional source that sustains the existence and quality of Life, and which the entity then mutates into lower two- and one-dimensional visible and physical effects.

The psychic energy of very young and uncorrupted children makes them particularly vulnerable. This is because they have not formed egos as yet, and within whom Spirit has not yet been consciously embraced. The consequent abuse of pre-adolescent children, including sexual abuse and torture, defies what we comprehend as normal or even believable, yet examples of such have been attested to. There have been and still are, exposures of various satanic rings engaged in such practises; for example, the 2016 Washington DC Pizza-gate affair[3]. One need but look at the numbers of missing children every year to see the severity of the situation.

The larger public remains mostly ignorant of the reality of this. They may hear of the terrible and traumatic fate of this or that child in the mainstream media, but the enormity of these acts is so incomprehensible, that most of this gets erased or branded as conspiracy theory. Hence, few contemporary people ever consider the actuality of this situation (which is not too unlike the phenomena surrounding covid & vaccines).

This then leads us to the motives. When we try to determine these along contemporary principles, we may find it inexplicable from many a perspective; including ones of physical and material reward. There is, however, besides a well-known sex-trade, also a documented[4] trade in blood,

---

[1] Parasite-induced behavioral modification occurs when a parasite alters the behavior of its host to benefit the parasite's survival, reproduction, or transmission. Among human beings, there is increasing evidence that microbes and parasites can subtly shape human emotions, decisions, and mental health.
[2] Once the psychic energy of a person is tapped into, their prana, qi or life force will gradually diminish, with a similar effect as when blood is drained from the body.
[3] Although it has been generally censored from the mainstream media, the Pizza-gate scandal that went viral in 2016, was about the New York City Police Department discovery of a paedophilia ring linked to members of the White House.
[4] The trade of human organs, tissues, and body products, usually for transplantation, according to the World Health Organization, occurs outside of national medical systems. As there is a global need or demand for healthy body parts for transplantation, which exceeds the numbers available, there is a viable black market.

organs and body parts for the purpose of extending life, and where naturally, those from young bodies are valued. Although I am quite certain this occurs among some of the super-rich and powerful, I believe that the stronger motivator and more frequent transgressions are linked to the 'harvesting' of psychic energy. These arcane deeds, which include acts of cannibalism, are not just perpetrated to extend life, but also in grotesque rituals, with as its aim to ensure re-birth in positions of power, repeatedly.

I understand that this subject is for many a very complex subject to grasp or accept. From a personal perspective, when, some time ago, I researched these processes, it was for me a very sinister, bleak and somewhat depressing experience. Beside reviewing the descriptions in books and studies on mysticism and legend, scripture, history, and those of whistleblower accounts, I also made a logical assessment of the science of harvesting and channelling forms of psychic energy, which included modern and ancient design and architecture of high profile places[1]. At times, it took me a through a long and dark tunnel, and although this was mostly an intellectual study, it definitely left some scars, as some of these things one cannot 'unknow'!

Now, in most contemporary circles, these transgressions are automatically blamed on that sector of humanity's 4 – 6% who have a psychopathic nature, but I do not believe this is accurate. The reason is that the psychopath, although he or she is unable to feel or care, has therefore no such instinctive need or desire. Having studied *the effects* of this phenomenon, I cannot but feel that this dark feature is able to capture and infect the mind of all people; especially those who are unaware of these tendencies, who become mesmerised by the promises of charlatans, and then docilely subjected into such conspiratorial rings within rings.

Between the seemingly growing complacency of the general public towards such crimes and the corresponding rising chaos, it almost seems as if a 'Rapture' of sorts is imminent[2]. It also seems that we may be tasked to bear witness and learn, as there is seemingly little else we can do at this time. Hence I find it helps me tremendously to spend time interacting, thinking, writing, and speaking with family, good friends, and good people across all walks, and to see Creation and Reality from different dimensional angles as well. As a point of light, here is one of such angles – a long but enlightening 2 ½ hour exchange between Rupert Spira and Donald Hoffman, and beautifully orchestrated by the interviewer. I enjoyed listening to it and did so several times.
https://www.youtube.com/watch?v=rafVevceWgs

With much love and best wishes,
John

PS. The interview between Rupert Spira and Donald Hoffman is lengthy, but I find it offers a veritable higher dimensional view on science and

---

[1] Most temples, cathedrals, churches, monuments, and locations that house government, academia, and entertainment, incorporate this science.
[2] The Rapture is a Christian reference to a separation of believers from non-believers, at the end of times.

spirituality. They confluence with each other perfectly, and I find the observation of this confluence enlightening to my psyche. The realities described in the testimonies of interviews such as those of Reiner Fuellmich – as important as this knowledge is – it is not healthy to dwell on them too much. As real as they are, they belong to the one- and two-dimensional worlds, where we do not reside, and thus we cannot realistically do anything to change them. I find the same when I study the negative influences of pharmaceuticals – not just side effects and the calculated harm of many of the vaccines, but also how the spread of opioids (legally distributed) continues to destroy the soul-journeys of tens of millions of people. Hence, taking a higher dimensional perspective enables me to take a regular breath of fresh air, in between the deep dives.

On Sunday, August 24th, 2023, Vidyananda wrote:

Dear John,
Hari OM.

Thank you for your detailed analysis. As usual, I find it very useful and insightful.

The dark force reminds me of the sixteenth chapter of the Bhagavad Gita, which explains the distinction between the path of light and the path of darkness: two possible paths that we can follow. Interestingly the path of darkness is called 'asura', which, quite literally means 'no light'. Then one can understand that as an individual enters into this path, with increasing darkness (or ever decreasing light), any action is possible, as they have cut themselves off from the Light. Yes, it is rather disturbing to know about this; and one wonders what would happen if people realized this and who is involved.

The only redeeming feature is that darkness is not the total absence of Light, it requires Light to exist, and hence even in the greatest darkness, there is the glimmer of Light that enables redemption and healing. Who knows what we have been through and done in previous births? Once a devotee asked Swami Sivananda whether he could tell him what the devotee was in a previous birth. Swami Sivananda replied, "You would not handle that knowledge!"

Maybe not much can be done, or maybe there is a momentum building up that may bring about change! Even if we cannot do anything, I believe the power of prayer is more powerful than we may think: so that is what we can do, not only for the children but also for the perpetrators. Theirs would be an extremely painful awakening!

Thank you for the link, which I will watch.

Yours in Prem and Om,
Vidyananda

On Saturday, August 26th, 2023, Vidyananda wrote:

Dear John,
Hari OM.

I just watched the Discussion you sent me. Wonderful!

Suddenly a thought struck me that maybe what is behind all the Evil that we see, is the Fear of Death. The Possession, as you call it, is an illusory belief in creating immortality. The control of others through Lockdowns etc also is an illusory attempt to preserve life.

Just a thought.

Let us celebrate Being!

Yours in Prem and Om,
Vidyananda

On Sunday, August 27th, 2023, John wrote:

Dear Vidyananda,
Hari OM.

Thank you for sharing your insights; I enjoy receiving them and they are equally valuable!

When I observe our combined views on this phenomenon, what seems to emerge is the inevitable Path-of-Choices that is part of mankind's journey to become one with the Divine Whole.

It was also interesting to read your comment on the necessity of prayer for the children but also for the perpetrators and align this with Swami Sivananda's response to the devotee about a previous incarnation, and not being able to handle such knowledge. Additionally, it reminded me of some of the teachings in Theosophy, which describe the two thresholds one must ultimately be prepared to cross. The first one is karmic-like, whereby one must take note and, if need be, take account or make amends, of everything one has encountered and encounters across the path of one's life. This one is said to be relatively easy to face and understand. The second threshold, however, is so monstrously horrible, that only a few are able to cross it (at first); it is whereby one must face the darkness inherent in one's own nature.

On the video of Spira and Hoffman: I was glad to hear that you enjoyed the interaction between these two profound minds within their disciplines. Regarding your response on this, I completely agree. It seems true that the Fear of Death is what drives the Possession. This I see as synonymous with the fear of exposure; that is, when the Light exposes the dark force, this is a form of Death for the dark force. Negative behaviours that contribute to the dark force, such as the *blatant, shameless and obvious* censorship and propaganda that we currently see, and which is rooted in this dark force, thus cease to exist when challenged by the Light of Truth. In this way, the dark force 'Dies' and only Truth and Truthful acts that are sincere and compassionate, go on to resonate throughout the ages. It is to the

Possession therefore worse than the death of its biological host, because where they can otherwise continue to exist from host to host, when Truth exposes the lie *that is them*, it is forever, including the reality of their past existence. If we envision this, from the perspective that Truth is all there ever is *and was*, then for such entities, such exposure is truly terrifying!

Thus it seems that this Fear of Death reigns strongest in such a dimensionally limited Possession. The human beings who are caught up in its 'spell' and who serve it through their negative actions, are likely to only begin to think of Death when, for example, they become terminally ill. Until then, they fan the flames of Chaos, and likely fear falling out of favour by the Possession when they cease to be of value to it, more so than their own actual Death. Hence the inexplicability of their desperate acts becomes transparent.

It is at this point perhaps interesting to note a confluence here: *If the process of illumination implies the non-existence of the three-dimensional self, which is how our space-time reality becomes illusory, we may realize that it was made manifest through our five senses, which in turn served a Higher Mind that exists outside of the brain* (as per Spira and Hoffman..?). In other words, it is when we become aware of the Self outside of our physical-biological three-dimensional limitation, that the transcendence to higher dimensions and consequent merger becomes apparent![1]

As such, while the Divine Pendulum between Chaos and Order continues its perpetual swing, with a little prayer, the celebration of Being is indeed veritable!

With love, high regards, and best wishes,
John

---

[1] Due to the complexity of this statement, following is the editor's elucidation of it: "Since Illumination implies a letting go of the three-dimensional self which is evident in space-time and made manifest through our five senses; then that which exists outside this three-dimensional self is the Higher Mind or Consciousness, experiencing this. In other words, once we become aware of the Self outside of our physical-biological three dimensional limitation, we transcend and merge with that Consciousness."

22

Opinion

The following exchange is largely a continuation of the earlier mentioned (Chapter 17) comments on the Schiller Institute. This entails a review of different socio-economic systems within which or whereby, people could co-exist free from the conflict observed in almost every current society.

On Wednesday, August 23rd, 2023, John wrote:

Dear Vidyananda,
Hari OM.

I forgot to respond to one part of your earlier email, where you wrote: "Vani is currently visiting Uma in Barrydale, which has come a little into the limelight, as it seems to be on the radar for the OneSmallTown movement. Are you aware of this movement?"

I did look into this but got caught up in the follow-up exchange.

I am relatively familiar with Michael Tellinger's work over the past 10 - 15 years, especially on very ancient civilizations[1] and the presence of a reptilian or non-human influence presiding over the financial systems and the authoritarian rule of mankind. Tellinger is a solid warrior for his causes, and I think he has made a decent living out of it. I resonate with many of his findings, but at a certain point, he reaches what I would call 'a dimensional limitation' to understanding. To move beyond this limitation requires an acceptance of the Divine or Universal / Cosmic laws.

The OneSmallTown concept sounds, in principle, like a good idea, and a possible solution to many of the problems in South Africa. I do fear that some of the ideas also carry seeds for potential corruption in them - especially if / when the idea grows in influence and strength. People are people, and most that enter such arrangements do so with the best of intentions but often find themselves embattled with others that simply see things completely differently to them.

I saw this in Tulbagh when we, as a small group of 6 or 10 hospitality operators, got together to synergize our region's hospitality operations. At first, it was informal, fun, and quite productive. I would refer to it to Terri as the "knitting club" because I often sat there, as the only man with a bunch of ladies, drinking tea and eating scones while some of them were doing their knitting at the meet!. In time however, more and more joined us and eventually, the group appointed a chairman (who became somewhat

---

[1] Tellinger discovered among other, Adam's Calendar, aka the Blaauboschkraal stone ruins, an ancient stone structure located in Mpumalanga, South Africa, believed to be around 75,000 years old.

tenacious), and a secretary. Then a constitution with rules and schedules was set up, by which several of the original 'knitting club' members were banned, as they did not 'comply' with its rules! I had by then left the party, as I saw where this could lead, and did not wish to partake in the unpleasant conflict that would inevitably arise. (In addition, I do not like to suffer foolishness which, in the past, seldom made me many friends – I thus had to leave them, to keep them as friends).

As it is, I fear the OneSmalltown concept, if it becomes too organized, may likely follow a similar trend. The added concept of a 'currency' that they planned to introduce (I forgot the name), would lead to collectivism, which leads to materialism, and from this, the whole rise and fall merry go round restarts again!

With love from your somewhat pessimistic or realistic friend,
John

On Sunday, August 27th, 2023, Vidyananda wrote:

Dear John,
Hari OM.

Thank you for this feedback, which confirms my thoughts as well; especially since it also has somewhat of a centralized financial (and hence power-) structure. And since this would be in the hands of a few (who have computer tech knowledge) it lies open to abuse. Hence I am not too fond of this aspect, and therefore the project.

However, the concept of a self-sufficient community seems to be a good way to go. But this was how things were in the past also. Then these communities fought each other, formed alliances, and eventually became countries. It seems that humanity is just running around in circles.

Change, as you well know, can only happen within oneself. If that change happens, then naturally the world would be a better place. But this cannot be engineered, as it is impossible to bring about fundamental spiritual change in another being.

So, I guess when it comes to society (in whatever form) we can only do our best, and maybe choose to live where it is least bad.

I certainly do not find you pessimistic. Always uplifting to be with you or communicate with you. As Swami Venkatesananda said, "Neither pessimist nor optimist. Clear the mist and see the reality."

May we be granted that vision of the Real.

Yours in Prem and Om,
Vidyananda

23

A Backward and Forward Glance on Current Status Quos

In this exchange, various subjects previously discussed were reviewed, both from a perspective of causality and interconnectedness, as well as their deeper meaning in the Creator's All and Everything. The reader must forgive, when repetitions on certain elements are observed; besides the fact that there was no agenda or other that determined the content of the correspondence between John and Swami Vidyananda, many an observation was elucidated along the course of their exchange.

On Friday 27 October 2023, John wrote:

My dear friend Vidyananda,
Hari OM.

I trust you, Vani, all at the Ashram, and our dear friend Uma in the Barrydale Outback are well!

All is well with us. We have settled into our new house and completed the necessary furnishing. We are still awaiting the shipment of our things from SA, but this is scheduled to arrive this week. Strangely enough; we realized that we have lived without all of these items (about 30+ boxes of books and personal paraphernalia) for 20 months, and wonder why we went through all the trouble of shipping these? The answer seems obvious (to me); it is simply our way of keeping a materially-identified ego - that must cling to 'things' – even whilst we purposely re-create an entirely new external surrounding and environment. I find that the intentional deception of my ego calms it, making the thinking less noisy, such changes less stressful and the experience more interesting!

Terri and I have happily settled into our respective routines, with Terri working hard at finishing her studies and me dividing my day between reading, writing, and studying topics of interest. At the moment these include the ancient and philosophical mysteries that I find interact with science and mathematics (this, whilst trying to learn Hrvatski - which turns out to be a very complex language). I also try to spend a few hours a day on physical chores and beautification around the house; I find that the stonework, bricklaying, plastering, paving, carpentry, painting, and other tasks keep my body-mind aligned and its practical skills honed!

There are still a few other projects whose seeds are waiting to germinate – some of these I think I previously discussed with you a bit - but they remain in the hands of others. Somehow I also sense the presence of a Higher Guidance in these matters, as once they begin, our lives will likely take a considerably new and different course.

In August Nick, and in September Matt, returned to their respective realities in Spain and the Netherlands. All is well with them. Nick came home this week for a short time off before his exams start next week. The timing of this was nice as we also have Terri's parents (Glynn and Steve) visiting us. We decided that it was easier and more economical to fly them here rather than for us to visit SA in December - especially now that we have sold our car there. But besides that, it was also something they really wanted to do - whilst they still could!

Before these latest visits, our friend Jeroen from Amsterdam visited us (I believe you two have met). As I wanted to take a little break and as Terri needed to catch up on her studies, I picked Jeroen up at Split Airport (on the mainland), and from there, we went on a little road trip into the mountains of Bosnia-Herzegovina. This entailed a spectacular drive through interesting, historical, and breathtaking scenery. Although the people there have little and suffered much during and following the Balkan wars, we found them to be beautiful, generous, and hospitable. Bosnia-Herzegovina is a complex region; it is divided between three distinct groups - Catholic Croatians, Orthodox Serbs, and Muslim Bosnians – their differences are very easy to exploit by those with political power and alternative agendas. It remains therefore, a potential conflict flash-point.

Of interest perhaps, is that when we were driving in the Bosnian mountains, on an old and little-used dirt road between the towns of Konjic and Mostar, we ran into a joyful old "Baka" (grandmother), travelling around with her very large flock of sheep. A very large dog was doing its job keeping the herd together whilst quietly placing itself between us and the sheep. The dog needed no instructions through words or signs to know what to do, and appeared to pay us little attention, even though it kept a weary peripheral or psychic eye on us! I had actually seen these amazing Yugoslavian (Sharplaninatz) dogs before - in the mountains of North Macedonia - and also with an equally joyful and friendly old Baka who had three of these connected and protective beings looking after her and a large flock of goats[1].

It has been a while since you and I corresponded; and, it is my guess, that we are both keeping a wary eye the ongoing and deteriorating developments in the authoritarian, geopolitical, and economic arenas. This is even more so in light of the East vs West theatrics that are now complemented by the horrific but equally orchestrated events in the Middle East. One can of course lengthily analyze each of these events across many different angles, but I suspect you understand that I see none of these as a conflict between people but rather as events occurring between *duelling but interlinked* Entities. These Entities are hidden within media references to 'developments' and each one has a story. To me, however, what remains

---

[1] As described earlier, on Tuesday, March 1st, 2022

clearly visible within all of these stories, is a connecting thread that serves the same old, but deeper and more hidden, entity, whose only purpose is to cause Chaos. It is within Chaos that the Entity thrives, gorging itself on the fear, anger, and suffering of the helpless, the affected and afflicted - *on both sides!* Even the considerable schism that has arisen among contemporary people worldwide, who are actively taking opposing sides, and seen either 'fighting for' or 'fighting against', in one form or another; all serve 'it' as well.

I find that when I raise my one dimensional awareness from the tragedies on the ground, to above that of a birds-eye-view, I find that this madness and its resultant suffering remains a feature of Creation's Whole. I believe this is especially evident when I see how Chaos is allowed to perpetuate like a wildfire, to such extremes, *and with no actual physical or profitable outcome even possible.* This, amidst the preposterous censorship and information controls, and the blatant corruption in so many sectors, that is openly visible, and yet ignored by so many!

As much as one may be able to identify the cunning design in this, to me it is still causal; being the effects of an unawakened many, who do not awaken, and who are unlikely to do so. This is because they, in turn, seek to fulfil their inner wish for enhancement in the physical, material, financial, popular, technological or similar, realms. Consequently, these ones are quite unable to see that evil factually exists among them, let alone to see that it is in the form of a conscious and intelligent entity that can transmit itself from host to successive host, generation to generation, and which is, in a way, 'immortal'. As the great many adore and serve one or many such entities, one may even say that the greatest trick the Devil ever pulled was not convincing man that he did not exist, but rather, that he convinced man that he was God...

But all this you and I have discussed (in some form or length) on previous occasions. From my side, however, I continue to sense a gentle whisper that says all is still exactly as it is meant to be. When there is such Darkness then somewhere there is also the Light that made it manifest. And if Darkness were ever to succeed in extinguishing the Light, then by proxy, it would cease to exist. Further, if this occurred, then all would (almost miraculously) return to normal because, in the non-existence of Darkness, the *timeless* Light will be as if It always was, which It is and ever must be!

On another note, and one that may explain what motivates or attracts some of these authoritarian entities responsible for fanning Chaos; I recently reviewed the workings, writings, and recordings of Viktor Schauberger[1], and at the same time, unrelated to him, those of Robert Edward Grant[2]. I ended up combining these readings with a review of the history of Tsarist and Communist Russia across the last 1000 years; this was in contrast to the

---

[1] Viktor Schauberger (1885-1958) was an Austrian forest caretaker, naturalist, philosopher, inventor and scientist.
[2] Robert Edward Grant is an inventor, entrepreneur, and thought leader in fields ranging from medical technology, cryptography, sacred geometry, mathematics, and music theory.

light work discovered by Grant and Schauberger, as well as that of Spira and Hoffman that we previously discussed. I could not but also observe how the earlier-mentioned dark features of humanity were and are omnipresent. This, too when reflecting on the mysterious and occult works of Da Vinci, Shakespeare, and others, such as the necromancer, John Dee[1], as well as how many of these works are connected via encoded geometry to numerous aspects of the equally mysterious Egyptian Giza Plateau. There was a source of knowledge and power inherent in that place; but this power was only available to certain initiated ones. It is said that besides Da Vinci, Alexander, Plato, Napoleon, and even (supposedly) Moses and Jesus ventured to Giza before performing their greatest works. If this is so, one can see why many of the deep and brilliant ones would practice their skills in the occult, away from seeing eyes; I guess then there are a great many that we do not know of!

Having reviewed its nature and its effects for some time, I believe that this power is channelled through the psyche and its character (or effect) is astral. As a result, it is dual in its design with neither part controllable by the ordinary man. Instead, the dark side controls those who think they work it, by shaping the effects of their 5 basic senses, and influencing what they perceive and believe is 'real'.

I feel that a very large part of what causes the dilemmas we see in the world, resides in the fact that those who embrace this *earthly* 'power', are usually unbalanced by it in their daily *earthly* existence. As a result, they are unable to perceive their higher intuitive and spiritual senses. Hence, unskilled and careless meddling with these powers, as the 17th century wizard John Dee experienced, and especially when done so from within powerful collectives of people, is something that can be catastrophic in many ways, and should not be taken lightly.

Thus, I will leave you with these views to (if you wish to, of course) chew, digest, and play with! There is, of course, no rush and no pressure to reply to this lengthy "glance", but it is always good to hear from you and to hear or read your thoughts. Your observations on the status of things are to me, after all, amidst all the other vectors of review, always of great value!

Please send our love and best wishes to Vani and Uma.

Best wishes,
John

On Saturday, 28 October 2023, Swami Vidyananda wrote:

Dear John,
Hari OM.

I am very happy to have received your email. I have been intending to write to you but...

---

[1] *John Dee and the Empire of Angels*, by Jason Louv. Dee (1527-1608) was an English mathematician, astronomer, astrologer, occultist, and alchemist. As an advisor to Elizabeth I, he spent much time on divination, and Hermetic philosophy.

I am glad to note that all is well with you, Terri, and the boys (or men?). Please send them our love. Also, lovely that you had that beautiful journey with Jeroen. Yes, we met at Welbedacht during one of my visits.

Life here at the ashrama continues more or less the same as always: we keep up with our spiritual life as best as we can, enjoy our Sunday walks, and also keep a little attention on 'world events'. I also managed to finally do a visit to the Namaqualand flowers near Garies and the Namaqualand National Park. Spectacular!

Before COVID, I was never interested in world events. Since that event, I felt it is good to have some understanding as some of the world events impact us directly. So, I have kept up with watching some talks and documentaries, although I must say that we are running out of things to watch or read, as much of it is repetition. And the thing with repetition is not only that one ends up hearing the same explanations, but one realizes that history does repeat itself indeed, albeit in different guises. There will always be the power-hungry and heartless people who will do anything to get their aims. And as you correctly point out, it is not merely an individual thing, they are driven by cosmic forces of darkness, which the Bhagavad Gita calls Asura Prakritti (the nature of darkness or non-light). And those who are attuned to this force will enter into ever-increasing darkness and therefore are capable of ever-increasing evil. The saving factor is this: there is no absolute darkness, and the Light is even present in that darkness, although very faint; but that faint light is enough to bring that person back on the path of light, even if it should take lifetimes. I guess the one thing we need to do is to ensure that we remain on the path of light, which incidentally the Bhagavad Gita calls Daivi Prakritti: the path of Light or Divinity. If we fight the evil, we shall get tainted; so the best is to remain pure.

Yes, the Middle East conflict is of course on our radar. What was a little amazing was that I was listening to some talks by Swami Venkatesananda in which he referred to the Middle East conflict and gave some very interesting insights. I had never before noticed Swami Venkatesananda mention these conflicts, and of course, the conflicts are not the subject of the talks and just illustrations. However, I thought that the synchronicity was astounding. One thing that struck me was that some people had emotional reactions to this conflict, whereas no one had ever mentioned anything about all the other previous conflicts. This indicates to me that the conflict is revved up to get people to take sides and support the war. I offer a more zoomed-out view so that they can see the bigger picture and remain calm.

It certainly appears that evil is out of control. According to another scripture called Bhagavatam, evil has to reach a point at which humanity in desperation reaches out to God for help. It is when the Grace of God is called upon that the Divine Forces restore the balance. It seems to me therefore that we are to witness a lot more because we still feel that we can do something. And as long as the 'I' feels it can do something, the Divine remains a witness only.

In my understanding evil is 'immortal' in the sense that as long as there is a creation, the force of evil exists. However, when the creation is temporarily withdrawn and God alone exists, then there is no more evil. There is also no more good. God alone exists. And maybe from 'God's perspective' that is so even now?

Can you explain your sentence please: "One may even say that the greatest trick the Devil ever pulled was not convincing man that he did not exist, but rather, that he convinced man that he was God..."

I agree with you that the psychic realm is dualistic. It is an enhanced and refined use of the mind and senses, which always function (and can only function) dualistically. This is one of the reasons why the Yoga Masters discourage the use of psychic abilities, as they can serve as a distraction from the path of Enlightenment.

I have also noticed that we need to be vigilant to remain on the path of Light. By condemning the 'evil', by judgment, by fighting evil, we easily become evil ourselves. And also, we have to be careful about considering others as 'unawakened' and ourselves as 'awakened', as this can easily lead to arrogance, which again is the entry into darkness. I have noted in quite a few 'awakened' podcasters this dangerous trait. I pray I don't fall victim to that.

I noticed also how important it is to not get caught up in all this. It is good to know what is happening, and that all these happenings are really a kind of illusion, especially in the way they are presented to make us believe and act in certain ways. But we must make sure these events do not preoccupy our minds because it is most important to focus on the Divine.

So, thank you again for initiating another conversation. I am fairly pathetic when it comes to writing. Please know that you and Terri are frequently on our minds and always in our hearts. You are our dear friends.

Love to Terri and You.

Yours in Prem and Om,
Vidyananda

On Tuesday 31 October 2023, John wrote:

Dear Vidyananda,
Hari OM.

Thank you for your fast response, and as always, its depth and consideration. I received it just before leaving for an overnight to Split with Nick, and it was pleasant contemplating your thoughts and observations along the drive back. He is back in the Netherlands now and I am back at my home since the beginning of last week with Steve and Glynn[1]. It has been an interesting few weeks sharing the house with them as naturally, we are all very different in almost every facet of being.

Their timing was great, it being not as touristy now and the weather is still nice - sunny but not hot. It is also olive time here, and unlike SA with its large corporate-style farming, most farms here are small and family-operated. Consequently, the local families can be seen everywhere across the

---

[1] Terri's parents, who visited Croatia

island, over the little stone walls, and into the terraced groves, harvesting their olives. It is a multi-generational effort; from toddlers to grandparents, and the processing into oil or for eating is also done so. At the same time and while much of the world now celebrates Dia de las Muertos / Day of the Dead / or Halloween with costumes, here it is All Saints celebrations, and the graves of the departed are honoured with flowers, candles, and family reunions. All these naturally also give the younger generations a very solid family-orientated and stable base, within which much of their culture is rooted.

I find this stable base lacking in many of the Western (or 1st-world) environments, where family values are seemingly being intentionally diluted and even discouraged. Even the somewhat illogical gender-type confusion, that is currently propagandized by state politics, academia, media and entertainment, appears to be part of this sinister plot ... and it is the idea of such a plot that I would like to add to our current discourse! On this, if I may, I would like to reply using excerpts from your letter:

You wrote: *"it is good to have some understanding as some of the world events impact us directly"*

The Miraculous never ceases to amaze me. This is especially so every time I re-discover its beauty and perfection – even in things that are considered bad, catastrophic, or unfortunate. Subsequently, I find it important to remember and understand that my search for answers to life's mysteries, including that of humanity's inexplicability, is not caused by a desire to 'FIX' anything. I would rather wish to entertain that it is to understand, in its entirety, both the light and dark sides of things. This is because without such understanding it may not always be feasible to find love that is truly unconditional, because in the end, a thing is what it is - because it is. Only by seeing it as such do I believe one can accept that-what-is, unreservedly! It is, from my perspective, from this place that one enters a reality where one can accept the existence of both the sinner and the sin.

That said, and having established this point of view as the 'canvas of my current painting', I can more consciously enter (without getting emotionally caught up), into a reality of Self and its opposite - that of the Collective. I believe that a search for the merger between these two 'impossible-to-merge-opposites', may offer guidance to the emergence of a new 'being'.

Hence for this, the spiritual life and a balanced understanding of the world is important. This view could be expanded on by considering the butterfly effect[1], as all world events do impact every one of us, to some extent or other. I have found that many people have a misinterpreted understanding of the co-existence of these two (the spiritual life within an understanding of the world), tend to become *emotionally* focused, which leads them to often be unable or unwilling to see an expanded view. Consequently, they see the effects of events but remain unaware of the ultimate causes. The recent events of, for example, Covid, Vaccines, the war in Ukraine, and the upheaval in the Middle East, are all such 'effects', and to me, the more I

---

[1] The phenomenon whereby a small change at one place in a complex system can have large effects elsewhere.

study these, the clearer, deeper, and more historic the causal picture becomes.

You wrote: *"as long as the 'I' feels it can do something, the Divine remains a witness only"*

While I understand and agree with this view, it could be debated along the lines of which one comes first. Being omnipresent, the Divine is always there, but do we act or do we wait and leave things to run their course, or is there a place somewhere in between? One may, after all, also observe reality as one that we co-create, meaning that not doing anything may lead to docility, laziness and sleep, which in turn may give rise to an even more brutal forms of authoritarianism.

"To be or not to be[1]"; to speak or to remain quiet; to do or to leave it be? Personally speaking, as I was not born without a bouquet of practical abilities, these have always been natural questions in me and subsequently, I sometimes feel I can do something. As a result, I have also pondered the alternative question, being; does the Saviour only come when He / She is needed or called upon? Or is He / She / or They perhaps already among us? Perhaps, instead of being in the form of a single being, the Saviour arrives in the form of many seeds that are spread out among millions of Seekers?

You wrote: *"Can you explain 'One may even say that the greatest trick the Devil ever pulled was not convincing man that he did not exist, but rather, that he convinced man that he was God...'"*

It is my understanding that in addition to those who are in the Know, like perhaps the enlightened Saint or Guru, there are those I classify as Seekers and Believers. The difference I see between these two is that the Seeker follows the path of the Knower, but the Believer can often be made to follow whatever appears as true and relevant at a particular time.

That said, I entirely agree with your view on us not knowing if we are 'awakened', or if others are 'unawakened', but perhaps my use of this word was misunderstood. When I use the term being 'awake', then I mean 'awakened to the existence of a higher purpose', being the path of transcendence or Higher Being, and in service of the Divine, but not (necessarily) enlightened as such (as yet).

Among those who, in this context, I consider as Believers, there are some who descend from this path of 'spiritual self-awakening' and who become the mere followers of rules, from where they may drift even further away and become enforcers and rule-makers. These are the ones who become 'trapped' within suggestive one- and two-dimensional realities, realities defined by dogma in the strictest sense, and where the intuitive higher dimensional or spiritual practice is unlikely to penetrate and take root by itself – *by natural means*. These 'traps' are usually found rooted in innocent cases of good intentions, poor taste, or unwise choice-making, but which, over time, become ingeniously and purposely designed to do just that – traps that create seemingly attractive and smart-looking choices. Often, these

---

[1] Quoted from Shakespeare's Hamlet.

'traps' are so cunningly designed by the Asura Prakriti that they convince people to the extent that they believe they are on the Daivi Prakriti and serving God.

Last but not least, a comment on "the immortality of evil"

Many of the events we are witnessing, the brutality that is beyond human comprehension, the intentional corruption surrounding gender identification, the steep increase of child abuse (of the worst kind), and the various other abnormal conditions, *cause me to question the contemporary acceptance of such things; that these things are accepted or seen as normal is the greatest mystery.* It is an agenda that does not serve life, or the accumulation of wealth and power, it only serves itself.

As such, I cannot but repeat and emphasize my belief that these Possessions are conscious, intelligent, and immortal entities that feed off the low-vibrational life-force of those who exist in low dimensional realities. This may sound like I believe we live inside some sort of mind-prison, but that is only partially true. It is true when one says that, as long as we remain in the Light it cannot touch us, but this still requires a constant measure of work on our self-awareness.

This is because 'it' is cunning, and knows how to hide, especially in the shadows of others who we allow to come close to us, and whom we will trustingly invite into our midst and our homes. it is like a veritable Trojan Horse, and as such we must remain vigilant!

Therefore, I agree with your view that the psychic and astral realms must be treated with utmost caution. Further, we must observe ourselves and our reactions and interactions with others and events. I noticed, for example, how many 'spiritual' podcasters are becoming quite adamant in suggesting we 'fight', 'sue', or 'avenge', as it seems to me, only when we cease to acknowledge the existence of the demon's calls or 'traps', can it cease to exist.

In closing, I again hope that with these topics I have not gone too far into the proverbial twilight zone – and if I have, please let me know! I intended to keep my response short, but alas, once I got going, that was it. I do however believe we live in an extraordinary time; one that is unlike anything that has occurred in our recorded history - and I am happy and blessed to be able to openly discuss these times with you.

I will leave it at that and instead, as always, send you and Vani all my love, high regards, and best wishes.

John

On Thursday, 16 November 2023, Swami Vidyananda wrote:

Dear John,
Hari OM.

This time I have taken a little long to reply due to various work commitments at the ashrama. Thank you for YOUR in-depth insights, which are always stimulating.

Wonderful to be in an environment where some of the traditions are still being observed. Although I do not consider myself a traditionalist as such, I do see the value of tradition, especially if it is wisely lived and the spirit behind the tradition is well understood. Traditions are meant to kindle the spirit. For this, they are very valuable. Discarding them can lead to disastrous societies, as we find ourselves in now. Under the delusion of 'Freedom,' many people are utterly confused and degraded, and therefore steeped in greater and greater suffering, and therefore not freedom.

You are most welcome to use the excerpts, and I hope that it is likewise alright to extract some 'themes'.

Fixing the world: It is becoming more and more clear to me that any attempt at fixing the world only makes it worse, or at best is a movement from one form of unhappiness to another form of unhappiness. All the 'fixes', be they religious, political, social or scientific (and these distinctions are really arbitrary) always seem to require a total mass adoption of the 'fix', which is of course not possible, because any 'fix' will be to the detriment of someone, usually the ones accused of the initial problem. And every 'fix' brings with it so many more of its problems. Even in our own little lives, we may have noted that any solution to a problem brings more problems.

So, I agree that understanding does not mean that one fixes anything. Actually, the understanding is the 'fixing', in the sense that if there is the correct understanding, then the action proceeding from that understanding will also be correct. But the question arises, "What is correct understanding?" Correct understanding cannot be of the mind, as it always operates in duality and is limited to thought. Correct understanding has to be beyond mind and intellect. It must come from the Soul.

Action vs no action: The Bhagavad Gita gives a very interesting teaching regarding action in response to events, whether they are the daily events of our lives, or political events, such as a war. You are quite correct that we cannot remain actionless. Leaving the solutions to the Divine does not mean 'actionless-ness' though. We do have faculties and these are to be used. However, as instruments in the hands of the Divine. We are to be instruments of the Divine: let the Divine prompt the action, not the ego or the mind. Yes, anyone can say, "The Divine prompted me to act," and use it as a justification, or even be deluded into believing they are instruments. So, this requires sincerity. I have to be sincerely looking into myself whether the action is prompted by the ego or the mind, or whether the action is prompted by the Divine. As long as we are not certain, it is safe to presume that our actions are still ego-driven and that more effort is to be made to be in tune with the Divine. (By ego I do not mean arrogance, but the basic ego principle of individuality).

I don't think that we can merge the collective and the individual through thought. The underlying already-existing Unity of the individual and the collective has to be discovered. Like space, there is something that is already uniting each individual to the collective; and that we need to discover.

Swami Venkatesananda had an interesting way of looking at the word individual. He thought of it as a contraction of the term: indivi(sible) dual.

Devil quote: Thank you for clarifying your point. Yes, I agree with you regarding the rule-followers and that they do so because they believe they are making a choice that is attractive, and if not pleasant, then wise and for the greater good. What is interesting to me, is that science seems to have taken over the role of religion now. People follow 'the science', whatever rules 'science' dictates and they believe that this is for the greater good. They don't realize that just as religions got corrupted over time to suit certain powers-that-be, so science is now being corrupted for the same purpose. Just as religion ceased to be true religion, science is following the same fate. Thank God that in both fields there always remained the sincere and true ones, of whom humanity may only become aware later in history. These are the seekers, which you call 'awakened'. They are awake because they do not blindly follow rules, nor blindly reject them, but continuously seek the Truth.

The ongoing evil: Yes, the Asura Prakriti is as eternal as the Daivi Prakriti. It all depends on the degree to which one is more dominant than the other. According to some of the Hindu scriptures, we find ourselves in that phase in which darkness and unrighteousness are in the ascent. They use interesting imagery. A cow represents righteousness. Over time her legs are severed by a quarter each time. In our current age, she only has one-quarter of her legs left and is crying pitifully, as even the last quarters are under threat. And when we read of what the 'demons' did in ancient times, then we realize that demons do not necessarily come with horns. They appear in human garb. Humans become demons, and then perform demoniacal deeds.

I read an interesting article by a disciple of Swami Venkatesananda, called Swami Narayani. I never met her as she passed away before I came to the Yoga path, but had heard a lot about her. She was a remarkable homeopath and healer, with amazing success. Her main focus was serving the poor and she never charged for her treatments. Everything ran on a donation basis and she had complete faith in the Divine. In this article, she writes that if a person has very strong negative thoughts/emotions/feelings these create an energy force that begins to have a life of its own, and this force also extends outward. When I read this I immediately thought of your expression 'possession'. Energy has built-in intelligence. So, humans create energy forces that will certainly influence the world in various degrees, and these forces act as if independent due to that in-built intelligence. And if individuals share the same or similar energy forces, then I guess that these combine to create stronger forces. And then those who are open to those forces are influenced by them.

I think that we are mostly influenced by those external forces that correspond with our inner energy forces: if they are negative, then we attract that; if they are positive, then we attract that.

It is also interesting that Swami Sivananda[1] wrote that it is due to the few

---

[1] Swami Sivananda was an enlightened Yoga Master who founded the Sivananda ashram as well as The Divine Life Society in order to guide seekers in the path of yoga. He was the guru of Swami Venkatesananda. https://en.wikipedia.org/wiki/Sivananda_Saraswati

enlightened beings that the world is still in one piece. It is their energy force of love and peace that holds the planet. They may not intentionally do so, but can a light do anything but remove darkness, even if it does not intend to do so?

When I was a teenager a psychic teacher taught me to always surround myself with white light as a form of protection. Also, she taught me that the dark forces cannot be in the aura of love. Hence love the dark forces.

And then, how do we 'protect' our near and dear ones? I think we can only share with them our understanding. In my experience, some will listen, others will not.

Yes, strange times indeed. And the more I look at this, the more it feels like I am watching a soap opera with the goodies and the baddies. And even the goodies begin to fight amongst one another, as in the Fuellmich saga for example. One realizes that we cannot take sides but we must continue our endeavors to discover the Truth, not so much the truth of events, but that Ultimate Truth. If we can be connected to that Truth, all our actions will be of that Nature.

I hope that my sharing does not sound too much like a sermon. Please forgive me if it does.

Yes, Love to all of you precious friends.

Yours in Prem and Om,
Vidyananda

24

All the World's a Stage?

"All the world's a stage" is the opening line of a famous monologue from William Shakespeare's play As You Like It. The speech compares life with a theatrical performance and humans to actors playing roles on a stage.

On Tuesday 28 November 2023, John wrote:

Dear Vidyananda,
Hari OM.

I trust all is well with you, Vani, Uma, and all at the ashram. All is well with us here and Terri is writing the last of her final exams today - and perhaps we will go on a little road trip later in the week to celebrate the end of her 3 1/2-year study-trek. Winter is here and things are rapidly cooling down, despite the dystopian globalist narrative of 'global warming', and it has brought the first snow and frost to the Balkans early; we feel it here with an icy cold north-easterly wind.

(This cold wind is known as the Burra, and unlike the warmer southerly Yugo wind, the locals are very superstitious about this one; supposedly – according to my lawyer – even a judge in court will be more lenient to an offender if he learns that the offending act was not premeditated and occurred whilst the Burra was blowing!).

Thank you for your last, very detailed and deeply considered response. It did not sound like a sermon to me at all, quite the contrary - it was (in my view) the sharing of your considerable knowledge, as observed from your quarter. In fact; where perhaps I tend to describe my observations from the reactive and interactive economic and geopolitical world, of which I am familiar, it seems to me that you can better describe the subject matter from a focused, order-disciplined, and uncluttered spiritual perspective, combined with your considerable teachings of course. Neither of our worlds are without the occasional twists, bumps, and challenges that influence these views, but I believe that our combined worlds (besides having to be lived and experienced separately), are able to offer us a more complete view at least when compared with a view from only one of them. Food for the Soul! Thus, besides your friendship, I am additionally very appreciative of your ability to share your insight and wisdom on such a level.

I agree with everything you mentioned in your last, and there is little I can add that would not be mere confirmation and repetition of what was already said. I also noted your profound observation that for a great many, their new god is science, which is artificial. Its overly academic and sponsored nature has subsequently led it to become corrupted in many fields. In this, I can see signs of certain centers of attention, such as those of academia, entertainment, and even selected charity organizations and sectarian forms of religion. This again indicates to me that, without a conscious pursuit for Truth and the spiritual path to guide us, the individual path becomes visibly reactive, mechanical, polar, and predictable, which makes it programmable, like an automated machine.

This 'programmable automation' could be considered as the next piece of the puzzle though, one that became more defined for me when you wrote: "*The more I look at this, the more it feels like I am watching a soap opera with the goodies and the baddies*". It begs me to re-consider if the perceived reality of our experience is a construct? For centuries, even millennia, man has tried to copy and improve on Great Nature, everywhere. Today it even seems as if man is instinctively or subconsciously trying to copy or improve himself with robotics, AI and Virtual Realities. In the pursuit of Singularity[1], technology is supposedly expected to be such that we would experience life as if in one of these 'games' or virtual programs, and we would not know the difference! That said, if I observe how our present day-to-day is often filled with intriguing coincidences and occurrences, many of which seem to be beyond normal, then I add to this the presence of what appear to be coded formats in much of our reality, whether DNA, geometrical, mathematical and fractal patterns, or even the presence of canonicals in both quantum- and macrocosmic formations... I wonder if perhaps we are already in such a construct?

What would your thoughts be on that?

With love and best wishes,
John

On Friday, 1 December 2023, Swami Vidyananda wrote:

Dear John,
Hari OM.

We are all well, and Uma is currently visiting us for a few days. I hope that Terri's final exams went well (which I'm sure they did), and that the two of you have a splendid holiday. The Burra sounds very onomatopoeic. I pray that you stay warm.

Your observation that we may already be in a construct is an intriguing one, and is dealt with in some of the Vedanta scriptures, which compare the universe to a dream. Just as we create a dreamworld when asleep, Consciousness also creates the dream, which we call the world. It is possible that we are able to dream because Consciousness can dream.

---

[1] The concept of Singularity refers to a future point when technological growth becomes uncontrollable and irreversible, leading to profound changes in human life, particularly through the merging of human intelligence with artificial intelligence. It was originally predicted to occur around 2045, resulting in machines that surpass human intelligence, but due to the exponential increase in development, this date is said to have advanced to 2029.

And then there is day-dreaming! I wonder whether what we call normal thinking is not really daydreaming. And this daydreaming includes academia, ideologies, etc. We create our own creations within the Universal Creation. And these creations cause all the suffering since they are based on ignorance of the nature of the Original Creation.

Now, back to the Vedantic view of the creation being the dream of Consciousness. This merely suggests that the Creation is not truly matter but essentially Consciousness-Energy and nothing but Consciousness-Energy. But this has to be realized through spiritual inquiry.

First, we enquire into the nature of our own creations, to discover their essential 'unrealness', and when that is realized, then the Cosmic Nature is enquired into, and the Vedantic Sages say that we shall then discover the Essence, being Consciousness-Energy, which is in fact non-dual.

The challenging part of course is to realise that we are having our own creation (or constructs as you call it), which is not only individual but also collective. This it seems to me is the most difficult step, and yet the most essential. It requires a constant vigilant inquiry into our minds.

So often I think of the movie Matrix. Also, I believe that some scientists have recently postulated that we are living in a simulation. I heard this only in passing, and don't know how he meant it. Did you hear of this?

By the way, I consider your insights not merely geopolitical, but also spiritual; albeit that they have that flavour in them. But these are very useful to me.

I am off to the Sri Adi Sankara Ashrama in Johannesburg for their 40-year anniversary tomorrow until Wednesday. Have a blessed trip and Love to Terri and You.

Yours in Prem and Om,
Vidyananda

On Tuesday 26 December 2023, John wrote:

Dear Vidyananda,
Hari OM.

My apologies for this slow response. I wrote most of the below during the week following my receipt of yours, but then, when I revised the various details and observations, I noted various complex points that remained hard to define in order to understand or realize… Hence, this is a somewhat revised response!

It was nice to hear that Uma came over during your absence; I trust that you returned safely from the Ashrama in Johannesburg and that the celebrations were enjoyable!

We returned from our little road trip as well; it was nice to get out for a few days. While SA is a stunning country, so too are the Balkans and much of Central Europe. We took a few days to see the first snow in the picturesque lakeside town of Bled in Slovenia, followed by a night in Zagreb, the capital of Croatia, where we enjoyed the Advent Celebrations. Here, like in many of the older parts of Europe, even in sub-zero temperatures, every part of the old city was stunningly decorated with countless lights and trims, and with stalls, people of all ages and music everywhere. In addition, Nick took a series of trains from NL, and travelled across Germany, Austria, and Slovenia, to arrive on Terri's birthday and join us for Christmas.

As for our epic-reality topic...

Thank you for your in-depth review of this reality-construct question/ concept; again, your Vedanta perspectives on this topic add a considerable facet to the growing mosaic of my perceived reality..!

On dreams: my review on these, is that we do not all experience the same when in the dream state. Whereas, for some, their dreams resemble very disturbing or life-realistic experiences, I find my dreams to be more of a collated reality that is assembled by my memory-supported and stimuli-translating brain trying to re-create sense from the echoes of my thoughts and observations. This, whilst I, as the observer, who – being asleep – is now separate of the observed 'reality'. Hence, I do not think too much of my own dreams or dream-state, not even the more lucid dreams, dreams within dreams, or ones with life-realistic experiences. I do, however, believe that there are also those for whom the dream experience is quite different, and they may receive guidance, or counsel. Others, on more destructive paths, may encounter a psychic inner-voice or higher self that tries to access their pre-occupied 'I'.

As for daydreaming; I remember feeling a resonance when reading Ouspensky mention that his teacher (Gurdjieff) remonstrated him for daydreaming. Gurdjieff felt that daydreaming was something that provided an easy out for complex mind situations - and that this was why it was more prevalent among adolescents with limited life experience.

The view that our reality – or rather our *experiential* reality – is a construct of sorts, is one that is narrated in a variety of quarters. There are several scientists and technocrats who claim that they are still waiting for someone to prove that their reality is NOT a construct – and it is not difficult to see why these views carry weight. As you wrote "*Creation is not truly matter but essentially Consciousness-Energy and nothing but Consciousness-Energy* "; as such, one could deduce that a 'construct' would not have to be 'virtual', such as that which technology already provides many variants of. A construct could perhaps also be made manifest through, or under, the influence of higher dimensional thought.

This 'higher dimensional' is, for example, explained in G.I. Gurdjieff's teachings[1]. He described this as a "Ray of Creation", which entails a sequential order of Creation, with fewer laws to exist by as one follows its hierarchical order. In this way, the Divine is only subject to the law of the Divine Him/ Herself, whereas human beings are subject to 48 or 96 laws depending on one's dimensional state of awareness. Accordingly, humans are still quite far from the Creator. Accordingly, one may surmise that our

---

[1] George Gurdjieff was a philosopher, mystic, spiritual teacher, composer, and dance teacher who taught a method called "The Work" or "The Fourth Way".

star, the Sun, and the Starry Systems such as the Milky Way, encompass *other-dimensional* Organisms or Beings of an angelic, aetheric or spiritual nature, that guide humans along the laws within the mechanism we perceive as our perceived reality.

This is an interesting perspective but a complex topic to realize using a limited dimensional mind. Even through deductive reasoning (syllogism) when observing reality with an unbiased mind, it becomes impossible to maintain a sense of *factual* reason and logic when considering the gazillions-to-one odds of an accidental or evolutionary formation of the dozens of phenomena that you and I have reviewed at some lengths over the years. These include not just the elemental parts of matter – such as the planet and people – but also Time and the cyclic nature of all things to do with people, including their civilizations.

If I go in a direction that is opposite to my own epic experience and observation of the so-called 'civilized world', it is difficult to believe I am awake within an actual 'non-dream' reality. This feeling becomes even stronger when I witness the self-destructive and absurd reality manifested by intelligent and informed people.

One may choose to blame these 'policies' on the power of financiers, combined with deep-state elements which are portrayed by a political elite that were willing to trade their souls for their careers. To me, however, only an acknowledgment of what I call the Possession, allows me to somewhat understand this. What I observe substantiates my feeling that the rate at which much of our civilization is 'progressing' is actually more of a reversal or teetering towards Chaos. At this current trajectory, and without some form of higher intervention – by which, of course, I do not mean the WEF or any other acronym for an organized collection of people – our current global civilization will likely end in the not-too-distant future, only to be revived a few thousand years hence, when the Living Earth has removed the last remnants of its present memory and machinery.

Considering this view, it would seem plausible that the human experiential reality is 'programmed' to exist as an inescapable pendular motion that includes both perpetual Order and perpetual Chaos. It is therefore unlikely that the individual man will ever become the interstellar voyaging being that many contemporaries imagine or dream him to be – and perhaps this is meant to be so. Perhaps our Creator gave manifest to this very limited, finite and dual construct for its sole purpose to be the production of transcended beings, through a pendular, cyclic and centrifugal-like process!

The way my head spins thinking of this, makes it certainly seem feasible!

With that, I shall close this letter and this year by saluting you my good friend, with love and high regards, and wishing you, Vani, Uma, and all at the ashrama a most joyful and blessed festive season, and with all that is good and light-filled in 2024!

Best wishes,
John

On Monday 2 January 2024, Swami Vidyananda wrote:

Dear John,
Hari OM.

A blessed New Year to you and Terri. May it bring more Wisdom and Love.

No need to apologize for the late reply. Seeing the depth of conversation, one needs time to read, reflect, and respond. Always a joy to receive your emails.

I was also away for a week's retreat on a farm called Kleinfontein, which is in the Cederberg Rocklands area. Very beautiful!

The dream state is the combined mind and energy fields. Mind of course has multiple dimensions, from mere sense impressions to psychic phenomena. From the Yoga/Vedanta perspective, we do not pay much attention (or not any at all) to these (even the psychic phenomena) because all of this is still in the purview of non-reality. The only purpose of being aware of this is to be aware and therefore not attached to the mind, no matter how 'profound' an experience seems to be. Otherwise, we get caught up in delusion.

Everything within the mind is delusion (illusion, construct), etc. How do we know? By observing the mind itself. Scientists etc who do not regard the universe as a construct are most likely not observing their own minds, therefore they are not able to see the constructs (which include the scientific paradigm) created by their own minds, as well as what we may term the Cosmic Mind. God, who is Universal Consciousness, being Consciousness, creates through thought. The universe including ourselves are thought forms, and because we are made of that consciousness, we too have the ability to create through thought. As you say, it is a matter of degree. The Angelic realms are the subtler thought forms that are nearest to Universal Consciousness in their subtlety, whereas our thought forms are more gross. Of course, through spiritual practice, our thought forms also become angelic, although, as mentioned above, that too has to be transcended.

Because humanity is stuck in the thought realm, it is spiraling into a destructive pathway, because when thought is unchecked by pure awareness, it creates more and more delusional thought patterns, but because it is thought that creates these delusional patterns, they appear as science and reason and logic. And since modern science has dispensed with God (i.e. Consciousness), it is unable to curb the downward trend.

So, I agree with you: unless there is a Divine Intervention, humanity shall witness great destruction. If we can go by the scriptures, then a Divine Intervention shall occur, but only if the prayers are desperate.

In the meantime, I guess we have to try our best to refine ourselves and get rooted in pure consciousness so that we can live from that dimension rather than thought.

Again my wishes of Love to you and Terri,
Vidyananda

25

Domination

On Friday 16 February 2024, Vidyananda wrote:

Dear John,
Hari Om.

I pray that you are well.

Today your lovely wife Terri will be visiting us this afternoon. We look forward to seeing her, but we will be sorely missing you!

I am interested to know about your trip to Katmandu. Is it for a spiritual purpose that you are going there with your colleagues? I hope I am not intrusive.

I wanted to share a thought with you, which is just another piece of the puzzle that we have been discussing. I was listening to a talk by Swami Venkatesananda, in which he stated that the only 'evil' is domination.

We can clearly see this within our own relationships: as soon as we try to dominate others, there is conflict. Even if we think that we are doing good to the other insisting they behave in a certain way, the very act of imposing is violence.

Not to speak of the social and political level. Of course, there are those people who want to be rulers for the sake of dominion and personal power. But I was also thinking about the do-gooders. All those people, who believe that their ideology, philosophy, etc will save humanity or improve humanity, end up dominating others to enforce their ideology, etc., resulting in the opposite of their initial intentions: instead of creating a better world, they make it into hell. When anyone wishes to implement ideologies etc, they have to dominate over others in order to implement these. And this of course results in conflict.

I am reminded of a personal incident when I was a student, in which I did exactly that: by trying to convince the other person that the world had to change, I started acting violently toward them (I was trying to illustrate that violence was bad by actually acting violently!). And this was toward a loved one! It was a painful, humiliating, and eye-opening event. When you try to convince others of evil and try to convince others of the remedy, that attempt to convince itself is violence.

So, it appears to me that any attempt at changing the world for the better necessarily ends up in violence, and therefore not a better world.

How ironic!

I am interested to hear/read your response!

I pray you have a fruitful time in Katmandu.

Yours in Prem and Om,
Vidyananda

On Sunday 3 March 2024, John wrote:

My dear friend Vidyananda.
Hari OM.

Thank you for your patience in awaiting my response; I am sorry for the loss of your friend[1], but I trust this finds you and Vani and all otherwise well!

In response to this email: firstly, you are of course not intrusive in asking me about my trip; on the contrary, I feel honoured by your interest in my journey!

I have been in Nepal with three friends/ colleagues/ fellow 'pilgrims', and to them, I have mentioned you, on several occasions; they agree that you would likely be a veritable asset to our little group!

Jacques is from Brazil and has helped many with his shamanic work for the past 20+ years and has done so, all over the world. This includes breathwork and plant-based ceremonies. He also guides groups on the Camino in Spain and combines this with breathing ceremonies and meditations.

André is qualified in acupuncture, physiotherapy, and Chinese medicine, and operates a health-centre with his wife in the Netherlands, where he very successfully applies mostly energy healing (from a distance).

Jeroen is a beautiful soul and friend, who has been on a considerably complex journey over the past 10 - 15 years, prior to which he was in charge of strategy in the Netherlands police. Having left that somewhat conflicted field, he now works as a consultant for many organizations that experience internal and often psyche-related issues.

Our trip to Nepal can be described in many ways, and although I do not think the word 'pilgrimage' is suitable or fair to pilgrims, I guess it can be considered, more or less, as a description! As you've seen by the photos, we've trekked and visited (and meditated in) numerous monasteries, nunneries, sacred caves, and other sites. We've also spent considerable attention on collectively studying the living spirituality that is so very present in these parts, and I believe I have been able to trace some of this back to the powerful, inherent natural energies of the region, which the Divine seemingly applied in its creation. When I saw the majestic and massive mountains, that were created by tectonic movement, or by fire (as in

---

[1] A good friend of Swami Vidyananda had recently died (of what appeared to be a massive blood clot or stroke) during a hike with Vidyananda and some friends. Although the event was very traumatic, the friend's blessing was that he died surrounded by friends who sang and prayed on his behalf. On Vidyananda's request, John offered a prayer on the friend's behalf in Pashupatinath, a well-known holy place in Kathmandu..

cosmic electrical currents[1]), or by water, the following words came into my consciousness:

> The earth pushed,
> Fire formed
> Water washed
> Wind shaped
> God wished

As to your question on domination.

My understanding of the phenomenon of domination is that it would not necessarily be evil, as it would depend on the purpose(s) of such domination. In my own practices, I came to realize that subjection to domination, which is based on deferral or better expressed as laziness, is an integral part of domination. And the one cannot exist without the other!

Sometimes forms of domination, I believe, can be justified. An example of this occurred when I dominated certain situations during the 2017 hurricane, and some people looked to me for this. Further, during other dangerous moments in earlier and later years, where life, limb, or fortune (accountability) were at stake, I did the same. Hard words and the use of strength or force (not violence though) were at times simply necessary tools. Many (most) people, as we've seen, are rather submissive and even docile, and will instinctively follow the one with the loudest mouth or largest promises, even when they know that these are unrealistic. To bypass unnecessary or costly stupidity-caused losses, temporary domination is then called upon.

As to your (now long-past) experience of trying to use violence to convince others that change was necessary; I do believe that sometimes, being on the far side of the wiggly fine line that separates ignorance and hypocrisy, which we all must walk, is a veritable experience in itself. We know that to discover one's 'self' one must occasionally lose one's 'self', and to realize the experience of awakening one must occasionally fall asleep (one seldom notices one's transition into sleep).

Whereas I know that you already realize this, I describe it as such because domination is, in my view, not something that has material, military, financial, political, emotional or intellectual qualities, but rather it has a life-like energy of its own that increasingly dominates the minds of those who participate in it. This, in my view, is another form of the Possession I referred to in our past exchanges.

When in a collective, individuals allow their collective to be dominated, and further, when that domination no longer serves the purpose of its individual participants but only itself, then this is when, in my view, the potential for evil arises. But even then however, before it can be considered evil, one

---

[1] Cosmic electrical currents are based on the observations and hypotheses of Immanuel Velikovsky and a variety of modern scientists. These interplanetary electrostatic discharges occurred in times of recorded human memory when the Solar System's order of planets changed, and affected in particular, the Earth, Mars and Venus. See *Worlds in Collision,* by E. Velikovsky and *The Saturn Myth,* by G. Talbot.

should consider why it is what it is, and how it became so. This is because it is only natural for a collective domination to become evil when its existence is considered necessary by its individual participants who may be ignorant but nevertheless unconscious and unaware of the effects. As such, this 'natural' process can also be considered part of God's design, and therefore not evil.

Evil, in my view, only occurs when a low dimensional force/ or entity, initiates low vibrational energy upon subjected, unaware and / or helpless beings, and uses the consequent negative energies of fear, anger, pain, envy, etc, to feed its cold and dark inhuman heart.

I hope my view on this makes sense. I believe it is similar to that of Swami Venkatesananda, just from the angle of one who has had to dominate for a living at times!

With best wishes.
John

On Wednesday 13 March 2024, Vidyananda wrote:

Dear John,
Hari OM.

Thank you for sharing your thoughts on 'Domination'. As always this provokes deeper reflection; hopefully not only to understand the world around us, but also the world within us.

Your point on being susceptible to domination is an important one. We cannot be dominated by another unless we have the weaknesses that you mention. Additionally also one requires courage to stand up to someone who wishes to dominate us; or the ability to slip out of such a situation. Mother Yogeshwari was excellent at this. I hardly ever saw her confront anyone, but she would never yield to domination and quietly get on with her life.

And of course, those people who subject themselves to domination have the characteristics that you mention, and therefore being dominated is inevitable. Maybe they even desire it, as it is an easy way out of having to think.

The above points relate obviously to the one who is subject to being dominated. As for those who dominate:

Reflecting upon your points, I realize that certainly at times, such as emergencies, it would be natural for someone to dominate, or as I would put it, take charge; and if necessary in a forceful way. This may be necessary and beneficial in certain circumstances. However, these circumstances are limited by time; and when the circumstance is over, the 'domination' should end. However, it becomes problematic when this conduct continues beyond the limitation of the initial circumstance. It is then that domination will lead to negative results and become an 'evil'.

Some people do wish to constantly dominate over others, whether in the domestic, social, employment, or political scene. These are people who want others to behave according to their ideas and wishes; and will try all kinds of means to achieve this, sometimes very subtle and appearing as goodness.

However, they are also dominated: by ideas, ideas that appear to be their own but actually have been imbibed from the outside. This may relate to the Possession that you talk about.

Just a few more thoughts that had arisen.

Yours in Prem and Om,
Vidyananda

On Sunday 17 March 2024, John wrote:

Dear Vidyananda,
Hari OM.

Thank you for your perspectives!

It seems we are, as in most things, seeing the phenomenon of Domination, in its entirety, along a similar vein. Whereas the causes and effects of Domination may seem, to us, relatively logical; the one undeniable characteristic that stands out is your observation that those who dominate: *'... are also dominated: by ideas, ideas that appear to be their own but actually have been imbibed from the outside."* These individuals often believe they are powerful and in control because they are very clever, but little do they realize that it is the darkness they serve. This, at least until the darkness has absorbed their hearts, and reduced their choices to a point where they find themselves between a rock and a hard place! Often enough, this realization may only come when they have run out of purpose and run out of that most precious of commodities: Time.

I do believe that many of the dominant ones started out with the best of intentions, but then, with a plethora of powers and choices, they lost track of these. Whereas this occurs in the obvious and predictable political and authoritarian places, it exasperatingly occurs only too often in domestic scenes, too.

With love and best wishes.
John

26

On the Automaton and the Religion of Science

John wrote to Swami Vidyananda while on a trek in the Himalayas of Nepal. While some would call this a 'pilgrimage' because it involved visiting temples, monasteries, shrines, and other holy places, John considered it more as an orientation (as the journey did not entail the altered lifestyle typical of a Pilgrim).

Due to being out of Wi-Fi proximity for extended periods, John was limited in his ability to respond to letters; as such, the following responses were applied to parts of emails, which led to the following chronology of exchanges that follow subject matter rather than dates.

On Friday 16 February 2024, Vidyananda wrote:

Dear John,
Hari Om.

I attached two short articles that I wrote. They are for your amusement!

Yours in Prem and Om,
Vidyananda

Is Science a Religion?

"Is science a religion?" is an interesting question.

A definition of the word 'religion' given in the Merriam-Webster Dictionary is: "institutionalized system of religious attitudes, beliefs, and practices."

Is science becoming institutionalized? What are some of the characteristics of a religious institution? It usually has an authority figure(s). It has a dogma/doctrine. It demands obedience.

When we listen to scientists (especially in the fields of medicine and climate change), we may see that the above characteristics have become apparent in science institutions. The priests (authority figures) have been replaced with 'expert scientists'. The religious dogma has been replaced with 'the science says'. Obedience to religious authority has been replaced with 'following the science' or 'following the experts'.

In both cases, we are asked to follow blindly what the authority says.

Also, the religious dogmatic institution sanctions any opposing views to its dogma. This is also reflected in science: there it is called 'misinformation', 'disinformation', and even 'mal-information'; and those who have a view other than the 'official' view are heavily censored. Much of the hype regarding 'misinformation' etc in social media is actually about censorship. And just as in religions, people who were of other persuasions were labelled 'sinners' and were persecuted, are we finding a similar trend now? Maybe we should ask those scientists who question the 'official' science.

Furthermore in regards to 'sinners', Swami Venkatesananda pointed out that the concept of sin and the redemption of sin is necessary for religious domination and authority. How about medicine? Sick people are necessary for the medical domination of medical institutions, such as pharmaceuticals. Is it possible that just as religious institutions labelled certain people as sinners, that medical institutions are labelling healthy people as sick? Are children hyperactive, or is school the wrong environment? There are probably many other such examples.

Furthermore, how much of scientific 'knowledge' is actually belief? How much of what we accept as knowledge is actually pure belief? Is it not interesting that many scientific 'truths' have never been proven: such as the existence of viruses, such as evolutionary theory, or the apocalyptic climate change to come. Most of these accepted 'truths' are actually theories ("a plausible or scientifically acceptable general principle or body of principles offered to explain phenomena" – Merriam-Webster). How is this different from religious belief?

Another definition in the same dictionary is: "a cause, principle, or system of beliefs held to with ardour and faith." Do we observe this in regards to scientific 'truths' (or rather beliefs) such as Climate Change? Is it not interesting that in a similar manner in which Christians are expecting an apocalypse, so are the climate change proponents? In both cases fear and obedience are created, and a lot of hype; and more significantly social change.

These are just some thoughts that have come to mind, which I think are valuable to think about. After all, science is now very much used to guide (or rule) humanity. It informs our thinking and behavior.

Will there be a time when people will be as skeptical toward science as they are of religions?

On Tuesday 5 March 2024, John wrote:

Dear Vidyananda,
Hari OM.

Thank you for sharing your articles with me. Instead of being amused, however, I am (as can be predicted with relative accuracy) 'automatically' triggered to comment! That is because I believe that the physical (body-mind) part of my being is an automaton. Everything it does, feels, thinks, and speaks, has no cause of its own, but is merely the effect of a preceding cause. (Some of these causes – such as my meeting Terri and you, for example, may be considered as Divine Intervention or karmic by design, but then these, too, are to me, still considered as preceding causes.)

As such, the automaton in the physical me will automatically – like a stream of water - always take the easier path, or that of least resistance. In my view, it is programmed to do so, biologically, to preserve energy, so that it can do more and go further, with less.

To add to this line of thought; consequently, I believe I can apply my higher senses and thoughts to more noble or worthy things, rather than to have them occupied with the more crude or rudimentary necessities.

The physical being, subjecting to the automaton state, is therefore, in my view, part of our Creator's design, and thus an inescapable part of me.

But this inescapable Divine design has a caveat...

When the metaphysical part of 'me', that is the observer of myself in 'me', observes that automaton state, what is being observed, changes!

By metaphysical part, I do not refer to my thoughts, as these, and the memory banks they operate from, are cognitive components and thus part of the physical being, and thus also part of the automaton. The part of me that I consider metaphysical would, at its 'root', begin with the taking note of the observer of myself in me. It is the observer's very act of observing, or '*paying* attention' to the physical reactive being, that then changes what is being observed. It is just like when an animal or person knows when he, she or it is being observed. (Coincidentally, I believe the power of our attention is a veritable and substantial form of energy).

To me, it is evident, that through constant and conscious observation, the physical, emotional or sensory, and thinking centers of my being, begin to lose their respective or individual dominance. Instead, they begin to function in harmony with each other, and the whole, which is greater than the sum of its parts; like cells and organs in our bodies which function to support the whole body. In this harmony, something new and beautiful then emerges; it is a kind of organism that functions without thoughts, but functions instinctively. In this way, the higher senses, no longer occupied with rudimentary thoughts and functions, begin to sense and observe the higher dimensional intuitive influences, and to respond to them. It is only then, in my view, that my being has separated itself from the automaton state.

I guess, however, that when one sees the consequential, almost magical, flow of energy that follows the direction of the attention-power, is often directed by many (if not most) people, in the opposite direction. This means that it does not manifest that new and beautiful intuitive being, but rather one that gives rise to another denser, darker, parasitic, narcissistic, and self-absorbed 'master'.

These thoughts, in response to your writing, are for many people, not always easy to absorb. This is especially true if they happen to be struggling with one of those, what I call, rudimentary or necessary aspects of day-to-day life, that occupy their attention to such an extent that there seems to be no room for quiet observation of the self. I agree that the reliance on automation, in such cases, merely increases the dependency on it, and this is then further applied to increase profit or entertainment, pleasure fulfilment, and so on. These, rather than making room for meditation, contemplation, the practice of yoga, art, time with loved ones and good friends, or simply being on the mat. (Also, for that matter, making room for the exploration of those paths and teachings of the true, high, and holy, or in the presence of Great Nature's immensely enhancing elements).

With love and best wishes,
John

On Saturday 16 March 2024, Vidyananda wrote:

Dear John,
Hari Om.

Thank you for sharing your thoughts, which I wholeheartedly agree with.

The automated way of living by depending on external automation is an extension of the automated entity that we are on the physical/mental/emotional level.

And, quite right, it is only through self-observation that we can transform to higher dimensions, which enable us to live spontaneously, creatively, and spiritually freely; thereby transcending the automaton in us.

I guess one of the steps towards this is to become aware of the automaton life we live.

Yours in Prem and Om,
Vidyananda

On Thursday 7 March 2024, John wrote:

Dear Vidyananda,
Hari OM.

I am writing from a very special place; a guesthouse, called Yangrima, located on a 2600m high mountain top in the Helambu mountain range, just below Nepal's towering Himalayan Langtang range.

At sunrise, with indescribable views, I contemplated and meditated on the question: "Is Science a Religion", and for your equal amusement I offer my findings below!

My first comment to the question of whether Science is becoming a Religion is that, if/ when this occurs, then it would be as an effect of an underlying cause. In this case, the cause would be one's desire to believe in something for its own sake, combined with the power of belief itself.

My second comment is that, in my view; Yes, Science is a form of religion, but only for the one- and two-dimensionally oriented people.

This is because these ones seek identification in denser, more physical and measurable attachments; these include material things, and social acknowledgment, but also knowledge through information. These same one- and two-dimensionally oriented people, fear the loss or lack of these attachments, and spend much of their time – when within their lower dimensional states – trying to avoid any decline of them. *To them a decline would be akin to being unnoticeable or forgotten by their god.*

Hence, the authoritarian elements within and around organized societies and individuals will manipulate information, scientific and other, by adjusting its content. The aim of this, is to subject these one- and two-dimensional majorities into states of fear-based existence, by which they then become docile, manipulatable, and easy to guide in order-based systems. The purpose of this, when observed along a series of consequential effects, is to absorb life force by acquiring the energy that comes from the attention of the one- and two-dimensionally oriented, but that is reprocessed in a similar low dimensional form.

My analysis may seem like a bleak one, but then ultimately, this process is dependent on the choices that individuals make along their path of life. Creation, it seems, is infinitely forgiving and patient, because It still continues to give every individual the opportunity to re-choose; it is only *in the lower one- and two- dimensional worlds or realities that,* after a great many illogical and bad choices, the bouquet of choices remaining becomes noticeably smaller.

This then leads to my third comment, which is; No, Science is not a Religion, but simply a Tool for those who have turned away from the illusory one- and two-dimensional realities, and who have embraced a three-dimensional one (Being one that is based on things like mathematics, geometry, and provable reason and logic). The three-dimensional reality, is one that can, from my perspective, ultimately lead to enlightenment. Enlightenment is possible, in the case of Science, when Truth is relentlessly applied in the study of Science, even if this requires overruling generally accepted fundamental laws and conditions. The removal of such 'burdening limitations' makes the three-dimensional reality lighter, which enables one to go further, deeper, and higher – until it becomes at one, with Spirituality!

My fourth (and last!) comment would be that, to a higher dimensionally aware person, Science that is based on material, measurable or Space-Time orientation, *is dependent on what the physical senses can detect,* and thus, is in itself, physical. From a higher or metaphysical dimensional perspective, the physical is no longer fundamental, and thus to these ones, Science becomes a dreamworld, or akin to a re-programmable virtual reality headset…

These views are however (probably) quite complex to get past the guardians of the lower dimensional egos that tend to defy and deny anything that cannot be configured. This is because, no matter how convincing or obvious, acknowledging the existence of such higher and defining dimensions, would dissolve the very dimensional reality over which they reign.

Hence, I thought your article was very relevant. I also noted how, within it, you posed relatively 'simple' and obvious questions that one should consider asking oneself, and which those who have come to question their reality or accepted truth, can use to ignite their own process of illumination!

With love and best wishes.
John

On Tuesday 16 April 2024, Vidyananda wrote:

Dear John,
Hari OM.

Thank you for your profound insights into the question of science and religion.

I also had a response from another person and have been contemplating her response, which however was more traditional.

One thing that struck me is that we tend to associate religion with blind belief and obedience to authority. This I feel is a distortion of what religion truly is. The word 'religion' actually means to re-unite, the very same meaning as the word 'yoga'.

If we understand this, then even from the higher dimensional levels we can see that religion and science (if both practiced sincerely) are the same, in that both aim to realize the Ultimate Reality, albeit through different pathways; although as they both reach the higher dimensions, the paths become the same due to the subtlety and oneness of that Ultimate Reality.

Interestingly, Krishnamurti calls a religious mind one that investigates the Truth relentlessly.

I hope you are well and I thoroughly enjoyed our video conversation the other day.

Love to you and Terri,
Vidyananda

On Wednesday 24 April 2024, John wrote:

Dear Vidyananda,
Hari OM.

Thank you for sharing your review with me.

I sent you an email yesterday, within which I forwarded a letter I had written to a friend who is a self-declared atheist. The letter was in response to a question from him on why or how it is that one becomes spiritual and what spirituality may mean. In my letter, I described the power of the Himalaya and its natural geographic energies that act as an amplifier of spirituality, along with the harsh life-conditions there, as a motivator. I did this (explained it as such) because there are so many different ways to translate "being spiritual" that I feel, if one tries to explain it to a mind-that-is-made-up in another way, it is automatically debated or marginalised.

In addition, to consider religion as an authority that one must adhere to, I believe, would also resonate with this, as this view is opposite to that of those who (truly) happily choose to embrace their religion.

You wrote: " 'religion' actually means to re-unite". I agree of course, but to some this "re-uniting" is a physical process that requires a central entity such as a church, mosque, ashram, or organised congregation of sorts. Even the word religion is in itself subject to such review. To most minds, it will be translated according to beliefs associated with their dimensional level of awareness (dimensions as referred to in my earlier mail). These beliefs are then repeated and re-interpreted or translated according to an ever-decreasing or limiting focal point. To try and convince one who sees only one or the other, or a part thereof which must 'look right', even if it doesn't, is, as we have found, futile.

In my view, any religion or form of belief must ultimately be translated *individually not collectively* and must be done so, *not by the head but by the heart*. And yes, I agree, the relentless search for Truth comes from the heart; the head simply requires some form of justification – even if it is fabricated!

Perhaps the use of the term 'religion' has had its time and must be let go of. Today's intensive re-interpretation of doctrines and scripture (as well as their various translations) seem to have become mutated teachings used by false prophets and pseudo-prophets with agendas and who wield such power over their subjects. One cannot help but wonder if religion is the butter knife that has been weaponized to become a sword. Perhaps, in the dimensionally entangled world of today, we must consider throwing away the butter knife. (Like throwing away the proverbial baby with the bathwater, but with the bath itself[1])? This would leave the masses like those of biblical Babel[2], whereby a misinterpreted doctrine did more damage than an absent one, and consequently, the people were left to find their own one, on their own.

From a higher dimensional perspective, science and spirituality do serve each other. It is, after all, science that enabled us to obtain methods of sharing support, gathering knowledge, as well as creating forms of communication, translation, and ease of travel, etc; and spirituality, miraculously fills in the numerous metaphysical blanks. It is regrettably humanity's dependency on the organized entities (of science and spirituality), as "concepts of necessity" that give the ego the means and reason to worship these as the preferred medium. Hence, perhaps it is necessary to compare science with spirituality but within a three-dimensional physical context. The higher dimensional Spirit and Its realization is, after all, one that exists free of time and space, both within and without.

Anyway, it was indeed very good to speak to you on Signal as well, and I would like it if we could do that again, sometime. What are your dates for going to the United States? Perhaps, if you would like to and if it is convenient, we can schedule another video-call around those.

---

[1] An idiom to express the elimination of something good or of value, when removing something unwanted or harmful.
[2] The Tower of Babel, is a parable in the Old Testament's Book of Genesis, explaining the origin of different cultures caused by the natural divisions among people, within an ever-ascending civilisation.

Best wishes,
John

On Tuesday 30 April 2024, Vidyananda wrote:

Dear John,
Hari OM.

Thank you for your further thoughts on the religion-science topic.

I feel that what you say about religion is what is actually happening in science. The Covid and Climate Change narratives and their consequences just being two examples.

Of course, there are good scientists too, just as there are good religionists.

Just as religion was/is used as a weapon and as a form of control, so is science. I have a feeling in the future science may begin to have the same reputation that religion has now.

Can we throw out the baby with the bath water? That depends on what we mean by 'baby'. If the baby is God or the Soul, then certainly not. That is what has been done in our secular world, which has led to.... well, I don't need to tell you!

The problem is that we focus on the bathtub and the bath water instead of the baby. If the baby is kept foremost in view, then the bathtub and bath water cannot take precedence.

I don't know about the masses: whether they follow religion, science, or anything else, as long as they remain asleep, they are asleep, no matter what the system or even no system. Can we wake them up? Not sure, but *we* certainly must remain awake.

Yes, a video call would be great. My USA trip got cancelled, so I am available, maybe tomorrow, as it is a public holiday in SA?

With Love,
Vidyananda

27

Talk on AI

Swami Vidyananda forwarded John a YouTube link to a talk by J. Krishnamurti, in which (at Chennai, formerly Madras, in 1981) he predicted the rise of the machines and computers that would supersede humans in everything, including the process of thinking, philosophy, rituals and so-called beliefs, and other. In this talk Krishnamurti questions what will be left when human sorrow, fear, pleasure, anxiety, immense loneliness, and so on – all of which are created by people – are no longer experienced. What is left, he says, is Time, biology, psychology, and the physical, and its natural decay.

By this question, the purpose of a human being is defined, as he either turns to pleasures and entertainment, where scientists and priests become the entertainers, or he chooses to turn his attention inward, to self-observation.

On Tuesday 16 February 2024, Vidyananda wrote:

Dear John,
Hari Om.

Now that you are on your pilgrimage and unable to answer my emails, I am writing a few to you. I pray that you are having much joy and learning on your pilgrimage to Nepal.

I shared the following talk by Krishnamurti. I thought that you might also be interested, as it deals with AI (although he does not mention that word): https://www.youtube.com/watch?v=jD1bQ6_OMAg

Yours in Prem and Om,
Vidyananda

On Wednesday 6 March 2024, John wrote:

Dear Vidyananda,
Hari OM.

Thank you for sending me the Krishnamurti link; it was indeed quite prophetic, and his assessment of its effectiveness was spot on. In addition, I observed a phenomenon that we have discussed before, and which I note with emphasis, here in Nepal.

In many towns here, there is a clear and noticeable period of time when people built and organized their homes, businesses and communities – including their places of worship – with love, care, and enthusiasm. This period is then followed by a time of neglect and decay. Like you, I am, of course, familiar with such states of existence in so-called 'developing' territory; I see the decay in various areas of preceding generations, ranging from states of broken furniture and appliances around the house, to neglected gardens and public areas. Often, this decay could have been prevented with just a little money, and some enthusiasm and care. Here, I note that much of this decay began about 5 to 10 years ago.

Personally, it seems to me that the most valuable commodity that all human beings are born with, is the energy emitted by/ from their Attention. Today we see how this attention is hijacked by the sensory devices, much of which is represented by screens. Many of these screens function with A.I., which aims, not necessarily to sell you anything, not even airtime such as it used to be with telephones, but to absorb the low vibrational energy that our Attention emits, and usually in forms of fear, anguish, desire, etc. This, for example, in lieu of the high vibrational energy that can lead us on the sacred path of creativity and care.

It is a somewhat sad state of affairs, and it is exceedingly complex to become aware of this, as often, I too, find myself unwittingly caught up in screens. It is only when I awaken again, that I can then zoom out, and from a higher dimensional perspective see their effectual nature in the greater wheel of a cyclic human civilization.

Artificial Intelligence is of course not a cause, but simply another effect that lies rooted in inherent laziness. However, the presence of A.I. in society, will, as per JK's words, be the cause of future effects, and I sigh deeply and heavily when I consider what these will do to human life, especially in consideration of the absurdities we are familiar with at present.

Still, one thing I am certain of though, is that even within all this, Creative Spirit will be found among those who choose to seek and embrace it!

With love and best wishes.
John

On Friday 16 March 2024, Vidyananda wrote:

Dear John,
Hari OM.

Yes, all Attention is absorbed in the screen. It externalizes our attention, and therefore makes us blind to what is actually within us, and also acts as an effective pacifier (the one that we put in babies' mouths).

As most of humanity does not want to look at their inner demons, it gets absorbed in the world of the screen; and if the screen can be integrated into oneself, that would be 'marvellous' because then we would be even more distracted.

But what struck me most in Krishnamurti's assessment is the fact that we are utterly lonely. There is a lot in that statement. AI is the new entertainment to distract us from that loneliness. It is very difficult to face the loneliness; and yet, if we wish to grow spiritually, it has to be done.

Yours in Prem and Om,
Vidyananda

28

Thoughts on the Astral world

On Thursday 20 June 2024, John wrote:

My dear friend Vidyananda,
Hari OM.

I trust this finds you, Vani, Uma, and all our good friends well!

Terri and I are well, and although months may pass without a word from us, we think of, and talk about you often! In between doing so, however, we remain occupied with our respective routines and projects. Having obtained her degree in psychology, Terri has started her honours and I keep busy on my own (domestic) projects of various studies and writing. Additionally, I try to spend a few hours a day doing manual work – as besides it being necessary, I find physical productivity with visible results quite meditative (a little like gardening I suppose, except not as 'demanding'). We are also blessed knowing that our sons are comfortable in their respective zones; Matt's yacht is currently in the UK for a 6-month refit, and Nick completed his thesis and will graduate next month. He plans to then come home for a little break, before commencing with his (as yet) unknown phase of professional life. It comforts us to know they are both strong, smart, independent, and mobile, especially in a decaying global economy, where the drums of war, and acts of ignorance in Europe (and the greater 'civilized' world) are of some concern. The fact that they (the boys) are not politically or ideologically aligned adds to this comfort!

As you may recall, Terri and I worked on the translation and editing of a friend's book that was originally published in Dutch. The book, titled "Laboratory of the Spirit", is about the principles, characteristics, and techniques the author, Andre, applies for healing. Like the Ayurvedic practise of working with the whole, he similarly uses a combination of Traditional Chinese Medicine, acupuncture, physical therapy, and (astral) energy. It was not an easy book to translate. This, largely because we persevered to translate and complement the author's message without losing the deeper, multi-faceted, and multi-dimensional content and meaning, which is often lost in the translation. It was also important to us that contemporary readers, from all walks of life, would be able to follow it, and within this be able to discover/understand how every component or aspect of the self affects the holistic whole.

The book's purpose is to introduce the reader to a comparative study of modern medicine and alternative forms of healing and benefits, and how one can do much of the healing process by oneself. Terri and I tackled this project together, with me focused on the translation and meaning, and Terri looking after the grammar, and ensuring the text was not like my usual writing, but rather more flowing, less layered, and easier to follow. Still, translating and describing, in coherent, easy-to-follow language, a text that covers the physical, emotional, mental, astral, and societal realms, as well as allowing for readers to find in these a sense of psychic self-awareness, was a complex, testing and enhancing challenge for us!

Words aside, this friend (with whom I travelled to Nepal in February) is a veritable healer, and a man who functions from a core of compassion and unconditional love. The realms and the energies he works with, however, are not, as you and I have discussed in the past, without challenge or peril. Consequently, after 30+ years of working with these energies and assisting thousands of people with a large spectrum of maladies and complaints, he now tires more quickly and must begin to tread cautiously and to see fewer 'sick' people. Hence, I 'felt' called to offer him some attention, which is one of the reasons I opted to assist him. Now that (after 3 months) the book-process is kind of done, I will see where our paths next guide us. We do plan to meet in the Netherlands with a few (like-orientated) colleagues to do some work (on ourselves and each other) in mid-July, but beyond that, the path is, as yet, undefined!

During this work, with my focus directed on the workings of the energetic elements we are immersed in and their astral origins, I observed how this metaphysical and entity-filled other-dimensional realm is where many (if not all) physical, emotional, mental and energetic maladies and/ or complaints are ultimately rooted. I realized that this was not something that most of those who are affected or afflicted would acknowledge, let alone willingly access and enter for their healing. And yet, it seems that, due to its occult nature, as in to-the-eye hidden, it leads to much of the otherwise inexplicable absurdity we see around us.

Some may say that the societal events that permeate the various facets of our civilization, merely follow the pendulum swing of the inevitably causal reality; we have discussed this before. This is because it is a pendulum that is powered by the unconscious and docile behaviour of people, and we can do *little* about this. However, 'little' in my view, does not mean nothing. Besides prayer, I believe there are also certain _passive_ corrective measures one can consider undertaking; informing people by placing information 'out there' that is not laden with emotion, is one such measure. Along with this non-emotional information (I feel), is the need for a practical awareness of the existence of the metaphysical astral world. This I consider to be a mirror image of the spiritual world: it being god-<u>like</u> but not God. I do believe it may be of benefit to recognise it for what it is and what it is not, and to consider whether or not it has influence in the field of medicine. Only too often have we seen people succumb to medicine or suppressing techniques as a 'cure' for psychic experiences – these maladies could have been effectively healed without mechanical or chemical intervention. We have also seen how many are unable to differentiate between the messages and the influences of (angelic) helpers, guides and intruders (sought or unsought). Naturally, this also aligns with my views and writings on the Possession or 'capture' of the psyche of people, which I consider as the most destructive of influences and which has infected many, and considered as 'normal' within societies and our civilization as a whole...

Now, all that said and stated, I am respectfully aware that you are very familiar with these things, including Ayurveda, and also that in our previous discussion, we agreed on caution against blindly interacting with the astral world. However, as a large part of humanity (it seems) is quite immersed in its expanding influences, would you share your thoughts on possible passive but corrective measures; how would your (and your guru's) teachings reflect on this?

As always, with best wishes and high regards,
John

On Thursday 18 July 2024, Vidyananda wrote:

Dear John,
Hari OM.

Finally! And thank you for your patience!

I pray that you and Terri are well! And that you are both engaged in your various projects. Has Nick graduated already? Since your email, it has been almost a month. Yes, they are wonderful boys (actually men!) and we pray that their common sense prevails and that they have the inner strength to remain rooted in their Selves.

Congratulations on completing the translation, which I gather was not an easy task. So much gets lost in translation due to the lack of vocabulary. Maintaining the spirit and meaning takes a lot of discipline. Well done!

I agree that our illnesses stem from the astral body and that real healing has to happen on that level. I am unsure of what your knowledge of the Yogic/Vedantic understanding is of the astral body, so please permit me to explain that at the risk of repeating something you know already.

Yoga/Vedanta acknowledges three bodies: physical, astral, and causal. The physical body is obvious. The astral body consists of energy (prana), mind, and senses, as well as intellect (buddhi). The causal body consists of bliss but also contains the seed impressions gathered from various lifetimes. The soul however transcends these bodies, is unaffected by these bodies, is pure consciousness; but exists within these bodies despite the transcendence.

The goal of yoga is (as you know) enlightenment, which really means transcending these three bodies and discovering and re-uniting with the Soul or Pure Consciousness (which is one with God). In the process of this journey, healing takes place naturally, as the practices of yoga also purify the three bodies de facto.

However, it may also be necessary to engage in some specific practices to remove these impurities. For this asanas, pranayama[1] and introspection can be used. Asanas and, more so, pranayama purify the channels of prana so that the prana[2] can flow harmoniously. This will then reflect a healthy body. The mind can also be healed through prana because thought

---

[1] These are Yoga Physical Exercises and Breathing Exercises.
[2] Prana refers to energy which comes through the breath.

is prana in motion and if the prana becomes steady (in the sense of rhythmic and harmonious), then the mind can be purified as well.

Through introspection (or direct observation) we can become aware of our thought patterns. This direct observation (which does not involve thought) can totally dissolve our negative thought patterns, which is real healing.

However, these are all practices that we do for ourselves. It can only be done by oneself. At best we can teach others how to do this, but they need to do this for themselves.

Healing others through psychic means is generally discouraged, for two reasons: (1) the results of healing others lead to depletion of prana and the possibility of ill health and (2) it can prevent one from enlightenment as one can get absorbed in the healing and thereby neglect one's journey of enlightenment.

So, the yogis discourage any work on the subtle realms as long as we are not enlightened. The enlightened Masters may or may not work in the astral realms, depending on the Divine Will.

From another perspective, the enlightened ones by default bring light and healing into the astral realm due to their enlightenment. What can enlightenment do other than spread light and healing? Light spreads light even if it does not intend to. Hence enlightenment is considered the most important goal.

So, to summarise, we would not engage ourselves in any work on the astral realm, other than teaching others what they can do for themselves. First, there must be total healing (which is enlightenment) within oneself. Then let the Divine guide one.

We must correct ourselves first.

Yours in Prem and Om,
Vidyananda

On Friday 2 August 2024, John wrote:

Dear Vidyananda,
Hari OM.

I trust this finds you, Vani, Uma, and all at the ashram well, and in good spirits!

As you guessed, Nick graduated, and on the 13th (of July), Terri and I took a slow drive to the Netherlands to attend his graduation ceremony and to drive him back to Croatia afterwards. It so happened, that the timing perfectly and beautifully confluenced with a retreat I had scheduled for myself, quite a while ago, with the colleagues from my trip to Nepal. The two events were obviously not scheduled or related to each other, and not only did they not overlap, but with two days in between they neatly followed each other. In addition, Matthew was able to get a few days off and fly in from Falmouth, on flights and schedules that fitted all (including his budget) smoothly, without stress or force enabling the four of us to spend a few quality days and evenings together. My retreat followed Nick's ceremony, which allowed him a few days to calmly complete the complex process of demobilizing a 4-year university stay, including his lodgings, material things, and social life. Every element followed the next in time, and it seemed as if it was written, including my retreat, which in itself was very constructive, and also including our various departures. I completed my retreat on Monday morning and was able to rendezvous with Nick a few hours later that day. We then loaded the car in no time and departed and had a very pleasant and harmonious 3-day drive through the hectic European summer traffic, back to Croatia. To make room in the car for Nick's things, Terri had by then flown back to Split, and with grace on her side as well as she skirted, with only a minor interruption, the major global internet interruption that simultaneously grounded and cancelled thousands of flights, stranding millions of people!

What was interesting, is that I noted how the perception of 'Time' can become quite illusory. This occurs once one removes one's attentive focus from memories and conditioning, and one realizes that the element of 'chance' in the orchestration of certain unrelated events is a mathematical impossibility! In my case, it became evident to me that, in its perfection, this whole trip and all its related and unrelated processes must have been written 'somewhere', in a 'place' where the closing event was already known before its unrelated opening occurred. This 'Knowing' must therefore have been present in a dimensional realm where 'Time' is not a factor!

In response to your email, it took me a while to send this. I wrote my reply shortly after receiving your mail but then delayed sending it for some time. This was because, after writing and reviewing my initial response, I found that I needed some time to contemplate the impact your email had upon my initial state of being, so that I could observe the response writing it, had invoked in me.

That said, thank you for your detailed and in-depth reply on the Astral world. In addition to the above-mentioned 'Time' riddle, the timing of your email could also not have been better, as its content was of considerable value to my work during this past weekend's retreat! I initially had little to add to your teaching, except to thank you for your profound, clear and substantial explanations. I completely agree that real (as in actual) healing can only be done by oneself, and that realistically we can only guide others to go inwards to do this - *if this is what they ask for.* However, as you know, this is at times complex, for even in the approach to guiding or teaching diverse peoples, there is (besides compassion) no fixed methodology. It seems to me that even before (a form of) yoga can be introduced, some worldly stabilizing factors are necessary.

This necessity is often amplified when life, time and especially trauma in individuals has redirected their already conditioned path, and buried the *real* Light under many layers – each with a large variety of well-established alternative, but often false idols.

I mentioned your thoughts on the Astral realm to my healer friend, and he agreed with what you wrote about the dangers of psychic healing. He said that it was therefore very important (when working with patients) to discern between the low-vibrational emotions of pity and unconditional love; (where pity tends to drag one into the potential toxic levels of such a suffering one, whereas selfless love elevates them to one's own). He did however say that, after about 3 decades of lovingly healing thousands of people, it was becoming exceedingly complex. The divas-of-darkness that seek to suppress the spiritual life/ light of contemporary people (and perhaps even biological life as a whole), through an artificial global order, are becoming increasingly overt and aggressive, and this made it exceedingly exhaustive for him. During the retreat weekend, which was spent with colleagues who are all quite experienced and familiar with these realms, we discussed these things, as well as the separation of religion and spirituality, the separation of science and nature, and the absurdity of belief systems that lead to the acquiescence, barbarism and indifference in the masses. [We need but look at the Western (EU, UK, and US-led) thirst for war – Ukraine, Middle East, China – it seems as if just about anywhere will do, as long as they can have war, and it seems the larger the war, the longer lasting and the more brutal, the better!]

That aside, our discussions and practices emphasized to me how the work of establishing environments that support enlightenment has become so very important. Although the path to the Light involves the work each of us does within, the act of assisting and enabling seekers to re-discover compassion for themselves and for others, seems as important, if not more so. Whereas one could say that the suffering and afflicted are already in Fate's hands, this work is perhaps more important for those whose minds are possessed and whose hearts, as a result, are closed or perhaps irreparably tarnished.

I believe most of us have felt and witnessed at one time or another, the indescribably harmonious effects of the Divine's work within. This is, I find, even more beautiful when observed in the compassionate interactions between people. And this, especially so, between people who do not know each other, who are perhaps on opposite sides of the spectrum, but who (in life) have little in common except the wish to heal, love and to find their truth. For these people, however, a suitable space or guided or assisted healing is often first necessary before this can occur.

Now, where these observations look at the world around us, I must now review them from my inner philosophical and personal angle:

As profound as that many of the teachings are, when I take the perception of 'illusory time' into account, I must consider that the Path (to Enlightenment) has many ways. This is becomes even more so when I note the presence of those dark corrupting elements in the astral world, and then find how, in this realm I am told to avoid, there are still paths to Light through shades of darkness.

It therefore seems to me that, through necessity or inevitability, I may still find my life's journey begin to change direction, and it treading towards and through the proverbial lion's den[1]. Then, instead of resting on past

---

[1] In reference to a perilous, and potentially compromising place

achievement and not risk exposing a certain state of 'attained enlightenment', I feel I may still be called upon to do just that. This may be because the Divine's purpose for me in this life has (at this point of its passage) a higher value than that which previously served my own perceived purpose of being, including that of my personal spiritual goal and 'life' itself.

These are complex thoughts though, and ones that are easily be misperceived. However, having recently left my old life of Nature's embrace, and now living in a place that is still peaceful but to which I am unlikely to become attached, my views on Life, have become clearer. These are equally complex and very unusual times, and within the prospect of ever greater travesties, 'from the one who has been entrusted with much, even more will be demanded.'[1] I hope this makes sense to you.

I could summarize this by saying that, *in my perceived reality,* I (being the ego that is called John, who is almost 60, and at an 'interesting' pivot point in life) find myself in the process of intuitively attaching thought and value to a path, that may be more active than the passive one I have been on for many years. I feel I must trust this intuitive process as, after all, for most (if not all) of the many 'unusual' experiences I have already encountered across the course of my life, especially those where I may have acted correctly, it feels it would be incorrect for this "I" to claim credit for much of it.

Although I am uncertain where all this will lead, it seems important to continue learning, to practice awareness, and to pray for guidance in discernment. Ultimately, we must acknowledge the Higher Power that guides us, even when the purpose or outcome is veiled.

With much love and best wishes,
John

On Monday 5 August 2024, Vidyananda wrote:

Dear John,
Hari Om.

We are all well, thank you. And I too pray that you, Terri, and the boys are well. From your account, I gather all are well. Congratulations to Nick and may he have a rewarding career.

Thank you for sharing your thoughts with me regarding your possible 'new' path. If I understood you correctly, you feel that your life path is taking you on a journey that entails helping others.

I don't think that this conflicts with the inner path. I would suggest that the 'active' spirituality requires the 'passive' as its foundation. For me, Mahatma Gandhi is a prime example. His Satyagraha (usually translated as 'conscious resistance') was based on Soul-power, which is what Satyagraha actually means. Being a 'spiritual warrior', as he called himself, was based on meditation and prayer. I feel that this is the essential foundation of any form of activism, healing or helping others.

---

[1] Quoted from The New Testament, the Gospel of Luke 12:48

We should keep up our spiritual practices and ensure that we are still growing spiritually and that we are established as much as possible in Spirit. From that space, we can do whatever work is required. And whilst engaged in our service, we should try to remain established in Spirit.

I feel that only then will there be truly any effect on others. We cannot shine light if our own light is dim. If our light is bright, then naturally we bring light to the world. Even the non-active yogi brings light to the world, merely by his/her en**light**enment.

Active or passive is God's directive.

I can visualize the 'spiritual warrior' John! OM!

I hope I have understood you correctly.

With Love and Blessings,
Vidyananda

AFTERWORD

During the course of 2025, as we worked on completing this book, we deliberated somewhat on how to close it – as in which letter to use last – and perhaps to try to end off on a 'high note'. However, as it is not really a book with a single storyline or topic, but simply a collection of letters with our thoughts and observations on a variety of topics, we decided instead in adding this brief Afterword.

Of course, there is no such thing as an ending with a high note, as this must then inevitably be followed by its ebb or low note! However, where we do not wish to be pessimistic about this, it is important to be realistic.

Life is largely a collection of choices and what we make of it, and where it is not a means to itself, or to an end, it can be considered as a type of 'school'. Unlike the compulsory lessons we are all accustomed to, if we can observe Life separate of all our familial and social tasks and necessities, there are a great many things we can do to enrich our experience of being, at little or no cost! Thus, to the exchanges in this book, where we began with a review of the beauty of the natural world and the interconnectedness of the world of matter, the most profound and miraculous review was that of Humanity, and in particular the role or path of the Individual essential Self!

Thus, in our analysis we discussed many things. Some of them to do with the world of people, some on politics and pandemics, some of them to do with society, individuality and spirituality, and then there were those comparative topics of duty versus responsibility, authority versus accountability, nature versus science, history versus mythology, and others. We pray that our conversation does not end here!

As such, we hope that some of these topics peaked your interest as they did ours, and that you were able to recognize that there is something quite miraculous in the co-existence of all of this.

In the gardens of the Blue Butterfly, October 2013

www.ingramcontent.com/pod-product-compliance
Lightning Source LLC
LaVergne TN
LVHW051728080426
835511LV00018B/2940